FLTK Programming Essentials

Definitive Reference for Developers and Engineers

Richard Johnson

Contents

5

Introduction

This book presents a comprehensive and detailed exploration of the Fast Light Toolkit (FLTK), a powerful and efficient cross-platform GUI library designed to facilitate the development of modern graphical user interfaces. Its focus lies in delivering a thorough understanding of FLTK's core components, architectural design, and advanced programming techniques, enabling readers to fully harness its capabilities for professional-grade application development.

Starting with foundational concepts, this volume delves into the architectural underpinnings of FLTK, elucidating its lightweight, modular structure and the event-driven programming model that forms the basis of its responsiveness and efficiency. Key aspects such as the widget lifecycle, event propagation, and rendering pipeline—including double-buffering strategies—are explored to provide insight into the internal workings of the toolkit. Memory management, resource handling, and multithreading considerations are examined rigorously, equipping developers with the knowledge to implement robust and stable applications that perform well across diverse system environments. Cross-platform portability is analyzed in detail, showcasing FLTK's mechanisms to ensure consistent behavior on Linux, Windows, and macOS platforms.

The text advances to a comprehensive guide on widget use and

1

layout management. Readers will gain expertise in standard UI components, advanced container hierarchies, dynamic layout techniques, and constructing custom widgets tailored to specific needs. Emphasis on styling, visual theming, accessibility, and internationalization ensures the creation of inclusive and adaptable user interfaces suitable for diverse users and global markets.

Handling user interaction is addressed through an in-depth study of FLTK's event system, covering fine-grained input event management, callback architectures, and stateful interaction modeling via finite state machines. Practical guidance on implementing drag-and-drop, gestural interfaces, and multi-touch input extends FLTK's usability to emerging interaction paradigms. Focus management, keyboard navigation, and accessibility compliance augment the user experience and facilitate broad adoption.

Graphics and rendering topics command significant attention, with comprehensive coverage of the FLTK graphics context, integration of bitmap and vector formats such as SVG, and smooth, flicker-free animation techniques. The fusion of FLTK widgets with OpenGL contexts is presented for advanced rendering scenarios. Additional treatment of image processing, post-processing effects, and performance profiling supports the development of visually rich and performant applications.

Architectural patterns for data binding and reactive programming in FLTK applications are detailed, including Model-View-Controller adaptations, bidirectional data synchronization, observer patterns, and undo/redo frameworks. This treatment ensures maintainable, extensible application architectures capable of handling complex user interactions and state management. Strategies for robust unit testing and integration verification further reinforce code quality.

System integration topics cover interfaces with native platform APIs, printing, clipboard access, networking, interprocess communication, and hardware peripheral support. Considerations of se-

2

curity, sandboxing, and permissions address vital concerns for deploying reliable and secure software.

For development workflow optimization, the book provides expert guidance on build automation using CMake, linking strategies, continuous integration pipelines, packaging, distribution channels, and post-deployment monitoring. These practices streamline the entire software lifecycle from development to delivery and maintenance.

Performance optimization is addressed through methods for memory analysis, CPU profiling, efficient event dispatch and redraw management, and adaptation to high-DPI and multi-monitor systems. Advanced threading and asynchronous techniques allow improved application responsiveness without sacrificing stability.

Specialized coverage of FLTK in embedded and modern system contexts demonstrates how to adapt the toolkit for resource-constrained environments, touch-enabled devices, and Internet of Things applications. Case studies detail real-world deployments, highlighting practical solutions and best practices.

The closing chapters focus on best practices for designing large-scale FLTK applications, advanced testing, security hardening, plugin extension architectures, and engagement with the open source community. A forward-looking perspective illuminates ongoing enhancements and how developers may contribute to the evolution of FLTK.

This volume is intended as an indispensable reference and practical guide for software engineers, UI developers, and system integrators seeking to master FLTK programming at an advanced level, enabling the creation of efficient, portable, and feature-rich graphical applications across multiple platforms.

4

Chapter 1

Deep Dive into FLTK Architecture

Explore the architectural heart of FLTK—where elegance meets efficiency. In this chapter, you'll uncover how FLTK's modular framework transforms C++ into a powerful cross-platform GUI engine. Behind every lightweight window and smooth interaction lies a deliberate design: discover the stories, engineering trade-offs, and best practices that enable FLTK to remain both nimble and versatile in the world of graphical programming.

1.1. Core Design Philosophy

The Fast Light Toolkit (FLTK) embodies a distinctive architectural ethos grounded in principles that prioritize minimalism, modularity, and an event-driven design. These principles collectively guide the construction of its interface, ensuring that the toolkit remains compact, efficient, and adaptable across multiple platforms without succumbing to feature overload. Understanding these guiding philosophies reveals the rationale behind FLTK's design decisions and illustrates how the toolkit successfully negotiates the often competing demands of functionality, performance, and scalability.

At the heart of FLTK lies the principle of *minimalism*, a deliberate strategy to keep the library lean. Minimalism here is not merely an aesthetic choice but a functional imperative. By limiting features to a necessary core set, FLTK avoids the common pitfall faced by many graphical user interface (GUI) toolkits: feature bloat. Every additional feature, while potentially increasing usability in a narrow context, invariably adds complexity to the codebase, enlarges the binary footprint, and introduces potential maintenance liabilities. FLTK mitigates this by providing a streamlined widget set that covers the fundamental building blocks required for user interfaces but intentionally excludes less common or specialized widgets. This restrained approach reduces dependency chains and keeps the overall footprint small enough to support deployment in resource-constrained and embedded environments.

Modularity complements minimalism by enabling extensibility without compromising the core's compactness. FLTK is architected as a set of loosely coupled modules that communicate through well-defined interfaces. It segments responsibilities among different classes and libraries-for example, separating drawing routines, widget management, and event processing. This modularity permits developers to selectively include or exclude components based on the application's needs, optimizing resource allocation. It further facilitates maintenance, as changes within a module are less likely to cascade into system-wide regressions. This compartmentalization also accelerates compilation and linking times, which benefits developers working in iterative, cross-platform environments.

Central to FLTK's architecture is its *event-driven* design, which aligns naturally with the asynchronous nature of GUI interactions. Unlike traditional procedural interfaces, FLTK employs an event loop that continuously listens for system and user events-such as mouse clicks, keyboard presses, and window messages-and dispatches them to the appropriate handlers within widgets. This reactive model decouples input processing from rendering and layout management, promoting responsiveness and smooth user experiences. The event-driven backbone also simplifies concurrency considerations, as all GUI updates occur in a single thread dedicated to event handling, preventing common race conditions and synchronization overhead.

FLTK's event model is implemented with a minimalist yet flexible approach. The core exposes a well-defined set of event types and a virtual method interface-most notably the `handle()` method on widgets-that processes incoming events. This design permits elegant customization by subclassing widgets and overriding event handlers, enabling tailored behavior without modifying the central library. Its lightweight event dispatching mechanism bypasses complex signaling frameworks or heavyweight observer patterns seen in other toolkits, ensuring minimal runtime overhead.

A direct consequence of emphasizing minimalism and modularity, while utilizing an event-driven backbone, is FLTK's advantageous *scalability*. The toolkit scales efficiently both upwards-by enabling the development of rich graphical applications-and downwards-by supporting lightweight embedded systems. The slim core avoids heavy runtime dependencies, facilitating swift cross-compilation and easy integration with native windowing systems such as X11, Win32, and MacOS Quartz. Its design ensures that incrementally growing an application's complexity does not exponentially inflate resource consumption or degrade performance, attributes critical for cross-platform consistency.

The avoidance of feature bloat also fundamentally influences FLTK's user experience. By focusing on essential widgets and straightforward interfaces, it sidesteps the cognitive overhead often imposed on developers by large, multifaceted frameworks. A smaller API surface area translates into faster learning curves

7

and more predictable application behavior. Simplicity in design also reduces the risk of subtle bugs related to intricate widget combinations or obscure features, leading to more robust software.

Architectural trade-offs emerge clearly when contrasting FLTK with more extensive GUI toolkits. For instance, while toolkits such as Qt or GTK provide comprehensive support for advanced widgets, theming, and extensive internationalization out of the box, they also entail larger binaries, steeper learning curves, and more complex build environments. FLTK deliberately relinquishes some of these capabilities in favor of a faster, lighter toolkit that excels in rapid prototyping, straightforward UIs, and embedded contexts. Consequently, although FLTK may require developers to implement specialized widgets themselves, this cost is offset by the agility and control provided by its tight foundation.

To exemplify, consider FLTK's graphical rendering strategy, which aligns with its design ethos. Instead of leveraging heavyweight graphics engines, FLTK incorporates a minimal OpenGL wrapper and basic software rendering paths. This guarantees broad hardware compatibility without adding bulk or dependencies. Moreover, the toolkit's transparent mapping of widgets to native system events and resources reduces abstraction layers, resulting in predictable, efficient rendering and input processing.

The toolkit's approach to cross-platform development further demonstrates its architectural intentions. By isolating platform-specific code to minimal, well-encapsulated modules, FLTK simplifies porting and enables developers to write platform-agnostic application logic. The platform abstraction layer intercepts native window messages and translates them into FLTK events while handling window management and drawing context allocation. This segregation is paramount to maintaining a compact codebase, allowing each platform adaptor to evolve independently without destabilizing the core.

8

In summary, FLTK's core design philosophy centers around maintaining a small, extensible, and efficient foundation driven by an event-loop architecture. Such a foundation imposes discipline on the toolkit's growth, forcing prioritization of essential functionality and eliminating unnecessary complexity. This philosophy not only curtails maintenance and distribution challenges but also empowers developers to produce responsive, portable applications with minimal overhead. As a result, FLTK serves as a paradigm of how restrained design and modular construction can achieve a versatile, high-performance GUI toolkit suitable for a wide spectrum of development tasks.

1.2. Widget Lifecycle and Event Queue

The Fast Light Toolkit (FLTK) adopts a robust and efficient approach to widget lifecycle management and event handling that ensures smooth graphical interface operation under varying user and system conditions. Understanding the intricate interplay between widget states and the event queue is essential for designing responsive and stable applications.

Widgets in FLTK follow a well-defined lifecycle comprising creation, initialization, event-driven interaction, and destruction phases. This lifecycle is tightly coupled with memory management strategies and event propagation mechanisms to achieve efficient resource utilization and responsiveness.

Widgets are instantiated through constructors that allocate the necessary memory and establish basic properties such as dimensions, labels, colors, and parent-child relationships. During the construction phase, widgets remain unattached to the display and cannot yet process events or render themselves. Initialization completes the widget's setup, typically through calls to member functions that configure callback routines and register the widget with the parent window or container.

9

FLTK organizes widgets into a hierarchical tree structure where each widget may have zero or more children and exactly one parent (except for top-level windows). The parent-child linkages form the basis of widget positioning, clipping, and event propagation.

The constructor of a widget usually invokes the base class constructor to properly chain initialization. For example:

```
Fl_Button* btn = new Fl_Button(10, 10, 90, 30, "Click Me");
```

Here, the Fl_Button constructor initializes widget geometry, label, and default callback pointers. Post-construction initialization often involves setting properties that govern widget behavior and appearance, such as color schemes or selection states.

FLTK manages widget lifetime largely through parent-child ownership semantics. Each widget is responsible for deleting its child widgets upon destruction, ensuring recursive cleanup without explicit user intervention. This design relieves developers from manual memory management and prevents leaks in typical UI scenarios.

Once a widget is added to a parent container, the parent assumes ownership. Consequently, deleting the parent widget automatically triggers destruction of all descendants in its widget subtree. This is achieved by the base widget destructor calling destructors on all child widgets.

It is critical to avoid deleting child widgets independently after the parent is destroyed or scheduled for destruction, as this leads to double deletions or dangling pointers. If manual control over widget lifetime is required, developers must detach widgets from their parents via remove() or nullify parental references before deletion.

FLTK relies on an internal event queue to serialize and dispatch user-initiated and system-generated events. The event queue mediates between the operating system's native event dispatch and the widget tree, translating generic input messages to widget-specific callbacks.

The event loop resides in `Fl::run()` or equivalent constructs, continuously polling and processing events until termination. On receiving an event, FLTK determines the target widget by hit-testing the event coordinates against widget geometries in front-to-back order.

Once a target is identified, the toolkit calls the widget's `handle(int event)` method with the event type. This function encapsulates a state machine that governs response to events such as mouse clicks, keyboard input, focus changes, and window resizing. Return values from `handle()` denote whether the event was consumed, dictating propagation behavior.

If a widget does not consume the event, FLTK may pass the event to its parent as a fallback, facilitating bubbling of events up the widget hierarchy. This mechanism enables interception and customized handling of unprocessed events at higher-level containers.

Callback functions constitute the primary mechanism by which widgets notify application logic of state changes or user interactions. Each FLTK widget maintains pointers to callback functions and associated userdata, enabling flexible handling without inheritance or complex event delegation.

Callbacks are registered using `widget->callback()` methods, for example:

```
btn->callback(on_button_click, (void*)extra_data);
```

The callback function signature must comply with:

```
void callback(Fl_Widget* w, void* data);
```

During event processing, invoking `handle()` will trigger the registered callback upon detecting relevant events (e.g., `FL_PUSH` for mouse button press). Callbacks execute synchronously in the context of the event loop, allowing immediate updates to application state.

Safe callback design mandates guarding against widget destruction within callbacks, as invoking member functions on deleted widgets leads to undefined behavior. A common pattern involves deferring destructive operations or posting flags for processing after event completion.

Because widget destruction implicitly deletes all child widgets, premature or circular destruction requests can lead to subtle errors. For instance, deleting a widget inside its own callback risks invalidating the call stack's state, potentially crashing the application.

A recommended strategy is to postpone destruction until after event processing completes. This is often implemented by posting a custom event using Fl::add_timeout() or setting a flag checked in the main loop:

```
void destroy_widget_later(Fl_Widget* w) {
    Fl::add_timeout(0.0, [](void* data){
        delete static_cast<Fl_Widget*>(data);
    }, w);
}
```

This approach ensures destruction occurs when the event loop is idle, preventing interference with ongoing callback execution.

When widgets must be removed dynamically from containers, the remove() method should be invoked to detach the widget from the parent before destruction. This prevents invalid parent pointers and enforces proper cleanup semantics.

Consider a typical usage pattern where application logic requires reacting to user clicks in a button nested inside a window hierarchy. The steps below exemplify lifecycle states and mechanisms:

- Create a window widget to serve as container.

- Instantiate child widgets (buttons, inputs) by specifying position and linking to the parent window.

- Register callback functions on each interactive widget corresponding to user actions.

12

- Enter the FLTK event loop via `Fl::run()`, where events are queued and dispatched.

- As the user interacts, FLTK detects input, identifies the targeted widget by hit-testing, and invokes their `handle()` methods.

- Callback functions execute synchronously, updating internal data or UI states.

- Upon window closure or application exit, deletion cascades from root windows down their respective widget trees, releasing all allocated memory.

This flow exemplifies FLTK's design philosophy: transparent memory ownership, flexible callback-driven interaction, and efficient event dispatch through well-encapsulated widget methods.

The event queue records asynchronous input and system events until they can be processed. Events are represented as integer constants, including:

- `FL_PUSH` and `FL_RELEASE` for mouse button actions,

- `FL_MOVE` for mouse motion,

- `FL_FOCUS` and `FL_UNFOCUS` for focus changes,

- `FL_KEYBOARD` for keyboard input,

- `FL_SHORTCUT` for shortcut key combinations.

User applications may define and post custom events via native methods but must ensure that `handle()` methods are extended to recognize such events appropriately. Proper event queue management includes calling `Fl::wait()` or `Fl::check()` in custom loops to process queued events.

FLTK's widget lifecycle and event queue framework informs several key principles for robust application design:

- Ownership semantics simplify memory management but require cautious detachment before manual deletion.

- The synchronous callback model facilitates immediate response but demands careful handling to avoid invalidated references.

- Event propagation via `handle()` return conventions offers flexible customization points.

- Postponed destruction via timeout callbacks or flag checks ensures thread-safe and consistent widget cleanup.

- Hierarchical widget registration and the event hit-testing mechanism guarantee coherent delivery of events to intended targets.

Mastery of these concepts enables the construction of reliable, performant graphical interfaces leveraging FLTK's lightweight and responsive architecture.

1.3. Rendering Pipeline and Double-Buffering

The FLTK (Fast Light Toolkit) graphical user interface library utilizes a carefully designed rendering pipeline to manage the drawing of widgets and windows efficiently while ensuring flicker-free output. Central to this process is the management of drawing contexts, handling paint events, and the use of double-buffering techniques, which together support smooth visual updates and responsive interaction.

Rendering within FLTK proceeds through a sequence of coordinated stages initiated by the arrival of paint events. These events signal the need to refresh or redraw certain screen regions, which may arise due to user interaction, window exposure, or programmatic updates.

- *Event Dispatch and Region Determination:* When the operating system requests a repaint-commonly through exposure or invalidate events-FLTK receives a paint event. This event contains information regarding the damaged region (the area that needs redisplay), which FLTK translates into a clipping box to optimize rendering.

- *Setting up the Drawing Context:* FLTK employs platform-specific drawing contexts abstracted by its internal graphics subsystem. These contexts encapsulate surface targets (window or off-screen buffer), clipping regions, and coordinate transforms. Before rendering, the drawing context is initialized or switched to the appropriate target, with the clipping box applied to limit drawing to the damaged areas.

- *Widget Draw Invocation:* Each widget in the visible hierarchy intersecting the damaged region receives a `draw()` callback. FLTK dispatches these calls in a depth-first manner starting from the top-level window to child widgets, ensuring that overlapping widgets render in the correct z-order. Widgets implement custom `draw()` routines to paint their graphical elements using FLTK's lightweight drawing primitives.

- *Draw Calls and Graphics Primitives:* Drawing commands within `draw()` include painting shapes, text, images, and other elements using FLTK's wrapper around native graphics APIs. These calls execute within the current drawing context, respecting clipping regions, color settings, and transformation matrices.

- *Buffer Swap and Presentation:* Upon completion of all widget drawing for the damaged region, the rendering pipeline proceeds to present the composed image to the screen. This presentation step involves exchanging or flushing buffers, depending on buffering strategy, in order to update the displayed content.

Drawing contexts in FLTK abstract platform-dependent device contexts (DCs), handling resource allocation, state preservation, and clipping. Upon paint event reception, FLTK creates or reuses a drawing context associated with the target window's graphical surface.

Critical to correctness and efficiency is the management of clipping regions that restrict drawing commands to painted areas, avoiding unnecessary computations. Contexts also maintain transformation matrices to support coordinate mapping, especially when widgets apply scaling or translation.

Developers extending FLTK's drawing capabilities implement custom `draw()` methods, which receive an implicit current drawing context. Within this context, they invoke graphics primitives while adhering to standard FLTK conventions: minimize global state changes, confine drawing to clipped regions, and avoid direct window system calls that bypass FLTK's drawing pipeline.

FLTK supports overlapping top-level windows and nested widget hierarchies. Managing these overlapping regions requires careful compositing order control and invalidation propagation. Paint events generated by the system often indicate exactly which regions of a window are exposed due to overlapping windows being moved, resized, or closed.

FLTK translates these exposure regions into clipping rectangles for each affected top-level window. Within windows, invalidation cascades down to child widgets intersecting the damaged region. The rendering pipeline guarantees that widgets overlapping in z-order are drawn sequentially with proper clipping and without overwriting each other. This process avoids visual artifacts such as partial redraws or ghosting effects.

Flicker in UI rendering is primarily caused by directly drawing to the visible screen buffer, where intermediate drawing states may become momentarily visible. FLTK employs double-buffering techniques to eliminate flicker and provide smooth visual updates.

The double-buffering approach maintains two pixel buffers:

- *Back Buffer:* An off-screen buffer where all drawing operations occur. Compositing of widget elements takes place entirely within this buffer.

- *Front Buffer:* The visible buffer displayed on the screen.

The rendering workflow using double-buffering operates as follows:

- Drawing commands triggered by paint events target the back buffer instead of the front buffer. This ensures no partial or intermediate image states become visible.

- Once all drawing completes, the back buffer is efficiently copied or swapped to the front buffer in a single atomic operation, typically by the graphics subsystem or windowing system's buffer swap functions.

- The front buffer update appears instantaneous to the user, offering a seamless visual transition without flicker.

In FLTK, double-buffering can be enabled or configured via widget or window flags. The internal implementation relies on platform-specific APIs for off-screen rendering surfaces, such as pixmaps or memory device contexts on X11 and Windows, or layer-backed views on macOS.

While FLTK's default rendering pipeline suffices for standard widgets, advanced applications often require customized drawing strategies that integrate smoothly with FLTK's pipeline:

- *Partial Region Redraw:* Drawing custom widgets to repaint only affected subregions improves performance. FLTK supports retrieval of the clip region during `draw()`, enabling developers to limit expensive drawing operations.

- *Double-Buffering at Widget Level:* Beyond window-level buffering, widgets can implement local double-buffering by maintaining their own off-screen pixmaps, compositing their content off-screen, then blitting to the parent context during `draw()`. This can isolate complex rendering code, reducing flicker at the widget level.

- *Deferred Drawing and Update Coalescing:* Deferring redraw requests and batching them reduces unnecessary paint events. FLTK's event system allows queuing redraws via `redraw()` calls that, combined with idle callbacks, optimize rendering frequency.

- *Integration with OpenGL and Hardware Acceleration:* FLTK supports OpenGL contexts which can be embedded within widgets. Rendering pipelines involving hardware acceleration must synchronize buffer swaps with FLTK's event loop to maintain flicker-free output.

Effective rendering in FLTK is the result of a layered approach:

- Precise event-driven identification of damaged regions minimizes irrelevant painting.

- Context-aware drawing allows scalable and modular rendering.

- Overlapping windows' compositing with clipping preserves visual coherence.

- Double-buffering eliminates flicker through off-screen composition.

18

- Extensible custom drawing strategies provide flexibility for diverse application needs.

The rendering pipeline and double-buffering mechanisms in FLTK combine to deliver high-performance, stable, and visually appealing graphical interfaces suitable for demanding cross-platform applications.

```
void MyWidget::draw() {
    // Retrieve the current clipping rectangle
    Fl_Widget::draw();

    // Access clipping region to optimize drawing
    Fl_Region clip = fl_clip_region();

    // Draw background only if clip intersects widget bounds
    if (clip.intersects(x(), y(), w(), h())) {
        fl_rectf(x(), y(), w(), h(), FL_WHITE);
    }

    // Custom drawing: draw a red rectangle with border
    fl_color(FL_RED);
    fl_rectf(x()+10, y()+10, w()-20, h()-20);

    fl_color(FL_BLACK);
    fl_rect(x()+10, y()+10, w()-20, h()-20);

    // If double-buffering enabled, drawing occurs on back buffer
    // Buffer swap is managed automatically by FLTK at end of
     paint event
}
```

Output:
The widget appears without flicker, with a solid white background
and a red rectangle bordered in black centrally placed inside the widget's ar
ea.

1.4. Resource Management and Memory Handling

The Fast Light Toolkit (FLTK) fundamentally espouses a lightweight and manual approach to resource management that aligns with its intent to serve both small utilities and complex graphical applications with minimal runtime overhead. Central to this approach is the explicit handling of ownership and memory allocation, which contrasts with modern frameworks that predominantly rely on automated resource management mechanisms. An in-depth understanding of FLTK's memory handling paradigms is essential for robust and leak-free GUI programming.

FLTK's design primarily follows a manual memory management model wherein widget allocation and deallocation are explicitly controlled by the programmer. Most widget constructors allocate resources on the heap, with the obligation to invoke the corresponding destructor or delete operation residing outside the library's automatic scope. For instance, instantiating a widget typically uses raw pointers:

```
Fl_Button* btn = new Fl_Button(10, 10, 80, 30, "Click me");
```

Here, btn owns a heap-allocated button widget and is responsible for its eventual deletion. The widget hierarchy does not imply automatic destruction of children; the programmer must carefully manage deletion to prevent memory leaks. This manual ownership model, while lightweight, requires strict discipline and clear ownership convention to avoid dangling pointers and leaks.

FLTK's memory model is further complicated by its use of C-style callback functions, which typically take widget pointers as arguments but do not manage their lifetimes. Callbacks must therefore assume valid lifetimes or employ external mechanisms to ensure pointers remain valid during invocation. This reliance on raw pointers underscores the importance of careful ownership semantics.

To mitigate the risks inherent to manual memory management, contemporary FLTK codebase and advanced applications increasingly integrate C++ smart pointers. Utilizing smart pointers introduces automated lifetime management and clarifies ownership intent, thus preventing common pitfalls such as double deletions or leaks. For example, using `std::unique_ptr` to encapsulate widget ownership provides exception safety and guarantees single ownership semantics:

```
#include <memory>

std::unique_ptr<Fl_Button> btn = std::make_unique<Fl_Button>(10,
    10, 80, 30, "Click me");
```

Since `std::unique_ptr` automatically deallocates the widget upon destruction, this pattern eradicates explicit `delete` statements and minimizes memory management errors. However, employing smart pointers within FLTK entails awareness of its internal event loop and callback mechanisms, often requiring the retention of raw pointers for callback registration while still owning the widget via smart pointers elsewhere.

Shared ownership scenarios can leverage `std::shared_ptr`, but this is generally discouraged except for specific use cases or complex widget interactions due to the increased overhead and potential for cyclical references. Importantly, neither `std::unique_ptr` nor `std::shared_ptr` natively support incomplete destructors for FLTK widgets, so custom deleters may be necessary when nontrivial cleanup is required.

FLTK itself does not provide built-in ownership transfer or automated resource tracking constructs. Therefore, strict ownership conventions are recommended: an application should clearly separate widget creation, ownership, and destruction responsibilities. For instance, a window object often assumes direct ownership of its child widgets and deletes them upon its own destruction, enabling safer hierarchical lifetime management.

Safe memory allocation practices within FLTK also encompass the consistent use of `new` and `delete` to match widget lifetime, avoidance of uninitialized pointers, and careful integration with the FLTK event loop, which may invoke callbacks asynchronously. In particular, allocating widgets on the stack is generally discouraged, as their lifetime may end prematurely relative to the window's event-driven lifecycle, resulting in use-after-free errors.

Techniques to avoid common memory pitfalls include:

- **Avoiding double deletes**: Multiple explicit calls to `delete` on the same pointer cause undefined behavior. Employing smart pointers or clear ownership transfer semantics prevents this.

- **Preventing memory leaks**: Every `new` call must have a matching `delete`. For dynamically created widgets that outlive the local scope, ownership should be transferred or tracked explicitly.

- **Handling exception safety**: Using RAII (Resource Acquisition Is Initialization) idioms with smart pointers ensures that objects clean up even during stack unwinding from exceptions.

- **Avoiding dangling pointers**: After `delete`, pointers should be set to `nullptr` or go out of scope to avoid accidental dereferencing.

An archetype of robust memory handling in FLTK programs embeds widgets in containers that manage their lifetime automatically. For example, a custom container class owning widgets via smart pointers can encapsulate creation and destruction:

```
class WidgetContainer {
    std::vector<std::unique_ptr<Fl_Widget>> widgets;
public:
    void add(std::unique_ptr<Fl_Widget> widget) {
        widgets.push_back(std::move(widget));
    }

    // All widgets automatically destroyed when container goes
    out of scope
};
```

Such a container guarantees collective cleanup and clearly delineates widget ownership boundaries. It also simplifies modifications, as the container abstracts individual widget lifetimes and facilitates batch destruction.

Another common pattern involves careful coordination between FLTK's linear widget hierarchy and external data structures to maintain ownership clarity. Since FLTK widgets maintain parent-child relationships (e.g., Fl_Group containing children), it is important to recognize that deleting a parent widget does not automatically delete its children unless explicitly programmed. Practitioners often override the destructor of Fl_Group derivatives to iterate over and delete children, thereby enforcing hierarchical resource deallocation.

Memory allocation efficiency is another dimension in FLTK's resource management. Because FLTK targets responsiveness and minimal resource consumption, excessive dynamic allocations or overuse of heavyweight smart pointer machinery may degrade performance. Wherever possible, static or stack allocation of small, transient objects should be preferred, with dynamic allocation reserved for widgets with lifetimes tied to the GUI lifespan.

Moreover, FLTK's internal handling of graphical resources (e.g., bitmaps, fonts) demands explicit release to avoid resource exhaustion. Typical patterns include:

- Ensuring Fl_Bitmap and related graphic objects are explicitly destroyed when no longer needed.

- Avoiding duplicated resource allocation by sharing handles or caching frequently used assets.

- Leveraging FLTK's limited internal reference counting mechanisms cautiously to avoid premature release of shared resources.

In multi-threaded environments, memory and resource management become more complex as FLTK is not intrinsically thread-safe. Widgets and GUI resource allocation must be confined to the main thread, and synchronization mechanisms must control cross-thread access to shared ownership objects to prevent race conditions.

Mastering FLTK's resource management involves a synthesis of manual management discipline supplemented by modern C++ idioms such as smart pointers. Clear ownership patterns, explicit deletion, and hierarchical lifecycle management remain fundamental. Employing these techniques mitigates common pitfalls like memory leaks, dangling pointers, and undefined behavior, thus enabling the development of stable, efficient, and maintainable FLTK applications, regardless of scale.

1.5. Threading and Synchronization

The Fast Light Toolkit (FLTK) employs a concurrency model that demands careful coordination between the user interface (UI) thread and worker threads to maintain responsiveness and thread safety. FLTK's event-driven architecture dictates a single-threaded UI loop responsible for processing input events, rendering widgets, and dispatching callbacks. Violations of this single-threaded UI rule-such as invoking FLTK API functions from non-UI threads-result in undefined behavior, including race conditions, data corruption, and application crashes. The concurrency model, therefore, must balance the need for responsive interfaces and concurrent computation while strictly mediating access to shared GUI resources.

FLTK's threading model designates the main thread as the *UI thread*, which alone must perform all UI-related operations. Worker threads are tasked with background computational workloads, such as data processing, I/O operations, or long-running calculations, to prevent UI blocking. Interaction between worker threads and the UI thread is feasible only through safe, well-defined synchronization mechanisms provided by FLTK.

Thread Safety Constraints and Locking

By default, FLTK's internal data structures and widget states are *not* thread-safe. This constraint necessitates explicit locking protocols when manipulating FLTK objects from threads other than the UI thread. FLTK offers a global lock mechanism, managed by functions Fl::lock() and Fl::unlock(), which protects the integrity of FLTK's internal state during multithreaded access. The lock serializes access to the internal event queue and widget properties, ensuring that concurrent modifications from multiple threads do not interfere.

However, the acquisition of FLTK's global lock must be performed judiciously to avoid negative side effects like priority inversion or deadlocks. Holding the lock for extended durations during computationally intensive tasks defeats concurrency benefits and reduces responsiveness. Moreover, callbacks executed within the lock context should avoid reentrance or blocking operations to maintain event loop fluidity.

```
// Example: Safely modifying widget state from a worker thread
void update_label_from_thread(Fl_Widget* label_w, const char*
    text) {
  Fl::lock();                    // Acquire FLTK lock
  static_cast<Fl_Box*>(label_w)->label(text); // Modify widget
    safely
  Fl::awake();                   // Wake up UI thread to process
    changes
  Fl::unlock();                  // Release FLTK lock
}
```

UI Thread and Worker Thread Interaction via Fl::awake()

Direct UI updates from worker threads are disallowed. Instead, FLTK provides the Fl::awake() mechanism to safely notify the UI thread from background threads. When invoked, Fl::awake() posts a special internal event into FLTK's event queue that triggers a designated callback in the UI thread. This enables deferred execution of UI modifications within the sanctioned UI thread context, avoiding race conditions and unsafe access.

The awake callback, registered via `Fl::add_idle()` or `Fl::add_timeout()`, must be structured as a small and non-blocking operation that processes the changes indicated by worker threads. Data transfers between threads should utilize thread-safe data structures or synchronization primitives outside of the FLTK locking scope before invoking `Fl::awake()`.

```cpp
// Worker thread signals UI thread to update
std::atomic<bool> data_ready(false);
void worker_thread_function() {
  // Perform computations...
  data_ready.store(true, std::memory_order_release);
  Fl::awake();
}

// UI thread idle callback processes the update
void ui_idle_callback(void*) {
  if (data_ready.load(std::memory_order_acquire)) {
    Fl::lock();
    // Update the widgets safely here
    // ...
    Fl::unlock();
    data_ready.store(false, std::memory_order_release);
  }
}

int main() {
  Fl::lock();
  Fl::add_idle(ui_idle_callback);
  Fl::unlock();
  // Start worker thread separately...
  return Fl::run();
}
```

This wake-up approach prevents blocking the UI thread and preserves responsiveness by ensuring UI changes occur asynchronously on the main thread.

Deadlock Avoidance and Best Practices

Deadlocks in FLTK applications usually originate from erroneous locking orders, prolonged lock holding, or circular waits involving

other mutexes. To minimize these risks, the following best practices apply:

- **Minimize Critical Sections:** Limit the scope and duration where Fl::lock() is held. Perform computation and
  non-FLTK-related operations outside the locked region.

- **Avoid Nested Locks:** Do not call FLTK functions that
  internally acquire the FLTK lock when already holding it,
  unless explicitly documented as safe. This prevents self-
  induced deadlocks.

- **Use Fl::awake() for UI Updates:** Never manipulate widgets directly from worker threads. Use Fl::awake() to defer
  UI changes to the main thread.

- **Thread-Safe Data Handoffs:** Exchange information
  between threads using thread-safe constructs such as
  std::atomic, std::mutex, std::condition_variable, or
  lock-free queues outside FLTK's locking scope.

- **Single Lock Ownership:** Avoid dependencies on multiple locks simultaneously, particularly when combining FLTK
  locks with application-specific mutexes.

Example: Responsive Status Update in a Multithreaded Application

Consider an application where a background thread performs a
time-consuming task while the UI indicates progress. The worker
thread updates progress data safely, signals the UI thread using
Fl::awake(), and the UI thread reads the latest progress asynchronously.

```
#include <atomic>
#include <thread>
#include <chrono>

std::atomic<int> progress_value(0);
Fl_Box* progress_label = nullptr;
```

```cpp
// Worker thread function
void worker() {
  for (int i = 0; i <= 100; ++i) {
    std::this_thread::sleep_for(std::chrono::milliseconds(50));
    progress_value.store(i, std::memory_order_release);  //
     Update progress
    Fl::awake();  // Notify UI thread
  }
}

// UI thread idle callback to update the label
void update_progress(void*) {
  static int last = -1;
  int val = progress_value.load(std::memory_order_acquire);
  if (val != last) {
    Fl::lock();
    progress_label->label(std::to_string(val).c_str());
    Fl::unlock();
    last = val;
  }
}

int main() {
  Fl::lock();  // Enable locking support
  Fl::add_idle(update_progress);

  Fl_Window* window = new Fl_Window(200, 100, "Threaded Progress
    ");
  progress_label = new Fl_Box(20, 40, 160, 20, "0");
  window->end();
  window->show();

  std::thread worker_thread(worker);

  Fl::unlock();

  int ret = Fl::run();
  worker_thread.join();
  return ret;
}
```

This example illustrates adherence to FLTK's threading requirements: the worker thread only modifies atomic data and calls Fl::awake(), whereas the UI thread safely updates the label within a locked section.

Considerations for Nested Event Loops and Idle Callbacks

28

The concurrency model complexity increases when nested event loops or modal dialogs are involved. Since nested loops process events on the same UI thread, they may reenter critical regions or callbacks holding the FLTK lock. Care must be taken to keep all widget modifications in nested loops consistent and avoid reentrancy bugs that can obscure deadlocks.

Idle callbacks should be brief and designed to execute only when necessary. Excessive processing or blocking within idle callbacks can degrade application performance or cause starvation of important UI events like redraws or input handling.

Summary of FLTK Concurrency Model Recommendations

- The UI thread solely manages all FLTK-dependent operations.

- Worker threads perform computational tasks without touching FLTK widgets or its event queue.

- Use `Fl::awake()` to signal UI updates for deferred processing.

- Protect FLTK state modifications by explicitly acquiring `Fl::lock()` and releasing it immediately afterward.

- Employ thread-safe data constructs external to FLTK locking mechanisms to communicate between threads.

- Prevent deadlocks by limiting lock scope, avoiding nested locks, and ensuring the UI thread remains unblocked.

These principles are critical to maintaining responsive, robust applications that leverage FLTK's lightweight UI framework alongside modern multithreaded programming paradigms. Mastery of this concurrency model enables the development of sophisticated graphical applications without compromising safety or performance.

1.6. Cross-Platform Portability Mechanisms

The Fast Light Toolkit (FLTK) achieves cross-platform portability through a carefully engineered architecture of core abstractions and interfaces designed to harmonize application behavior across Linux, Windows, and macOS. This harmonization relies on systematic isolation of platform-specific code, unified event management, and adaptable graphics backends, thereby enabling developers to write code once and deploy it seamlessly on disparate operating systems.

Fundamental to FLTK's portability strategy is the employment of a layered abstraction model. At the highest level, the public API exposed to application developers remains consistent and platform-agnostic, while beneath the surface, backend implementations selectively activate platform-specific modules. The toolkit's architecture bifurcates into *frontend* components responsible for widget definitions and layout, and *backend* components that encapsulate native system calls, event handling, and drawing operations.

Platform Abstraction Through Backends

The cornerstone of FLTK's isolation of platform-dependent behavior is the backend interface layer. FLTK defines an abstract set of interfaces representing core system services: window creation and management, event dispatching, input handling, and graphical rendering. For every supported platform-X11/Wayland on Linux, Win32 on Windows, and Cocoa (via Objective-C bindings) on macOS-these interfaces have concrete implementations dispatching to the native APIs.

This backend abstraction is structured around a small number of key classes and functions, such as the Fl_Window internals and event loop handlers, which carry the platform-dependent code behind an #ifdef-guarded implementation hierarchy. This conditional compilation strategy allows a single source base while maintaining optimized native interactions. For example, window creation on Windows invokes `CreateWindowEx` from the Win32 API; on Linux, it uses Xlib or XCB calls; and on macOS, it links against Cocoa's `NSWindow`.

Through a collection of virtual function overrides and platform-specific source files, FLTK enforces strict separation of platform logic. Widgets operate against an interface that abstracts device contexts and native widget handles, preventing direct embedding of platform-specific code in application logic.

System Event Management and Dispatching

Event handling within FLTK is centralized and abstracted to promote uniform behavior despite platform disparities in event models. The toolkit implements its own event loop that encapsulates and normalizes native system events into a common internal event type (`Fl_Event`).

Input events such as keyboard presses, mouse button clicks, motion events, and window notifications (resize, focus change, expose) are translated from native event data structures to FLTK's internal representation. This includes mapping key codes and modifiers into a consistent set of constants, regardless of underlying platform-specific values.

The event loop operates by querying the underlying system's event queue and dispatching processed events to the appropriate widget under the current mouse focus or keyboard focus. This dispatch architecture offers a platform-neutral event propagation model resembling the Model-View-Controller (MVC) paradigm, ensuring that user interaction behavior remains consistent across operating environments.

For instance, mouse wheel events are translated differently depending on the platform's native event structure and event granularity, but FLTK presents the application with a unified event type and delta values. This normalization is crucial for predictable application response and avoids the need for conditional event handling code in user programs.

Graphics Backend Adaptation

Graphics rendering in FLTK is conducted via an abstraction over the drawing backend, isolating application drawing calls from platform-dependent graphics subsystems. The toolkit originally employed software rendering through device contexts or pixel buffers exposed by the native APIs but has progressively incorporated leveraging hardware-accelerated backends as available.

On Windows, FLTK relies principally on the GDI (Graphics Device Interface) system to perform drawing into HWND device contexts. On X11 platforms, FLTK interfaces directly to Xlib drawing primitives, using GC (Graphics Context) objects, and may utilize shared memory extensions for performance. For modern Linux systems employing Wayland, FLTK leverages appropriate protocol implementations as available or falls back to XWayland compatibility.

On macOS, FLTK interacts with Quartz 2D and Core Graphics frameworks accessible through Cocoa, providing native anti-aliasing and compositing capabilities. The toolkit manages context creation and buffer flushing to accommodate macOS's compositor model.

This adaptive backend management extends to fonts, colors, and clip regions. Fonts are resolved using platform-native font subsystems, with mapping logic to select suitable font faces and sizes. Color management respects platform expectations for pixel formats and color depth, with conversions transparent to application layers.

Unified Widget Implementation with Platform Dependencies Encapsulated

Although FLTK provides a uniform API, certain widgets contain platform-specific optimizations or behavior adjustments within their implementations. This is handled by encapsulating platform dependencies inside widget methods or platform-specific subclasses, without exposing these differences in the public API.

For example, window decorations-title bars, resize handles, shadows-are either drawn manually or delegated to the native window manager depending on platform capabilities and user preference. FLTK allows toggling between native and custom decorations but in all cases ensures that the widget's API for window geometry and event handling is consistent.

Furthermore, the toolkit leverages platform-specific input method editors (IMEs) and accessibility APIs behind the scenes, transforming their idiosyncratic interfaces into a coherent set of signals that applications can consume without special coding.

Conditional Compilation and Build System Strategies

To manage cross-platform source code, FLTK extensively uses preprocessor directives to include or exclude platform-specific code chunks. The build system orchestrates the compilation of the appropriate source files and headers depending on target platform and compile-time options.

This conditional approach ensures minimal runtime overhead by excluding irrelevant code segments and promoting static linkage to native libraries. Optimizations such as function inlining and platform-specific calling conventions are preserved without compromising portability.

Source directories are organized by platform, and core platform-independent code is shared. The build configuration detects the operating system, compiler, and environment capabilities, enabling an adaptive compilation pathway. This modularity is pivotal for maintenance and scalability, enabling FLTK to support emerging systems and evolving native APIs.

Threading and Concurrency Model

FLTK's portability mechanisms extend to handling concurrency and threading differences between platforms. Given that not all supported systems manage GUI threading identically-for example, macOS requires drawing operations on the main thread-FLTK enforces an event loop threading model that avoids race conditions by design.

The toolkit encourages applications to perform all GUI interactions within the main thread, while background processing is delegated to auxiliary threads communicating via thread-safe message queues or callbacks. FLTK's internal locking primitives abstract platform threading APIs (such as Win32 Critical Sections, POSIX mutexes, or macOS dispatch queues) to provide a consistent concurrency interface.

This careful threading model preserves responsiveness and avoids deadlocks or inconsistent UI states across platforms.

Summary of Cross-Platform Mechanism Integration

In aggregate, FLTK's cross-platform portability mechanisms form a cohesive framework where:

- Abstract interfaces define the contract for system services such as windowing, events, and drawing.

- Backend implementations encapsulate platform-specific details through virtualized and conditional code paths.

- Event models are normalized, providing uniform input and window event semantics.

- Graphics operations adapt dynamically to differing device contexts and rendering subsystems.

- Widget behavior and window decorations integrate native platform features where beneficial but preserve API uniformity.

- Source code and build configurations leverage preprocessor directives and platform detection for selective inclusion.

34

- Threading and concurrency use cross-platform abstractions to ensure safe GUI operations.

This deliberate partitioning between interface and implementation allows FLTK to operate as a thin portability layer with minimal runtime overhead, yet extensive platform coverage. As a result, the toolkit empowers developers to maintain a single codebase with predictable behavior and appearance on Linux, Windows, and macOS, advancing the goal of write-once, deploy-everywhere in native application development.

Chapter 2

Comprehensive Guide to Widgets and Layout

Master the building blocks of FLTK interfaces by diving into its wide array of widgets and intelligent layout mechanisms. This chapter transforms abstraction into action, revealing how to assemble, customize, and sculpt interfaces that are both visually appealing and functionally robust. Whether you're crafting simple tools or complex interactive environments, understanding FLTK's widget and layout system unlocks expressive UI possibilities for all your applications.

2.1. Standard Widgets Deep Dive

The Fast Light Toolkit (FLTK) offers a compact yet powerful set of standard widgets designed to create responsive and visually consistent graphical user interfaces. These widgets form the building blocks for complex applications, affording developer control over appearance, behavior, and user interaction. The following detailed examination covers the fundamental elements: buttons, input fields, sliders, menus, and other frequently used widgets, elaborating on their core properties, event handling, and customization capabilities.

Buttons

The Fl_Button class serves as the foundation for clickable interface elements. It supports several visual styles, including normal, toggle, radio, and menu buttons, each providing distinctive interaction paradigms. Construction of a button requires specification of its position, size, and label, for example,

```
Fl_Button *btn = new Fl_Button(10, 10, 100, 30, "Click Me");
```

Core properties include value(), which for toggle and radio buttons reflects their current state (pressed or not), and callback(), a function pointer invoked on user activation. The set_down_color() method allows customization of the button's appearance when pressed, enhancing visual feedback.

Beyond the basics, Fl_Button supports text alignment with align(), enabling left, right, center, top, and bottom positioning of its label relative to the button frame. Flags are combined bitwise from FL_ALIGN_LEFT, FL_ALIGN_RIGHT, FL_ALIGN_TOP, and FL_ALIGN_BOTTOM. This permits sophisticated layout management without resorting to custom drawing.

Toggle behavior is enabled by assigning the button type via set_type(FL_TOGGLE_BUTTON). Radio buttons require grouping, facilitated through Fl_Group or by using the Fl_Radio_Button subclass. Explicit control over group exclusivity and initial active button streamlines interface state consistency.

Input Fields

Single-line text input is provided by Fl_Input, which supports typed text from the keyboard within an editable box. Parameters such as maximum character length can be set using max_size(), and input validation can be enforced by subclassing and overriding the handle() method or by connecting a callback to when() events.

For multi-line text, Fl_Multiline_Input and Fl_Text_Editor come into play, the former suited for simple textual data and the latter supporting syntax highlighting and selectable text features. These widgets inherit from Fl_Text_Display and internally manage the representation and editing of text buffers.

Input fields can toggle attributes like read-only mode via readonly(1) and display text alignment similarly to buttons using align(). Validation often involves attachment of user-defined callbacks on FL_WHEN_NOT_EMPTY, FL_WHEN_CHANGED, or FL_WHEN_ENTER_KEY triggers, making them reactive to user input changes.

Sliders

FLTK provides several slider classes, encapsulated by the abstract base Fl_Slider. Specializations include Fl_Hor_Slider, Fl_Vert_Slider, Fl_Dial, and Fl_Value_Slider. These control numeric input within a continuous or discrete range, ideal for configuration interfaces.

Sliders maintain minimum(), maximum(), and current value(), which can be set and retrieved programmatically. The resolution or step size, while not explicitly exposed, can be mimicked by processing slider events and snapping the value() to discrete increments.

Customization of sliders extends to the visual style through color attributes such as slider_color(), selection_color(), and color(). Tick marks and labels are rendered based on widget dimensions and properties but can be disabled if the interface demands minimalism.

Interaction with sliders is governed by their callbacks, typically triggered on FL_WHEN_CHANGED or FL_WHEN_RELEASE. The latter ensures that adjustments are only processed after user finalizes the selection, useful when underlying computations are resource-intensive.

Menus

The Fl_Menu_Bar widget presents a horizontal menu located traditionally at the top of an application window, supporting cascade menus and keyboard shortcuts. Menu items are defined through an array of Fl_Menu_Item structures or via the more convenient add() method with path strings specifying the hierarchical placement.

Menus categorically support labels, separators, checkable states, and radio groups. For example, a menu entry string might be specified as &File/&Open\tCtrl+O, indicating an underlined 'F' mnemonic in "File" and an "Open" command with a control key shortcut. This notation automates keyboard interaction, improving accessibility.

Context menus utilize popup() methods to display menus at arbitrary screen coordinates, responding to right-click or long-press events. Menu callbacks receive a pointer to the activated item, allowing precise determination of the user's choice.

The Fl_Choice and Fl_Menu_Button widgets provide dropdown menu interfaces for selecting a single item from a list, supporting both graphical and keyboard navigation. They extend menu behavior to embedded UI elements without commandeering screen menu space.

Additional Widgets

Fl_Check_Button and Fl_Radio_Button facilitate mutually independent and grouped toggle states, respectively. Both inherit from Fl_Button, preserving the general callback and labeling mechanisms while enforcing semantic behavior suitable to checkboxes and radio groups.

Progress indicators are handled by Fl_Progress and

Fl_Value_Input subclasses. The progress widget subclasses Fl_Widget directly and allows manual control over the fill level through value(). It supports both determinate and indeterminate progress indications, with configurable colors and minimum/maximum ranges.

Fl_Output serves to display non-editable text, ideal for status messages or computed output. It mirrors Fl_Input in visual presentation but disables user modification by default. This difference ensures that consistent font and alignment styling can be used without risking inadvertent input.

Scrollbar widgets, Fl_Scrollbar or embedded scrollbars within Fl_Group derived containers, provide intuitive vertical or horizontal navigation across larger content areas. Their properties include thumb size, value ranges, and callback routines responding to slider movement.

Customization and Event Handling

Each widget class inherits from Fl_Widget, gaining the ability to override input event handling through the handle() method. This is essential for advanced applications requiring modified user interaction or integration of novel behaviors.

Color schemes, fonts, and labels are highly configurable at the widget level. The color(), labelcolor(), labelfont(), and labelsize() methods allow visual tailoring that can harmonize the interface with corporate branding or enhance readability.

Tooltips, accessible via copy_label() or by using Fl_Tooltips, provide contextual help that appears on hover, improving usability without cluttering the interface. Tooltips are especially effective on widgets such as buttons and sliders with abstract or icon-only representations.

Moreover, FLTK widgets support explicit keyboard focus manipulation through take_focus() and related event codes, granting refined control over tab order and accessibility. This is fundamental in constructing user-centric applications compliant with usability standards.

Integration Strategies

Implementing responsive user interfaces with FLTK widgets involves structuring widget hierarchies within Fl_Group containers, controlling layout via manual positioning or external layout managers. Signal-slot connections between widgets through callbacks promote modular design, while widget-specific variables maintain state consistency.

Custom drawing is achievable via the draw() method, allowing developers to layer additional graphics atop standard widgets or to replace them with tailored renderings. However, maintaining standard widget ergonomics is advisable unless necessary to preserve application usability.

Interaction between widgets is often mediated by shared data models or controllers external to the widgets themselves, which synchronize inputs and outputs. This separation encourages a clean architecture supporting testing and extension.

Through careful use of the described properties, event facilities, and customization techniques, FLTK's standard widgets empower developers to craft applications that are both performant and user-friendly, striking a balance between simplicity and sophisticated control.

2.2. Complex Container Hierarchies

Effective construction of sophisticated user interfaces demands a comprehensive understanding of container widgets-primarily group, pack, and tab widgets-that enable modular, maintainable, and logically organized layouts. These widgets serve as structural

42

elements that orchestrate child components, enforce spatial relationships, and govern the overall behavior of the interface. Mastery of nested layouts and containment hierarchies is foundational for UI architectures that scale in complexity while maintaining clarity.

Group widgets provide an essential mechanism for logically partitioning the interface into related subsections. Typically, a group widget acts as a container that visually and functionally encapsulates its children. This encapsulation enhances semantic clarity and visual grouping by drawing bounding boxes or applying background styles, which guide users through the spatial organization at a glance.

When designing with group widgets, the primary considerations involve the appropriate scope and granularity of each group. Groups that are too granular may introduce unnecessary nesting that complicates the layout, while overly coarse groups risk diluting contextual relevance.

From an architectural perspective, group widgets simplify event propagation and state management. Events originating from child widgets can bubble up to their respective group container, allowing centralized handling when applicable. Likewise, groups can maintain collective state information reflecting the status of the contained widgets, enabling higher-level logic such as enabling or disabling an entire group conditionally.

Pack widgets function as versatile layout managers that organize their children in a sequential manner-either horizontally, vertically, or some combination thereof-based on packing parameters. Unlike absolute positioning, pack widgets allow dynamic resizing and reflowing of contained widgets when the parent dimensions change or when the interface adapts between form factors.

Efficient use of pack widgets requires insight into the packing algorithms and parameterization. Common parameters include:

- *Expand*: whether a child should consume any extra space available.

- *Fill*: whether a child should stretch to fill the allocated space.

- *Padding and margins*: fine-tune spacing between children and edges.

A core capability of pack widgets is their recursive composability. A pack widget may contain either terminal widgets or other pack widgets, enabling deeply nested, flexible layouts. This composability allows designers to interleave vertical and horizontal packing strategies to achieve grid-like or asymmetric layouts without direct coordinate management.

One must carefully balance flexibility and predictability when applying pack nesting. Overly deep hierarchies can incur performance penalties and debugging complexity, whereas insufficient nesting may necessitate manual adjustments elsewhere.

Tab widgets partition the interface into discrete panels accessible via a tabbed navigation mechanism. Each tab corresponds to a dedicated content pane, facilitating contextual switching without cluttering the display area. Tabs efficiently organize multi-view interfaces common in settings dialogs, editors, and data entry applications.

Implementation of tab widgets includes managing the active tab index, rendering tab headers, and associating each tab with its content widget tree. Internally, the tab container ensures that only the active tab pane is rendered and interactive, optimizing resource consumption.

Tabbed containers may themselves be nested within other container widgets, supporting complex multilayered interfaces. This capability enables scenarios such as tabs embedded within grouped sections or pack-driven sidebars containing tab sets.

Combining group, pack, and tab widgets requires meticulous planning to construct maintainable nested hierarchies that fulfill functional and aesthetic criteria. The general approach involves:

1. Defining high-level sections via group widgets, each encapsulating a major domain of interface elements.

2. Within groups, applying pack widgets to arrange components in sequences, respecting flow orientation and adaptive behavior.

3. Integrating tab widgets at appropriate points to isolate alternate views or modes without expanding screen real estate.

Consider a user interface composed of a master-detail data view with adjustable settings. The top-level container may be a horizontal pack widget splitting the window into a navigation pane and a detail pane. The navigation pane itself may be a tab widget with tabs correlating to different data categories. Each tab contains a group widget with settings grouped by common themes. Inside these groups, vertical pack widgets organize input forms.

Such a nested structure benefits from clear naming and encapsulation strategies. Assigning meaningful identifiers to containers facilitates programmatic access and event binding. Adhering to consistent layout conventions within and across groups streamlines visual coherence.

Parent-child relationships in container hierarchies govern ownership, event routing, rendering order, and lifecycle management. A container widget acts as the logical parent for its direct child widgets, imposing spatial constraints and coordinating input focus.

Accurate management of these relationships is critical in complex nested UIs. For instance, the destruction of a parent container automatically cascades to child widgets, ensuring memory and resource cleanliness. Conversely, adding or removing children dynamically requires the parent to re-adjust layout and repaint accordingly.

Event propagation typically flows from child to parent, allowing parent containers to intercept or augment event handling. This model supports use cases such as container-wide keyboard shortcuts or validation that depends on multiple child states.

Effective containment strategies in UI layout design contribute to code modularity, ease of maintenance, and performance. Several best practices emerge:

- Minimize unnecessary nesting by grouping logically related widgets while avoiding redundant containers.

- Use pack widget expansions judiciously to prevent unintended resizing and maintain interface stability.

- Defer heavy computation or complex rendering tasks within hidden tabs until they become active, reducing startup overhead.

- Leverage group widgets to encapsulate input validation scopes and state synchronization, simplifying event logic.

The choice of container widgets impacts not only layout but also rendering performance. Deep container trees may introduce cost in layout recalculation and repaints. Profiling the interface with representative workflows can reveal bottlenecks caused by container nesting.

```
# Create the main horizontal split container
main_pack = PackWidget(orientation='horizontal')

# Left navigation pane - tab widget with category tabs
nav_tabs = TabWidget()

# Tab 1: User Settings, containing grouped inputs packed
    vertically
tab_user_settings = GroupWidget(title="User Settings")
user_settings_pack = PackWidget(orientation='vertical')
```

```
user_settings_pack.add_child(TextInput(label="Username"))
user_settings_pack.add_child(Checkbox(label="Enable notifications
    "))
tab_user_settings.add_child(user_settings_pack)
nav_tabs.add_tab("User", tab_user_settings)

# Tab 2: System Settings, with grouped sections
tab_system_settings = GroupWidget(title="System Settings")
network_group = GroupWidget(title="Network")
network_pack = PackWidget(orientation='vertical')
network_pack.add_child(TextInput(label="Hostname"))
network_pack.add_child(TextInput(label="IP Address"))
network_group.add_child(network_pack)
tab_system_settings.add_child(network_group)
nav_tabs.add_tab("System", tab_system_settings)

# Add navigation tabs to left pane
main_pack.add_child(nav_tabs)

# Right detail pane - group with pack layout
detail_group = GroupWidget(title="Details")
detail_pack = PackWidget(orientation='vertical')
detail_pack.add_child(Label(text="Detail View"))
detail_group.add_child(detail_pack)
main_pack.add_child(detail_group)

# Set main container as root widget
root_widget = main_pack
```

```
# Expected visual layout description:

-----------------------------------------------
|          |                                   |
| Tabs     |           Details View            |
|          |                                   |
|----------|-----------------------------------|
| User     | Username: [____]                  |
| System   | Enable notifications []           |
|          | Network:                          |
|          | Hostname: [_____]                 |
|          | IP Address: [_____]               |
-----------------------------------------------
```

This snippet exemplifies a balanced use of container widgets: a horizontal pack for primary division, tab widgets for categorical navigation, group widgets for logical sections, and nested vertical packs for sequential layout. Each container preserves scope, layout properties, and functional clarity.

The interplay between group, pack, and tab widgets enables flexible, scalable interface designs. Key principles for leveraging complex container hierarchies include:

- Mapping UI semantics into container structures, promoting meaningful grouping with group widgets.

- Employing pack widgets for dynamic, orientation-aware layout management that responds gracefully to resizing.

- Utilizing tab widgets to segment interface real estate into manageable, context-specific panels.

- Structuring container hierarchies that reflect both visual and programmatic parent-child relationships, facilitating maintainability.

- Balancing containment depth to optimize resource use and user experience.

Applying these principles systematically fosters interfaces able to accommodate expanding functional requirements without compromising usability or architectural integrity.

2.3. Dynamic Layout Management

The Fast Light Toolkit (FLTK) provides a flexible layout system designed to accommodate the dynamic nature of modern graphical user interfaces (GUIs), where windows may be resized or their content changed at runtime. This capability is essential in creating adaptive, scalable applications that function seamlessly across diverse platforms, ranging from desktop environments with abundant display space to embedded systems with stringent resource constraints.

At the core of FLTK's dynamic layout management are automatic resizing behaviors, widget alignment strategies, and adaptive design principles that respond fluidly to window size changes. These mechanisms enable developers to construct interfaces that maintain proportionality, preserve margins, and adjust widget dimensions without resorting to static, pixel-based layouts.

FLTK employs a hierarchical widget structure where containers organize child widgets and manage their geometry. The primary containers relevant to dynamic layouts include Fl_Group, Fl_Pack, and Fl_Flex. Each container type contributes distinct behaviors for resizing and arrangement.

Fl_Group serves as the base container, organizing child widgets in a fixed region. By default, Fl_Group does not impose automatic resizing; child widgets must be manually sized or repositioned in response to window events. This functional simplicity allows for precise control when needed but requires extra code to achieve responsive interfaces.

Fl_Pack, a subclass of Fl_Group, simplifies layout by automatically stacking child widgets either horizontally or vertically based on its constructor parameters. It adjusts the position and size of children to fit within the group's area, optionally distributing extra space evenly or proportionally. The Fl_Pack container adapts readily to resizing in one dimension, making it ideal for toolbars, button arrays, and similar UI sections.

More sophisticated layout capabilities are provided by Fl_Flex, introduced in recent FLTK versions. Fl_Flex supports complex, nested layouts with flexible sizing policies for each child widget, including fixed size, proportional size, and minimum or maximum constraints. By exposing an API for specifying expansion weights and alignment modes, Fl_Flex enables developers to declare layouts that recalibrate smoothly when the parent window resizes.

Within these containers, widget alignment defines how

individual components are positioned relative to each other and the group's boundaries. FLTK supports alignment flags such as FL_ALIGN_LEFT, FL_ALIGN_RIGHT, FL_ALIGN_TOP, and FL_ALIGN_BOTTOM, which control the placement of widget content (e.g., labels, images). Proper use of alignment flags ensures visual harmony and can prevent artifacts such as truncated text or overlapping widgets during resizes.

Margin and spacing management plays a vital role in layout aesthetics and usability. FLTK container classes often provide interface methods to set padding between widgets and from widgets to container edges. For example, Fl_Pack supports the spacing() method to globally define uniform gaps between children, while Fl_Flex allows variable spacing on a per-child basis. Adapting margins responsively may require custom resizing code when using base containers; however, Fl_Flex can dynamically allocate space to margins in proportion to the layout's needs.

An essential objective in scalable UI design is to maintain component proportions relative to one another and to the available window area. FLTK facilitates this through weight-based sizing in flexible containers, where each widget can be assigned an expansion weight-a numeric value indicating the proportion of extra space that the widget may absorb during expansion.

Weights are particularly useful in scenarios such as split panes, where two or more areas divide the window horizontally or vertically. Adjusting expansion weights allows one pane to expand more than the other, preserving the relative importance of widgets while accommodating user-initiated resizing. The Fl_Flex interface supports these features with functions such as set_size_policy().

When fixed-size widgets coexist with expandable widgets, the layout manager respects fixed dimensions while distributing remaining space according to weights among resizable widgets. This behavior ensures stable UI elements like text fields or buttons remain legible and usable, even as surrounding panels resize.

Distinct display characteristics and resource availability in desktop versus embedded environments impact layout decisions. Desktop applications typically benefit from greater screen real estate, higher resolutions, and varied aspect ratios, which call for flexible, content-rich interfaces with adjustable toolbars, resizable dialogs, and multi-pane views.

Embedded systems, conversely, frequently impose strict constraints on display size, color depth, and CPU efficiency. Dynamic layout strategies become critical to optimize usability without compromising performance or clarity. Minimalist designs with clear margins and larger, purpose-built controls improve interaction quality on small touchscreens or low-resolution displays.

In both contexts, FLTK's lightweight design and responsive layout containers facilitate adaptive UIs. Leveraging Fl_Flex with appropriate expansion weights and margin settings allows interfaces to scale elegantly from compact embedded panels to expansive desktop windows.

Consider a common use case of constructing a data entry form that is both compact and scales gracefully with window resizing. Using Fl_Flex allows organizing label-input pairs in a structured grid with horizontally-resizing input fields and fixed-width labels.

```
#include <FL/Fl.H>
#include <FL/Fl_Window.H>
#include <FL/Fl_Flex.H>
#include <FL/Fl_Input.H>
#include <FL/Fl_Box.H>

int main(int argc, char **argv) {
    Fl_Window *window = new Fl_Window(400, 200, "Responsive Form
    ");

    Fl_Flex *flex = new Fl_Flex(10, 10, 380, 180);
    flex->horizontal(false); // Vertical stacking

    // Label - fixed width
    Fl_Box *label1 = new Fl_Box(0, 0, 80, 25, "Username:");
```

```
label1->align(FL_ALIGN_RIGHT | FL_ALIGN_INSIDE);

// Input - expandable
Fl_Input *input1 = new Fl_Input(0, 0, 100, 25);
input1->set_size_policy(Fl_Flex::EXPAND, Fl_Flex::FIXED);

// Label - fixed width
Fl_Box *label2 = new Fl_Box(0, 0, 80, 25, "Password:");
label2->align(FL_ALIGN_RIGHT | FL_ALIGN_INSIDE);

// Input - expandable
Fl_Input *input2 = new Fl_Input(0, 0, 100, 25);
input2->set_size_policy(Fl_Flex::EXPAND, Fl_Flex::FIXED);

flex->end();
window->end();
window->show(argc, argv);

return Fl::run();
}
```

The above example employs vertical stacking of horizontal pairs. Labels maintain fixed width and right alignment, ensuring consistent presentation, while input fields expand horizontally to occupy available space. This pattern adjusts seamlessly as the window widens or narrows, preserving usability and aesthetic balance.

Margins between the window border and contained widgets, as well as spacing between widgets themselves, influence readability and touch target size. Fl_Flex widgets include methods such as set_margin() and set_spacing() to finely tune these parameters.

```
flex->set_margin(10);    // Uniform margin of 10 pixels around
    all edges
flex->set_spacing(8);    // 8 pixels between child widgets
```

To achieve asymmetrical margins or non-uniform spacing-often required by branding or design constraints-a nested hierarchy of Fl_Flex containers may be deployed, each with tailored margin and spacing settings. This approach enables modular adjustment without complicating the global layout logic.

Although FLTK's container classes automate substantial layout recalculations, some scenarios require explicit handling of resize

52

events to accommodate custom behavior. This is often true when embedding OpenGL widgets or complex custom widgets where layout dependencies extend beyond simple container hierarchies.

Overriding the `resize()` method of a widget or window provides direct access to new dimensions after a resize and allows recalculation of child locations or internal rendering parameters. An exemplary override might look as follows:

```
void MyWindow::resize(int x, int y, int w, int h) {
    Fl_Window::resize(x, y, w, h);

    // Adjust child widget sizes manually if necessary
    child1->resize(x+margin_left, y+margin_top, w - margin_left -
      margin_right, fixed_height);
    child2->resize(...);

    // Trigger redraw or other updates as needed
    redraw();
}
```

While such manual intervention offers maximum flexibility, overuse may reduce maintainability. Prefer container-based strategies when possible due to their declarative and error-resistant nature.

In embedded systems, it may be necessary to limit layout complexity to ensure smooth rendering and responsiveness. Reducing the number of nested containers, minimizing continuous resize calculations, and simplifying spacing and alignment logic can all contribute to more efficient execution.

Profiling layout update times and monitoring memory usage during resize events help identify costly operations. FLTK's lightweight architecture suits these platforms, but prudent design choices enhance its benefits further, balancing visual adaptability with resource constraints.

Dynamic layout management in FLTK hinges on selecting appropriate container classes, utilizing expansion weights judiciously, and applying alignment and margin controls to maintain proportionality and visual balance. Employing `Fl_Flex` whenever complex, responsive behavior is needed streamlines development and enhances cross-platform adaptability.

Explicit resize event handling should be reserved for specialized widgets or when layout logic exceeds container capabilities. Awareness of platform-specific constraints ensures that adaptive designs retain both performance and usability across diverse deployment targets.

Through careful application of these principles, FLTK enables creation of user interfaces that respond gracefully to window dimension changes, enhancing user experience and interface robustness in a variety of technical contexts.

2.4. Custom Widgets Construction

The construction of custom widgets is a foundational skill for creating user interfaces that are both highly functional and visually distinctive. This process involves either building widgets entirely from scratch or extending existing built-in components. Mastery of the principles of inheritance and composition, together with disciplined encapsulation of logic and appearance, empowers developers to produce reusable, maintainable, and tailored UI elements suited to complex application requirements.

At the core of custom widget design lies the concept of *inheritance*, which facilitates the creation of new widget classes by deriving from established ones. Inheritance allows leveraging existing behavior and appearance while introducing new functionalities or modifying defaults. For instance, a base button class can be extended to form a toggle button widget by overriding event handlers and maintaining custom state variables that track toggled status. The derived widget class automatically inherits core button functionalities, including rendering and input handling, reducing redundancy.

Inheritance demands careful consideration of the widget lifecycle and event propagation mechanisms. Overriding key methods such as initialization, rendering, and input event callbacks must maintain consistent invocation of superclass implementations where appropriate, to avoid breaking fundamental widget behaviors. The following illustrative pseudocode fragment summarizes a typical inheritance pattern inheriting from a base widget:

```
class CustomWidget : public BaseWidget {
public:
    CustomWidget() {
        // Custom initialization
    }

    // Override paint method to customize appearance
    void paintEvent(PaintEvent *event) override {
        BaseWidget::paintEvent(event); // preserve base painting
        // Additional painting code here
    }

    // Override input handler to add custom logic
    void mousePressEvent(MouseEvent *event) override {
        if (/* custom condition */) {
            // Custom handling
        } else {
            BaseWidget::mousePressEvent(event); // delegate to
    base
        }
    }
};
```

Beyond inheritance, *composition* is an essential design strategy that promotes creating complex widgets through the assembly of simpler ones. Composition encapsulates smaller widgets as member variables or child components within a higher-level custom widget, coordinating their orchestration to achieve desired functionality. This approach enhances modularity and separation of concerns, as each subcomponent can be independently developed, tested, and reused across different composite widgets.

An example of composition is constructing a custom dialog widget that internally contains multiple pre-existing widgets such as labels, text fields, and buttons arranged using layouts. Here, the dialog delegates specific responsibilities like text input and button interactions to its subwidgets, while managing the communication and data flow between them internally. This clear partition of functionality mitigates complexity and improves maintainability.

Combining inheritance and composition often yields the most effective widget implementations. Inherited base classes provide a solid foundation of behavior and look-and-feel, while internally composed subwidgets fulfill specialized roles. This hybrid approach allows the encapsulation of distinct concerns at multiple levels of abstraction.

Effective custom widgets must isolate internal logic and presentation details from external usage, adhering to the principles of encapsulation. This separation fosters resilience against changes and simplifies integration in larger applications.

Encapsulation begins with defining public interfaces that expose only the minimal set of methods and properties needed for interaction. Internal state variables, helper functions, and implementation details are kept private or protected, preventing accidental misuse or dependency on fragile internals. For example, a custom progress bar widget should provide only methods to set progress values and configure appearance parameters, while how it translates these into rendered visuals remains hidden.

The appearance of custom widgets is encapsulated by implementing custom painting routines or leveraging style sheets and theming mechanisms. Painting should be deterministic and stateless with respect to the widget's rendering context, enabling consistent results across various device pixel densities and rendering backends. Common practice involves overriding low-level paint or draw events and utilizing dedicated graphics APIs or frameworks' painting abstractions.

Separation between logic and UI rendering simplifies both testing and future modifications. Business logic, state management, and event processing should be independent from graphical operations. This can be achieved by introducing model or controller classes that manage widget state and behavior, while the widget itself remains a thin view layer translating state into appearance.

```
// Example illustrating separation between logic and appearance
class LogicController {
    int progressValue;
public:
    void setProgress(int value) { progressValue = value; }
    int getProgress() const { return progressValue; }
};

class ProgressBarWidget : public Widget {
    LogicController controller;
public:
    void setProgress(int value) {
        controller.setProgress(value);
        update(); // trigger repaint
    }

    void paintEvent(PaintEvent *event) override {
        QPainter painter(this);
        int p = controller.getProgress();

        // Draw progress bar background
        painter.fillRect(rect(), Qt::gray);

        // Draw progress indicator
        int width = rect().width() * p / 100;
        painter.fillRect(0, 0, width, rect().height(), Qt::blue);
    }
};
```

Several best practices govern the construction of robust and reusable custom widgets:

- **Minimal Coupling and High Cohesion**: Widgets should encapsulate logically related responsibilities while minimizing dependencies on external components. Loose coupling reduces ripple effects of changes.

- **Clear Public API**: Define and document a precise public interface that exposes all necessary functionalities without revealing internal details. Consistent naming conventions and argument semantics enhance usability.

- **Respect Widget Lifecycle**: Properly manage initialization, resource allocation, and cleanup procedures to prevent leaks and undefined states. Leverage constructors, destructors, and event hooks systematically.

- **State Management**: Maintain internal states with thread safety and synchronization if needed. Encapsulate states behind accessors to control mutation and invariant preservation.

- **Accessibility Considerations**: Integrate support for keyboard navigation, screen readers, and other assistive technologies intrinsically within the widget logic.

- **Performance Optimization**: Optimize rendering paths, minimize repaints, and defer expensive calculations without sacrificing correctness.

- **Testing and Validation**: Provide comprehensive unit tests targeting both public API and internal states where accessible, to ensure reliability across varying inputs and edge cases.

Complex widgets often benefit from employing advanced composition strategies such as event delegation, property bindings, and the use of intermediate controllers or managers to coordinate communications among child widgets.

Event delegation centralizes event handling logic by forwarding or intercepting input events from subwidgets to designated handlers in the composite widget. This avoids scattering event processing code and simplifies debugging.

Property binding allows automatic synchronization of attributes between different widgets or between the widget and underlying data models. Reactive frameworks often provide signal-slot or observer pattern implementations facilitating this mechanism.

Controller components or mediator classes act as intermediaries managing the interaction logic among widget parts. By decoupling communication from visual components, these controllers enhance modularity and accommodate dynamic reconfiguration of widget composition.

Consider a composite widget designed to allow users to select colors via multiple input modalities: RGB sliders, a color wheel, and a hexadecimal input box. Each modality is implemented as a separate widget subclass, exposing a signal or callback upon changes.

The composite widget encapsulates these subwidgets, synchronizing their states to maintain color consistency. It employs a controller object that listens to changes from each subwidget, computes the unified color representation, and updates all inputs accordingly.

The rough structure can be outlined as:

```
class RGBSliderWidget : public Widget { /* emits rgbChanged(r, g,
    b) */ };
class ColorWheelWidget : public Widget { /* emits colorChanged(
    color) */ };
class HexInputWidget : public Widget { /* emits hexChanged(hex)
    */ };

class ColorPickerWidget : public Widget {
    RGBSliderWidget rgbSliders;
    ColorWheelWidget colorWheel;
    HexInputWidget hexInput;
    QColor currentColor;

    void setupConnections() {
        connect(&rgbSliders, &RGBSliderWidget::rgbChanged,
                this, &ColorPickerWidget::onRGBChanged);
        connect(&colorWheel, &ColorWheelWidget::colorChanged,
                this, &ColorPickerWidget::onColorWheelChanged);
        connect(&hexInput, &HexInputWidget::hexChanged,
                this, &ColorPickerWidget::onHexChanged);
    }

    void onRGBChanged(int r, int g, int b) {
        currentColor = QColor(r, g, b);
        updateInputs();
    }
```

```
void onColorWheelChanged(QColor color) {
    currentColor = color;
    updateInputs();
}

void onHexChanged(QString hex) {
    currentColor = QColor(hex);
    updateInputs();
}

void updateInputs() {
    // Update all subwidgets without triggering recursive
   signals
}
};
```

This example illustrates how inheritance provides specialized sub-widgets, while composition creates a sophisticated interface. The controller pattern mediates state synchronization and event coordination, encapsulated within the composite widget.

The design and construction of custom widgets require rigorous application of object-oriented principles such as inheritance and composition, combined with disciplined encapsulation. By thoughtfully structuring widget internals and their interactions, engineers can craft UI components that not only fit exact application specifications but also remain robust, extensible, and performant. The adherence to best practices in interface design, lifecycle management, and separation of concerns is essential to successful widget engineering and long-term maintainability.

2.5. Visual Themability and Styling

Modern software applications often require extensive customization of their visual appearance to align with brand identity, user preferences, or contextual requirements. Achieving a balance between rich themability and maintaining efficiency, cross-platform consistency, and maintainability remains a critical engineering challenge. This section explores advanced strategies for designing visual themability through appearance overrides, skinning techniques, and integration with style libraries, enabling the creation of visually distinct applications without compromising performance or portability.

Appearance overrides represent a fundamental mechanism for modifying the visual representation of user interface (UI) elements without altering underlying functional logic. Overrides enable developers to selectively redefine visual properties such as colors, fonts, borders, and layout margins on a component-by-component basis or globally, thereby facilitating flexible theming.

In large-scale systems employing appearance overrides, it is essential to establish a hierarchical model of cascading styles reminiscent of CSS, but adapted to native rendering pipelines. This hierarchical approach allows overriding styles at varying levels of specificity-for example, global application-wide themes, container-level styles, or individual widget adjustments.

A robust appearance override system typically includes:

- **Property Inheritance:** Visual attributes cascade from parent containers to child components unless explicitly overridden. This ensures consistency and minimizes redundancy.

- **Dynamic Resolution:** Overrides can be resolved at runtime, supporting dynamic theme switching without recompilation or restart.

- **Context Awareness:** Styles can adapt based on interaction states (e.g., hover, pressed, disabled), system settings (e.g., dark mode), or platform conventions.

- **Fallbacks and Defaults:** Mechanisms to gracefully degrade to default styles when specific overrides are absent.

Implementing efficient appearance overrides requires maintaining a style resolution cache or dependency graph to minimize re-computation during UI rendering cycles. This optimization is especially crucial in high-frame-rate, resource-constrained environments.

Skinning represents an advanced themability technique wherein the entire visual appearance of an application or component is redefined through the application of a cohesive set of graphical assets and style rules. Unlike isolated appearance overrides, skinning addresses the full spectrum of UI visuals, including backgrounds, controls, icons, animations, and layout metrics.

Key skinning approaches include:

- **Image-Based Skins:** Employ bitmap graphics or vector assets to style UI elements, allowing for rich textures, gradients, and unique artistic styles. However, this approach can introduce challenges related to scaling across device resolutions and maintaining performance.

- **Programmatic Skins:** Use code-driven rendering (e.g., vector drawing commands, shader programs) to create scalable and resolution-independent skins. This technique offers improved adaptability but requires more intricate development and testing.

- **Hybrid Skins:** Combine static assets with dynamic rendering to balance visual richness and efficiency.

Within a skinning framework, architectures often separate the skin definition from the core UI logic through interfaces or skin managers. This separation allows skins to be loaded, switched, or customized without recompilation, greatly enhancing flexibility.

An example of a skin definition schema might include:

```
// Skin description pseudo-code
Skin BlueOcean {
    BackgroundColor: #002F4B;
    Button {
        Normal: texture("button_normal.png");
```

```
        Hover: texture("button_hover.png");
        Pressed: texture("button_pressed.png");
        BorderRadius: 6px;
        FontColor: #FFFFFF;
    }
    ScrollBar {
        TrackColor: #004A7C;
        ThumbColor: #007ACC;
        Width: 14px;
    }
}
```

Efficient rendering pipelines within skinning frameworks optimize the rasterization of vector and image assets, employ caching, and selectively update only changed areas to maintain responsiveness.

Relying on native style libraries and UI frameworks is a strategic choice to achieve consistent themability across multiple platforms. Integration with these style libraries leverages their inherent support for platform-appropriate rendering, system-level theme adaptation (e.g., dark/light modes), and accessibility compliance.

Advanced integration strategies encompass:

- **Style Wrapping:** Abstracting native style APIs behind a unified interface, allowing for platform-specific style invocation while presenting a homogeneous theming layer to application code.

- **Style Synchronization:** Detecting and synchronizing with system-wide theme changes to adapt application appearance dynamically.

- **Augmented Styling:** Layering custom skins or appearance overrides on top of native style elements to enrich or alter default visuals without losing native look and feel.

Consider the example of integrating with a cross-platform GUI toolkit that exposes native widgets but supports style injection:

```
auto button = new NativeButton();
```

```
button->setStyleSheet(
    "NativeButton {"
    "  background-color: palette(highlight);"
    "  border-radius: 8px;"
    "  color: palette(text);"
    "}"
    "NativeButton:hover {"
    "  background-color: palette(highlight).lighter(120);"
    "}"
);
```

Here, the local palette variables adapt to the host environment, maintaining consistency with system settings. Furthermore, style sheets can define custom overrides layered upon native elements.

Achieving visually distinct applications while preserving system performance necessitates careful design choices:

- **Minimize Overdraw:** Optimize rendering paths to reduce redundant painting operations, a common pitfall when applying complex skins or multiple layered overrides.

- **Asset Optimization:** Leverage vector assets where possible for resolution independence and lower memory footprint; compress and cache bitmap images efficiently.

- **Lazy Evaluation:** Defer or batch visual updates triggered by style changes to avoid frequent re-layouts and repaints.

- **Responsive Scaling:** Design skins and overrides with adaptable layout frameworks to gracefully handle different device resolutions and aspect ratios.

Profiling tools specialized in UI rendering can identify bottlenecks introduced by theming mechanisms, enabling targeted optimizations. Memory usage should also be analyzed, particularly in applications employing multiple active skins or dynamic theme switching.

Complex themability pipelines must incorporate architecture

patterns that support extensibility and maintainability. Recommended practices include:

- **Modular Style Definitions:** Segment style and skin resources into reusable modules, allowing teams to update or replace themes independently.

- **Versioning and Compatibility:** Maintain version metadata for skins and style libraries, supporting backwards compatibility and incremental rollout.

- **Declarative Styling Formats:** Use declarative stylesheets or markup (e.g., JSON, XML, or domain-specific languages) over hard-coded style logic to improve clarity and facilitate tooling.

- **Automated Testing:** Deploy visual regression testing frameworks to catch unintended changes in appearance after style updates.

The use of themability frameworks that expose clear APIs for querying, modifying, and persisting style states ensures that appearance customization remains a well-defined and controlled procedure within the software lifecycle.

The combination of appearance overrides, sophisticated skinning methodologies, and seamless integration with native style libraries enables the construction of visually distinct, efficient, and consistent applications. Hierarchical style management systems underpin flexible overrides, skinning facilitates comprehensive look-and-feel transformations, and platform-aware style integrations sustain cross-platform consistency. Balancing these elements with performance considerations and maintainability practices ensures themability solutions remain robust under evolving application requirements and platforms.

2.6. Widget Accessibility and Internationalization

Modern user interface widgets must be designed to accommodate the broadest possible audience, ensuring usability across diverse abilities and linguistic backgrounds. Accessibility and internationalization are intrinsic to this objective. This section delves into critical techniques and standards—ARIA attributes, keyboard navigation, high-contrast accommodations, localization mechanisms, and right-to-left language support—that collectively contribute to universally usable and globally relevant widget implementations.

Accessible Rich Internet Applications (ARIA) Support

ARIA, defined by the W3C, specifies a set of attributes to enhance the semantic information available to assistive technologies, enabling non-HTML5 widgets or complex UI components to expose their roles, states, and properties clearly. ARIA roles such as `button`, `checkbox`, `dialog`, and `tabpanel` provide screen readers with the necessary context to interpret widget purpose correctly. The use of `aria-live` regions becomes essential for dynamic content updates, ensuring that changes are promptly communicated to users relying on screen readers.

Effective ARIA implementation requires meticulous management, avoiding redundancy with native HTML semantics, since excessive or incorrect ARIA can degrade accessibility rather than improve it. For example, native `<button>` elements inherently provide necessary semantics, so overwriting them with ARIA roles is unnecessary and may confuse assistive technologies.

Consider the following ARIA example for a custom toggle button:

```
<div role="button" tabindex="0" aria-pressed="false" id="
    toggleBtn">
  Show Details
</div>
```

66

In this example, `role="button"` identifies the widget as a button, `tabindex="0"` makes it keyboard-focusable, and `aria-pressed` reflects the toggle state. JavaScript logic should dynamically update `aria-pressed` on interaction to convey state changes.

Keyboard Navigation Considerations

Keyboards remain the primary input modality for many users, including those with motor disabilities or preferences for non-pointer devices. Widgets must therefore provide comprehensive keyboard operability. This includes making widgets reachable via the `Tab` key, maintaining logical focus order, and clearly defined keyboard interactions.

A consistent tab order is critical; the logical flow should match the visual presentation and interaction sequence. For composite widgets-such as menus, tabs, and accordions-additional keyboard controls include arrow keys, `Space`, `Enter`, and `Escape` to activate elements, move focus, or dismiss overlays.

Example keyboard interaction for a tab widget may include:

- `Tab` and `Shift+Tab`: Move among interactive elements outside the tab list.
- `Arrow Left/Right`: Navigate between tabs, moving focus and activating tab panels.
- `Home` and `End`: Jump to the first and last tab respectively.

Implementing keyboard navigation requires careful event handling and focus management. The widget must prevent pointer-only functionality and ensure all actions are performable via keys alone.

High-Contrast and Visual Adaptations

High-contrast modes are vital for users with low vision or color perception deficiencies. Widget designs must provide sufficient contrast ratios according to WCAG guidelines, typically a minimum of 4.5:1 for normal text and 3:1 for large text. Colors used for text, icons, and controls demand careful selection.

In addition to color contrast, many platforms support user-applied high-contrast themes, which may override default styles. Widgets should not compromise functional or visual clarity under such conditions. Use of system colors or CSS media queries (e.g., `@media` (`forced-colors: active`)) allows detection and adaptation to these forced high-contrast modes.

An example CSS snippet enabling high-contrast adaptation:

```
@media (forced-colors: active) {
  .widget {
    background-color: Highlight;
    color: HighlightText;
    border: 2px solid ButtonText;
  }
}
```

Moreover, widgets should avoid relying solely on color to convey information. Supplementing color cues with shapes, text labels, or patterns preserves meaning for color-blind users.

Localization and Text Internationalization

Localization is the process of adapting widgets for target languages, regions, and cultures, extending beyond simple text translation to encompass date formats, number formats, and culturally appropriate icons or UI metaphors.

Text strings embedded in widgets must be externalized for translation. Dynamic insertion of localized strings should preserve markup integrity and accommodate text expansion or contraction, which can impact layout and element sizing significantly. Employing Unicode throughout ensures consistent character rendering.

Integration with localization frameworks or libraries can be achieved via resource files (e.g., JSON, XML, PO files) with keys and translations. The widget code dynamically loads appropriate strings based on the user's locale.

Handling pluralization and gender, which vary widely among languages, often requires complex ICU MessageFormat or equivalent constructs to deliver grammatically correct strings dynamically.

Right-to-Left (RTL) Language Support

Supporting RTL languages such as Arabic, Hebrew, and Persian involves mirroring the user interface layout and directional flow. Widgets must respond appropriately to the `dir="rtl"` attribute at the document or component level, adapting visual alignment, iconography orientation, and control behavior.

Key transformations include:

- Flipping horizontal positioning-for example, aligning tabs to the right side instead of left.

- Reversing the order of items in lists or menus when indicated by locale.

- Adjusting padding and margin to maintain consistent visual rhythm.

- Mirroring directional icons, such as arrows pointing left instead of right, to maintain semantic clarity.

CSS logical properties such as `margin-inline-start` and `padding-inline-end` facilitate direction-aware styling without manual overrides, greatly simplifying RTL support. Additionally, JavaScript-driven layout calculations must be direction-sensitive, applying coordinate transformations as needed.

A code example demonstrating RTL-aware style using logical properties:

```
.widget {
  margin-inline-start: 1em;  /* Left margin in LTR, right margin
    in RTL */
```

```
padding-inline-end: 0.5em; /* Right padding in LTR, left
    padding in RTL */
}
```

Integration of Accessibility and Internationalization Strategies

Achieving a truly global and accessible widget requires integrating accessibility and internationalization considerations from the outset. Localization frameworks should support accessibility metadata translations, including ARIA labels and descriptions. Dynamic changes in text direction or language should trigger updates to ARIA attributes and keyboard navigation logic as needed.

Automated testing tools, including screen readers and accessibility analyzers, must be employed to validate proper functionality across assistive technologies and locales. Testing in high-contrast modes and RTL layouts uncovers issues early in the design process.

Ultimately, accessible and internationalized widgets elevate software inclusivity, enabling users worldwide to engage with functional, efficient, and enjoyable user interfaces, irrespective of ability or language. The confluence of ARIA standards, keyboard usability, visual accommodations, and multilingual support defines the state of the art for widget development in a global context.

Chapter 3

Advanced Event Handling and User Interaction Models

Unlock the true interactivity of FLTK applications by mastering advanced event handling and sophisticated interaction paradigms. This chapter takes you beyond basic callbacks, revealing the intricate choreography of user inputs, command flows, and reactive behaviors that power modern interfaces. Discover the patterns and strategies that turn passive widgets into dynamic, context-aware components capable of delighting users at every click and gesture.

3.1. Fine-Grained Input Event Management

The Fast Light Toolkit (FLTK) employs an event-driven architecture foundational to responsive and efficient graphical user interfaces. Mastery of its input event system is essential when developing applications requiring low-latency, precise handling of keyboard, mouse, and gesture inputs, especially in scenarios demanding simultaneous or complex user interactions. The ability to intercept, interpret, and respond accurately to these events ensures smooth user experiences and robust application behavior.

FLTK's event mechanism centers on the Fl_Event class and a set of predefined event constants representing various event types such as key presses, mouse movements, button clicks, and gestures. At its core, all input events funnel through the handle(int) method of widgets, where the event integer specifies the event type. Typical event identifiers include FL_KEYDOWN, FL_KEYUP, FL_MOUSEWHEEL, FL_PUSH, FL_DRAG, FL_RELEASE, and gesture-related events like FL_GESTURE.

Event Filtering and Interception

To achieve fine-grained control over input events, FLTK provides mechanisms to intercept events before they reach a target widget's default handler. This interception typically involves overriding the handle() function in a subclassed widget or leveraging the global event handler via Fl::add_handler(). For example, overriding handle() can be used as follows:

```cpp
int MyWidget::handle(int event) {
  switch(event) {
    case FL_KEYDOWN:
      // Inspect or modify the key event before default
      processing.
      if (Fl::event_key() == FL_Escape) {
        // Custom behavior for Escape key.
        return 1; // Event handled.
      }
      break;
    case FL_PUSH:
      if (Fl::event_button() == FL_LEFT_MOUSE) {
        // Custom mouse press processing.
      }
      break;
    // Additional event handling...
  }
  return Fl_Widget::handle(event); // Default processing.
}
```

72

This approach allows filtering of specific key codes or mouse buttons and deciding whether to consume the event or pass it upwards in the event chain. Returning a nonzero value from handle() signals to FLTK that the event has been fully handled, preventing further propagation.

Global event filtering can be implemented with a handler function registered through Fl::add_handler(), which intercepts all input events before widget-specific handlers:

```
int global_input_filter(int event) {
  if (event == FL_KEYDOWN) {
    int key = Fl::event_key();
    // For example, globally suppress the F1 key:
    if (key == FL_F + 1) return 1; // Event handled.
  }
  return 0; // Pass event to default handlers.
}

// Register in main initialization:
Fl::add_handler(global_input_filter);
```

Such filtering is critical for implementing application-wide shortcuts, modal input grabs, or nuanced behavior based on the current state without altering every widget's handle method.

Interpreting Keyboard Events with Precision

Keyboard events in FLTK provide access to both the raw key code and modifier state, enabling precise differentiation between key presses, releases, and character input. The functions Fl::event_key() and Fl::event_text() offer these data points, respectively. For low-latency text input scenarios, combining these yields complete context:

```
if (event == FL_KEYDOWN) {
  int key = Fl::event_key();         // Logical key code.
  const char* text = Fl::event_text(); // UTF-8 input.
  int modifiers = Fl::event_state();   // Modifier keys (Shift,
    Ctrl, etc.).

  // Example: Detect Ctrl+C for copy.
  if ((modifiers & FL_CTRL) && (key == 'c' || key == 'C')) {
    // Perform copy operation.
    return 1;
```

```
  }

  // For character input:
  if (text && text[0] != '\0') {
    // Insert character into buffer or text field.
  }
}
```

Attention must be given to modifier masks defined by FLTK: FL_SHIFT, FL_CTRL, FL_ALT, and FL_META, which can be combined bitwise. Because keyboard events are delivered asynchronously and in order, maintaining a state machine or buffering strategy can help handle rapid input sequences without data loss or UI blocking.

Mouse and Gesture Event Handling

Mouse input in FLTK distinguishes basic button pushes, drags, and releases while also supporting wheel rotations and advanced gesture events via system-level integration. The event types FL_PUSH, FL_DRAG, and FL_RELEASE correspond to mouse button press, movement with button(s) pressed, and release, respectively. The function Fl::event_button() identifies which mouse button triggered the event.

Utilization of mouse coordinates retrieved via Fl::event_x() and Fl::event_y() is essential for spatially-aware processing:

```
case FL_PUSH: {
  int bx = Fl::event_x();
  int by = Fl::event_y();
  int button = Fl::event_button();

  if (button == FL_LEFT_MOUSE) {
    // Begin drag or select operation.
  } else if (button == FL_RIGHT_MOUSE) {
    // Possibly open context menu.
  }
  return 1;
}
case FL_DRAG: {
  int dx = Fl::event_x();
  int dy = Fl::event_y();

  // Update drag operation.
```

```
    return 1;
}
```

The support for gesture events, though platform-dependent, is exposed through the generic `FL_GESTURE` event, enabling recognition of pinch, swipe, rotation, or tap actions. FLTK allows retrieval of gesture-specific parameters via functions such as `Fl::event_gesture_type()` and `Fl::event_gesture_value()`. For example, on a touch-enabled device, implementing pinch-to-zoom might involve:

```
if (event == FL_GESTURE) {
  Fl_Gesture_Type gtype = Fl::event_gesture_type();
  double gvalue = Fl::event_gesture_value();

  if (gtype == FL_GESTURE_PINCH) {
    // Adjust zoom factor based on gvalue.
  }
  return 1;
}
```

Since gestures may conflict or overlap with mouse events, strategies such as event consumption flags and temporal heuristics can prevent erroneous interpretations.

Custom Event Creation and Propagation

In some applications, the built-in range of event types is insufficient for specialized interactions requiring application-specific state signaling. FLTK facilitates custom event creation by defining unique event constants beyond the predefined range (typically starting at 1000 or higher to avoid clashes).

Handlers must propagate custom events judiciously to maintain the event system's integrity. A typical custom event dispatch might use `Fl::handle()` to inject the event into the system:

```
const int MY_CUSTOM_EVENT = 1001;

void send_custom_event(Fl_Widget* target) {
  Fl::handle(MY_CUSTOM_EVENT);
  // Alternatively, post targeting widget handle:
  target->handle(MY_CUSTOM_EVENT);
}
```

Widgets overriding `handle()` can then intercept this custom event by checking for the assigned event ID:

```
int MyWidget::handle(int event) {
  if (event == MY_CUSTOM_EVENT) {
    // Perform custom behavior.
    return 1;
  }
  return Fl_Widget::handle(event);
}
```

An important consideration is ensuring that custom events are well-documented and differentiated, particularly to avoid conflicts within large applications or libraries.

Handling Simultaneous and Complex Interactions

Managing multiple concurrent inputs, such as multi-touch gestures combined with keyboard shortcuts or simultaneous mouse button presses, demands comprehensive state tracking and conflict resolution. FLTK's event system, while not natively designed for advanced multi-touch in all configurations, allows augmentation through internal bookkeeping and layered event handling.

A common approach involves maintaining state variables for each input modality to track active presses, modifier keys, and gesture stages. For example:

```
static bool left_mouse_down = false;
static bool right_mouse_down = false;

int MyWidget::handle(int event) {
  switch (event) {
    case FL_PUSH: {
      int button = Fl::event_button();
      if (button == FL_LEFT_MOUSE) left_mouse_down = true;
      if (button == FL_RIGHT_MOUSE) right_mouse_down = true;
      break;
    }
    case FL_RELEASE: {
      int button = Fl::event_button();
      if (button == FL_LEFT_MOUSE) left_mouse_down = false;
      if (button == FL_RIGHT_MOUSE) right_mouse_down = false;
      break;
```

```
    }
    case FL_DRAG: {
      if (left_mouse_down && right_mouse_down) {
        // Interpret as simultaneous interaction, e.g., pan and
      zoom.
      }
      break;
    }
  }
  return Fl_Widget::handle(event);
}
```

This explicit tracking facilitates recognition of complex interaction patterns. Additionally, temporal filters leveraging timestamps from Fl::event_time() can help distinguish between quick sequential events and genuine concurrent inputs.

Event bubbling and focus-management strategies combine with such stateful handling to determine which widget receives simultaneous or overlapping input events, ensuring clean, deterministic responses.

Latency Optimization and Responsiveness

Latent input handling undermines usability especially for real-time applications such as graphical editors, games, or instrumentation panels. Within FLTK, reducing input latency is achieved by minimizing expensive operations inside event handlers and processing critical input synchronously.

Deferring nonessential computations with event-posting mechanisms or timer callbacks avoids blocking the event loop. Utilizing non-blocking drawing and invalidating only requisite regions maximizes frame rates. Furthermore, ensuring that handle() implementations avoid unnecessary event propagation overhead helps maintain prompt input dispatch.

Platform-specific input polling rates and driver configurations also influence the practical latency floor. FLTK's lightweight event handling architecture benefits from this as it introduces minimal overhead beyond what the underlying windowing system delivers.

FLTK's event system provides a comprehensive framework for low-latency, fine-grained management of keyboard, mouse, and gesture inputs. Through systematic event filtering, precise interpretation, flexible custom event creation, and coherent strategies for simultaneous input handling, developers can build responsive and feature-rich user interfaces capable of sophisticated interaction paradigms.

3.2. Callback Patterns and Command Routing

Event-driven systems fundamentally rely on effective callback mechanisms to decouple event sources from their corresponding handlers. Achieving robustness in such systems entails careful architectural considerations to enable modularity, maintainability, and scalability. The callback pattern, when combined with the command pattern and event routing strategies, provides a powerful paradigm to manage user interactions and asynchronous events with minimal coupling.

A core challenge lies in organizing callbacks to avoid monolithic handler functions that degrade readability and complicate future extensions. Employing command patterns enforces encapsulation of requests as objects, thereby promoting clear separation between event detection and event execution logic. This abstraction allows for flexible invocation, queuing, logging, and undo mechanisms, which are often critical in interactive applications.

Command Pattern as a Callback Mechanism

At the heart of the command pattern is the encapsulation of a request into an object that implements a common interface, typically with an `execute()` method. This encapsulation allows the invoker (event dispatcher) to trigger the command without knowledge of its actual implementation details.

The basic command interface can be expressed in C++ as follows:

```
// Command interface
class ICommand {
public:
    virtual ~ICommand() = default;
    virtual void execute() = 0;
};
```

Concrete command implementations encapsulate specific event-handling logic:

```
// Concrete command example
class SaveCommand : public ICommand {
    Document& doc_;
public:
    explicit SaveCommand(Document& doc) : doc_(doc) {}
    void execute() override {
        doc_.save();
    }
};
```

The invoker, often an event dispatcher or controller, maintains a registry of commands mapped to event types or user inputs. Upon detecting an event, it locates the corresponding command and invokes execute(), enabling polymorphic dispatching of event responses.

This approach distributes the responsibility for handling events across multiple command objects rather than a sprawling event handler. Consequently, the system gains modularity that enables independent development and testing of each command.

Event Routing for Scalable Callback Dispatching

Scalability in event-driven architectures demands sophisticated routing layers that direct events to appropriate handlers. Event routing introduces an abstraction between event sources and their destinations, enabling dynamic binding and resolution.

One prominent architectural style employs a *dispatcher* or *router* component that maintains a mapping between event identifiers (or types) and callback handlers (commands). The dispatcher listens for incoming events and forwards them to the registered commands.

A typical event router interface might be specified as:

```cpp
class EventRouter {
    std::unordered_map<EventType, std::unique_ptr<ICommand>>
      handlers_;
public:
    void registerHandler(EventType type, std::unique_ptr<ICommand
      > handler) {
        handlers_[type] = std::move(handler);
    }
    void routeEvent(const Event& e) {
        auto it = handlers_.find(e.type());
        if (it != handlers_.end()) {
            it->second->execute();
        }
    }
};
```

In this structure, the router decouples event generation from command invocation, improving modularity and supporting late binding or runtime reconfiguration by updating handler registrations.

For complex systems, event routing layers may support hierarchical or prioritized routing. For example, events may propagate through a chain of routers or handlers, akin to a *Chain of Responsibility* pattern, allowing multiple layers of processing or fallback handlers.

Maintaining Clarity and Modularity

Using command patterns and event routing promotes a well-structured codebase where user interactions are cleanly modeled. Key practices include:

- **Encapsulation of Side Effects:** Commands encapsulate all side effects and state mutations, reducing the cognitive load on the dispatcher and facilitating testing.

- **Loose Coupling:** By depending on abstract command interfaces, invokers and event sources avoid direct knowledge of implementation details.

- **Centralized Event Management:** Routers provide a unified layer to manage event-to-handler mappings, simplifying the addition or removal of event responses.

- **Expandable Command Registry:** Commands can be dynamically registered or deregistered at runtime, enabling plug-in architectures.

Practical Example: GUI Button Events

Consider a graphical user interface where multiple button widgets generate click events. By applying command and routing patterns, each button registers a command representing its specific response (e.g., OpenFileCommand, PrintCommand), and a centralized router dispatches click events accordingly.

The button class holds a pointer to a command and invokes it on click without knowing its internals:

```cpp
class Button {
    std::unique_ptr<ICommand> onClickCommand_;
public:
    explicit Button(std::unique_ptr<ICommand> cmd) :
     onClickCommand_(std::move(cmd)) {}
    void click() {
        if (onClickCommand_) {
            onClickCommand_->execute();
        }
    }
};
```

This modular design permits reuse of commands among multiple buttons and facilitates injection of new behavior without modifying the Button class.

The GUI framework manages event routing by assigning commands to buttons or event identifiers:

```cpp
EventRouter router;
router.registerHandler(EventType::OpenFile,
    std::make_unique<OpenFileCommand>(document));
router.registerHandler(EventType::Print,
    std::make_unique<PrintCommand>(printer));
```

When the user interacts with the interface, the router dispatches the events to appropriate commands, streamlining the event handling pipeline.

Extending Command Pattern for Parameterized and Asynchronous Callbacks

Basic command implementations frequently limit parameter passing or asynchronous considerations. To accommodate these needs, commands can be extended with parameter holders or by embedding context objects.

Parameterized commands may implement an execute method accepting a generic context or event data:

```
class ICommandWithContext {
public:
    virtual ~ICommandWithContext() = default;
    virtual void execute(const EventContext& ctx) = 0;
};
```

In asynchronous environments, commands can be designed as futures or continuations, returning control tokens or promises to integrate with event loops or concurrency frameworks.

This adaptability ensures that commands remain applicable for a range of complex event-driven scenarios, including UI responsiveness, network callbacks, or system notifications.

Architectural Benefits

The integration of command patterns with event routing significantly enhances the maintainability and scalability of callback-based systems. By isolating event handling into discrete command objects and managing invocation through centralized routing mechanisms, software architectures achieve:

- Improved modularity with clear boundaries between event sources and handlers.

- Enhanced testability through isolated command units.

- Flexibility in modifying event responses without impacting the overall event framework.

- Streamlined addition of new event types and handlers, promoting extensibility.

Such robust callback architectures form the backbone of modern interactive and reactive systems, enabling developers to systematically manage complex user interactions and asynchronous events with clarity and control.

3.3. Stateful Interaction and Finite State Machines

Modern interactive applications frequently require managing complex sequences of user actions that depend on prior inputs and contextual data. A robust conceptual and practical framework for such scenarios relies on explicit *state machines* embedded within widgets or entire applications. Finite State Machines (FSMs) underpin systematic modeling, enabling precise control over multi-step processes, context-sensitive behaviors, and reversible operations such as undo/redo actions.

An FSM is formally defined as a quintuple $(S, \Sigma, \delta, s_0, F)$, where S is a finite set of states; Σ is a finite set of input symbols representing possible events; $\delta : S \times \Sigma \to S$ is the transition function determining the next state; $s_0 \in S$ is the initial state; and $F \subseteq S$ consists of acceptable or terminal states. In interactive systems, states correspond to discrete contextual configurations or modes of a widget or application, while input symbols map to user-generated events (e.g., clicks, keystrokes, drag actions) and internal signals.

Modeling Multi-step Processes

Multi-step workflows naturally translate into FSMs where each step corresponds to a unique state. The transition function encodes the permissible progression, ensuring that only valid sequences activate subsequent UI elements or modify data structures. Consider a multi-step form widget with three sequential states: Step1, Step2, and Step3. Each step requires validation and user confirmation before transitioning to the next state.

```python
from enum import Enum, auto

class FormState(Enum):
    STEP1 = auto()
    STEP2 = auto()
    STEP3 = auto()
    COMPLETE = auto()

class MultiStepFormFSM:
    def __init__(self):
        self.state = FormState.STEP1

    def transition(self, event):
        if self.state == FormState.STEP1:
            if event == 'valid_input':
                self.state = FormState.STEP2
        elif self.state == FormState.STEP2:
            if event == 'valid_input':
                self.state = FormState.STEP3
        elif self.state == FormState.STEP3:
            if event == 'submit':
                self.state = FormState.COMPLETE
```

This code snippet embodies a simplified FSM where explicit transitions enforce a strict, linear user flow. Validation logic, while abstracted here, is critical to preserve state invariants and prevent premature advancement.

Context-sensitive Actions and States

When an application's behavior depends not only on the current step but also on diverse user contexts or environmental factors, FSM design demands augmentation with context variables or extended state machines, commonly referred to as *extended finite state machines* (EFSMs). These incorporate auxiliary data, allowing transitions to be conditional rather than purely event-driven.

For example, a drawing application may allow shape manipulation

84

modes contingent upon the presence of a selection or modifier keys. The FSM managing widget behavior could distinguish states such as Idle, Drawing, SelectionActive, and Transforming, with transitions conditioned on both user inputs and additional parameters, such as whether a shape is currently selected or keyboard modifiers are held down.

$$\delta : S \times \Sigma \times C \to S$$

Here, C represents a set of context variables. Implementing such conditional transitions requires careful modeling to avoid state explosion and ensure maintainable code.

Undo and Redo Mechanisms from FSM Perspectives

Undo and redo mechanisms introduce a bidirectional traversal over a sequence of states or actions, demanding more sophisticated management than simple FSMs provide. Conceptually, undo-redo stacks can be viewed as paths through an FSM, with backward and forward navigation along these paths corresponding to undo and redo operations, respectively.

A common implementation pattern involves two stacks: an undo stack holding prior states or actions, and a redo stack holding states or actions reverted by undo operations. When applying a new state-changing action, the redo stack is cleared, maintaining consistency of linear history.

```
class UndoRedoManager:
    def __init__(self, initial_state):
        self.undo_stack = []
        self.redo_stack = []
        self.current_state = initial_state

    def do_action(self, new_state):
        self.undo_stack.append(self.current_state)
        self.current_state = new_state
        self.redo_stack.clear()

    def undo(self):
        if self.undo_stack:
```

```
            self.redo_stack.append(self.current_state)
            self.current_state = self.undo_stack.pop()

    def redo(self):
        if self.redo_stack:
            self.undo_stack.append(self.current_state)
            self.current_state = self.redo_stack.pop()
```

This approach integrates seamlessly with FSM-driven UIs, where transitions correspond to discrete actions producing new states. Capturing sufficient state information to restore prior configurations remains a crucial consideration, often mitigated by storing inverse operations or state snapshots.

Best Practices for Designing Stateful Interactions

- *Explicit State Representation:* Encapsulating widget or application states as enumerated types or explicit classes simplifies reasoning and debugging. Avoid implicit state encoded solely in UI elements or scattered flags.

- *Single Source of Truth:* The FSM should be the authoritative source for the component's state and permitted transitions. UI elements and handlers synchronize to this source to ensure consistency.

- *State Transition Validation:* Enforce validation rules strictly within transition functions to prevent illegal states or sequences. This improves robustness and error handling.

- *Deterministic Behavior:* Ensure the FSM is deterministic, with unambiguous transitions for given inputs and states. This prevents race conditions and unintended side effects.

- *Minimal State Explosion:* For complex systems, use hierarchical or concurrent state machines (e.g., statecharts) to reduce combinatorial explosion of states.

- *Decoupling State Logic and Presentation:* Separate FSM

logic from the UI rendering code. This modularity supports easier maintenance, testing, and reuse.

- *Comprehensive Testing:* Implement exhaustive unit and integration tests to verify correct transitions, particularly for edge cases and error recovery.

Hierarchical and Parallel States

Hierarchical state machines extend FSM capabilities by nesting states, allowing a parent state to encapsulate substates. This approach aids in representing modes with common behavior, reducing duplication. Parallel states enable concurrent state regions, facilitating modeling of interactions that proceed independently yet simultaneously within a widget or application.

For example, in a media player widget, a hierarchical FSM may define a `Playback` state containing substates for `Playing`, `Paused`, and `Stopped`, while concurrently running a separate `VolumeControl` state machine managing mute/unmute and level adjustments. Interaction complexity increases, but modular abstractions enhance clarity and scalability.

Tool Support and Implementation Strategies

Numerous domain-specific languages, libraries, and frameworks support explicit FSM implementation in interactive applications. Examples include:

- Statechart frameworks providing graphical and textual modeling.

- Functional reactive programming patterns integrating streams of events with state transitions.

- Library support for immutable state updates enhancing undo/redo flows.

The choice of implementation method depends on application complexity, language ecosystem, real-time constraints, and developer expertise. A minimal custom FSM may suffice for simple widgets, while complex software may benefit from comprehensive modeling tools.

Contextualizing FSMs Within User Experience Design

Explicit state modeling fosters predictable, consistent user experiences by making transitions and state changes transparent and manageable. For multi-step processes, clear state demarcation aids users in understanding progress and sequencing. Context-sensitive behavior enhances responsiveness and reduces cognitive load by dynamically adapting controls and feedback.

Moreover, when undo/redo mechanisms are integrated with state machines, users gain confidence in manipulating complex data or workflows, knowing that unintended changes can be reversed safely. This combination directly contributes to robustness and usability in sophisticated interactive systems.

Encapsulating stateful interactions within finite state machines is a foundational technique for engineering complex user interfaces. The disciplined application of FSM principles enables predictable control flow, enforces valid user paths through multi-step processes, accommodates nuanced context-dependent behavior, and supports reversible operations. Adhering to best practices in design and implementation ensures that interactive systems remain maintainable, scalable, and aligned with user expectations.

3.4. Drag-and-Drop Infrastructure

Implementing an efficient drag-and-drop (DnD) infrastructure requires comprehensive coordination of event handling, precise data transfer protocols, and responsive user feedback mechanisms. These internal components must tightly integrate to facilitate smooth interaction between widgets or applications, ensuring data integrity while preserving intuitive and responsive user experiences.

At the core of drag-and-drop operations lies a sophisticated event coordination model. Dragging initiates a sequence of discrete yet interrelated events: `dragstart`, `dragenter`, `dragover`, `dragleave`, `drop`, and `dragend`. Each event serves a distinct role in the management of state transitions and user interactions. The `dragstart` event marks the beginning of a drag operation, during which the source widget registers the data payload and sets up necessary metadata such as allowed effects (e.g., copy, move, link). The `dragenter` and `dragover` events provide continuous signals to potential drop targets, enabling dynamic acceptance testing and feedback based on the cursor's position and modifier keys. The `drop` event finalizes the operation by transferring data to the target widget, while `dragend` ensures cleanup regardless of success or cancellation.

Accurate event propagation and cancellation are essential. Commonly, drag events employ event propagation models allowing listeners to intercept and handle or ignore events based on contextual logic. For example, a target must explicitly call methods analogous to `preventDefault()` during `dragover` to indicate it accepts drops. Failure to do so results in the drag operation being rejected by default, guiding the user visually with appropriate system feedback such as prompting "not allowed" cursors. Event handlers must be meticulously designed to avoid conflicts and unintended side effects, especially within complex widget hierarchies where multiple elements may qualify as drop targets.

Data transfer protocols define the mechanisms to serialize, encode, and communicate data reliably between source and target endpoints. At the application level, the drag source packages one or more data items into a structured data store, frequently referred to as a *data transfer object*. Each data item is associated with a MIME-type-compatible identifier, supporting extensibility and standards compliance for a broad array of content types including plain text, HTML fragments, images, and custom binary formats. By negotiating MIME types at runtime, drop targets can filter and process only compatible formats. This negotiation is critical when drag-and-drop operations span process or application boundaries, often facilitated by interprocess communication (IPC) channels or operating system clipboard services.

Data serialization must preserve fidelity and security. To ensure robustness, implementations incorporate fail-safe encoding techniques (e.g., Base64 for binary content) and content validations to mitigate data corruption or injection threats during transfer. For sizable or complex data, lazy loading or deferred fetching techniques reduce overhead by transferring only minimal metadata during the drag with full content delivered on demand at drop time. This approach enhances responsiveness and avoids blocking UI threads during prolonged operations.

User feedback during drag-and-drop is paramount for usability, leveraging both visual and haptic cues. The cursor icon dynamically updates to reflect the current drag effect, combining the pointer shape with modifiers to indicate validity and consequences of the drop, such as copying or moving data. Target elements highlight or animate to signal acceptance or rejection zones, providing intuitive spatial awareness. Furthermore, drag images-snapshots representing the dragged content-are rendered near the cursor, enabling clear visual continuity. Advanced systems incorporate drag shadows or semi-transparent thumbnails to maintain context without obscuring underlying widgets.

Beyond basic pointer feedback, accessibility considerations expand feedback channels. Keyboard-driven drag-and-drop schemes announce status changes via screen readers and provide tab-based focus management of potential drop targets.

Auditory or tactile signals may be employed, triggered by event milestones to accommodate diverse user needs. These inclusive design patterns are integral to comprehensive drag-and-drop infrastructure and reflect growing standards compliance such as ARIA drag-and-drop roles and properties.

Synchronization between source and target throughout the drag lifecycle is crucial for state management. For instance, when the drag enters a new target, internal states track acceptance criteria and update drag effects accordingly. If the user cancels the operation through gestures or system commands, rollback procedures ensure that resources are released and UI elements revert to original states. Likewise, the source widget often maintains a transient *drag session* object encapsulating information such as data types offered, allowed drop effects, and timestamp, enabling consistent state inspection by all event handlers involved.

The following pseudo-code illustrates a concise structure of the event handling sequence within a drag session:

```
class DragSession {
public:
    void startDrag(DataTransfer data, DragEffects effects) {
        this->data = data;
        this->allowedEffects = effects;
        fireEvent("dragstart", this);
    }

    void onDragEnter(Widget* target) {
        if (target->canAccept(data)) {
            currentTarget = target;
            fireEvent("dragenter", target);
        }
    }

    void onDragOver(Position pos) {
        if (currentTarget && currentTarget->isValidPosition(pos))
        {
            fireEvent("dragover", currentTarget);
            // Indicate allowed drop effect for current target
            setDropEffect(currentTarget->preferredEffect());
        } else {
            setDropEffect(DragEffects::None);
        }
    }
```

```
    void drop() {
        if(currentTarget) {
            currentTarget->handleDrop(data);
            fireEvent("drop", currentTarget);
        }
        endDrag();
    }

    void endDrag() {
        fireEvent("dragend", this);
        cleanup();
    }
    // Additional methods omitted for brevity
private:
    DataTransfer data;
    DragEffects allowedEffects;
    Widget* currentTarget = nullptr;
};
```

Data transfer objects commonly encapsulate multiple representations to optimize compatibility. For example, dragging an image might expose both the original bitmap and its URL. Drop targets then select the most suitable format depending on context: an image editing widget prioritizes bitmaps, whereas a web browser might prefer URLs for embedding. This flexibility fosters interoperability between heterogeneous environments.

Here is an abstract example of a structured data transfer using MIME types:

```
{
  "text/plain": "Example text",
  "text/html": "<b>Example text</b>",
  "image/png": "iVBORw0KGgoAAAANSUhEUgAAA..."
}
```

Managing drag-and-drop across application boundaries involves challenges such as sandboxing, security constraints, and differing IPC mechanisms. Operating systems provide native drag-and-drop APIs that abstract these details, but developers must handle edge cases including data format mismatches, latency in data retrieval, and cross-platform discrepancies. In some systems, drag-and-drop interacts with the clipboard; integration must ensure that ongoing drag sessions do not inadvertently clear clipboard contents or vice versa.

The reliability of drag operations depends on atomicity between event dispatch and data transfer. If a drop event succeeds without error, the source often executes a commit phase-for instance, deleting or moving the original data in a move operation. However, partial failures must be handled gracefully. Rollback and retransmission strategies, coupled with user notifications, enhance robustness in environments prone to interruptions or resource constraints.

An advanced drag-and-drop infrastructure consists of coordinated event sequences, standardized and extensible data transfer protocols, and comprehensive user feedback systems. Strong synchronization models and secure data handling practices guarantee functional correctness and user confidence. Designing such a system demands attention to architectural patterns that promote modularity, scalability, and cross-context interoperability.

3.5. Gestural and Multi-Touch Input Extensions

Extending FLTK (Fast Light Toolkit) applications to support advanced input paradigms requires sophisticated handling of gestural, multi-touch, and stylus data streams. These paradigms elevate user interaction beyond traditional mouse and keyboard events, enabling modern applications to harness the natural and intuitive capabilities of contemporary input devices. This section explicates techniques for integrating such input methods into FLTK frameworks and addresses challenges posed by device-specific input data, event management, and gesture recognition.

FLTK's native input model is primarily designed around mouse, keyboard, and basic touch inputs, necessitating augmentation to handle complex input gestures and multi-point contact. Multi-touch and gestural support fundamentally rely on recognizing simultaneous input points and interpreting temporal and spatial patterns in the input data. Consequently, extensions often require low-level access to raw device input or platform-specific event handling mechanisms, combined with higher-level gesture interpretation layers.

Integration begins by intercepting native platform events that encapsulate multi-touch and stylus input. On Windows, this involves managing WM_TOUCH messages; on macOS, processing NSEvent's touch and gesture events; on Linux, handling touch and gesture events from XInput2 or Wayland protocols. FLTK's event loop must be enhanced or supplemented with native hooks that provide raw touch points, pressure, tilt, and other stylus-specific data.

FLTK's Fl_Event structure and event callback model do not natively express multi-point touch or gestures. Thus, external handlers capture the raw events and convert them into FLTK-compatible events or custom signals. These custom events can be dispatched through FLTK's user event messaging system or sent directly to widgets interested in advanced input.

Fundamental to multi-touch integration is maintaining a data structure representing the current state of all active touch points. A common approach associates each touch point with a unique identifier provided by the underlying OS to track its lifecycle. For each frame or event occurrence, touch point states-including position, pressure, size, and orientation-are updated and passed to gesture recognizers.

A C++ data structure supporting extensibility to stylus data might resemble:

```
struct TouchPoint {
    int id;                     % Unique identifier per touch
    point
    float x, y;                 % Coordinates relative to window
    or widget
    float pressure;             % Pressure level from 0.0 to 1.0 (
```

```
      if available)
      float orientation;        % Stylus or finger orientation
      angle in radians
      bool isActive;            % True if currently touching
};
```

The input dispatching system accumulates a `std::vector<TouchPoint>` representing the current frame's contact points. Event handlers in FLTK widgets query these touch points to determine gesture state or direct manipulation.

Gestural input is inherently temporal, requiring multi-stage stateful recognition. Gesture detection schemes generally employ finite state machines (FSM) or continuous gesture interpretation algorithms such as template matching, neural networks, or probabilistic models. Common gestures include single-finger taps, double taps, long-press, pan, pinch (zoom), rotate, swipe, and stylus-specific interactions such as air hover or eraser toggling.

Implementing an FSM involves defining input event types, state transitions, and output gesture events. For instance, a pinch gesture can be recognized by tracking two simultaneous touch points converging or diverging. The FSM for pinch recognition typically transitions through these states:

- **Idle:** No active gesture detected.

- **GestureStart:** Two points detected; initial positions stored.

- **GestureActive:** Movement of touch points quantified; scale factor computed.

- **GestureEnd:** Points released; gesture finalization.

Each state transition is triggered by updates in touch point data. The FSM emits custom events or signals processed by application logic for UI updates, transformations, or user feedback.

95

Stylus devices provide richer input parameters such as pressure sensitivity, tilt, rotation, and button states. On platforms supporting Microsoft Pen Protocol (MPP) or Apple Pencil APIs, these extensions capture such characteristics to facilitate natural drawing, writing, and control.

Pressure and tilt can be mapped to line thickness and angle in drawing applications or to emulate variable brush effects. Stylus buttons often serve as modifiers (e.g., switch to eraser mode). Stylus hover events, when available, enable pre-contact interactions such as tool preview.

Stylus input can be incorporated by extending the `TouchPoint` structure or by creating a dedicated structure:

```
struct StylusPoint : public TouchPoint {
    float tiltX;               % Degrees or radians from vertical
      axis on X
    float tiltY;               % Degrees or radians from vertical
      axis on Y
    bool buttonPressed;        % True if stylus button is pressed
    bool inAirHover;           % True if stylus is hovering but
      not touching
};
```

Event propagation mechanisms must distinguish between finger touch and stylus input to provide appropriate feedback and behavior.

Tooltip extensions to FLTK incorporate platform-specific calls through native APIs:

- **Windows:** Capturing WM_TOUCH and real-time Windows Pointer Input (WM_POINTER) messages requires subclassing the FLTK window handle or injecting into the message processing loop. WM_POINTER messages provide enhanced data including pen and touch distinctions, pressure, and contact size, accessible via GET_POINTER_INFO APIs.

- **macOS:** Integration with the Cocoa event loop enables

96

extraction of NSGestureRecognizer-driven gestures and NSEvent properties for touch and stylus data, such as NSEventTypePressure and deviceID for finger differentiation.

- **Linux:** Using XInput2, multi-touch events (XI_TOUCHBEGIN, XI_TOUCHUPDATE, XI_TOUCHEND) provide device IDs, position, and pressure. Wayland compositor clients receive touchpoint arrays through dedicated protocols.

The bridging code encapsulates these platform differences, creating unified touch and stylus event abstractions for FLTK's event system.

Handling simultaneous multiple input points at high temporal resolutions demands efficient event buffering and processing. The native event loop must ensure minimal latency to preserve responsiveness in drawing or manipulation applications. Synchronization between native event callbacks and the FLTK event dispatch mechanism is critical to avoid inconsistencies or missed updates.

Double buffering of touch point states, combined with atomic or lock-free message queues between platform event threads and FLTK's single-threaded UI thread, is a common approach. Batched updates allow gesture recognizers to operate on coherent frames of touch input, improving accuracy.

A FLTK window subclass augmented with platform-specific touch event capture enables pinch-to-zoom functionality as illustrated below. The example abstracts from platform details and simulates the availability of a function getActiveTouchPoints() returning the current vector of active touch points.

```
class PinchZoomWindow : public Fl_Window {
private:
    bool gestureActive = false;
    float initialDistance = 0.0f;
    float currentScale = 1.0f;
```

```
    float distance(const TouchPoint &p1, const TouchPoint &p2) {
        float dx = p2.x - p1.x;
        float dy = p2.y - p1.y;
        return std::sqrt(dx * dx + dy * dy);
    }

    void updateScale(float scaleFactor) {
        currentScale *= scaleFactor;
        // Application-specific scale handling (e.g., zoom canvas
     )
        redraw();
    }

public:
    PinchZoomWindow(int w, int h, const char* title = 0)
        : Fl_Window(w, h, title) {}

    int handle(int event) override {
        switch(event) {
            case FL_ENTER_NOTIFY:
            case FL_LEAVE_NOTIFY:
            case FL_MOVE:
            case FL_PUSH:
            case FL_RELEASE:
            case FL_DRAG: {
                // Retrieve active touch points from extended
    input system
                std::vector<TouchPoint> touches =
    getActiveTouchPoints();

                if (touches.size() == 2) {
                    float dist = distance(touches[0], touches[1])
    ;

                    if (!gestureActive) {
                        gestureActive = true;
                        initialDistance = dist;
                    } else {
                        float scaleFactor = dist /
    initialDistance;
                        updateScale(scaleFactor);
                        initialDistance = dist;
                    }
                } else {
                    gestureActive = false;
                }

                return 1; // Event handled
            }
            default:
                return Fl_Window::handle(event);
        }
    }
```

```
};
```

This simplified logic highlights continuous tracking of two touch points to control a zoom factor. Real implementations incorporate smoothing, thresholding, and gesture cancellation criteria.

Advanced input support often requires extending standard FLTK widgets or creating custom ones that react suitably to multi-touch and stylus events. Widgets may override `handle()` methods to manage gesture states and provide visual or functional feedback such as inertia scrolling, pinch-to-zoom scaling, or pressure-sensitive drawing.

Application-level gesture callbacks can be installed using observer or signal-slot mechanisms aligned with gesture recognition modules. This modularity promotes separation of concerns, allowing core input processing to remain distinct from UI logic.

Incorporating multi-touch and stylus input also involves calibrating coordinate systems and normalizing device peculiarities. Touch screens and stylus sensors differ in resolution, accuracy, reporting ranges, and noise characteristics. Transformations mapping raw device coordinates to FLTK window coordinates must account for display scaling, orientation, and high-DPI settings.

Pressure and tilt values, if available, require normalization to consistent ranges for uniform application responses. Calibration routines may be necessary to guarantee precision critical for drawing or handwriting applications.

Augmenting FLTK applications with gestural, multi-touch, and stylus input capabilities expands the scope and sophistication of interactive software. This integration involves blending platform-native event handling, robust state management of multi-point contacts, and flexible gesture recognition frameworks. Careful abstraction reconciles device-specific nuances, enabling developers to craft responsive, immersive user experiences harnessing the full potential of contemporary input hardware.

3.6. Focus, Navigation, and Accessibility

Effective management of widget focus, keyboard navigation sequences, and the facilitation of accessible user flows constitute foundational requirements for modern user interface (UI) frameworks. These elements enable robust interaction paradigms that are inclusive of diverse user capabilities, including those dependent on assistive technologies. This section delineates the principles and best practices surrounding the orchestration of input focus, navigation mechanisms, and accessibility interfaces, with particular emphasis on visual focus cues, input focus policies, and the integration of accessibility APIs.

Focus Management in Widget Hierarchies

Focus represents the active state within a user interface that indicates which widget currently receives input events from the keyboard or other input devices. Accurate management of focus across widget hierarchies is critical to ensure intuitive navigation and consistent interaction. The input focus system typically distinguishes between two principal types:

- *Keyboard focus*, which determines the widget currently targeted by keyboard and accessibility input.

- *Pointer focus*, which tracks the widget currently under pointer devices such as a mouse or touch.

Keyboard focus must be exclusive-only one widget in the active interface may hold it at any moment. The process of setting and moving focus follows a deterministic sequence, governed by the logical structure and arrangement of widgets. Frameworks often maintain a global focus manager responsible for:

- Tracking the widget hierarchy and the currently focused widget.

- Managing focus traversal policies.

- Generating focus events to widgets that gain or lose focus.

A critical component is focus assignment during dynamic interface changes, such as activating new windows, dialogs, or switching between input modalities. By design, the focus manager enforces policies that avoid focus loss or ambiguity, thereby preventing user disorientation.

Keyboard Navigation Sequences

Keyboard navigation is the cornerstone for non-pointer-based interaction. Reliable and predictable keyboard navigation supports both power users and accessibility needs. The fundamental navigation keys-Tab, Shift+Tab, arrow keys, Home, End, Page Up, and Page Down-should function in a manner aligned with the interface's semantic intent.

Tab Order and Sequential Navigation

Tab order determines the sequence in which widgets receive focus when the user presses the Tab key. Specifying an intuitive and logical tab order is paramount for seamless user flows. The tab sequence usually aligns with:

- The visual layout from left to right, top to bottom in Western reading contexts.

- The logical grouping and nesting of controls (e.g., grouping related controls within panels).

Programmatic control over tab order involves assigning explicit tab indices or relying on container hierarchies. Avoiding tab traps-where focus becomes cyclically confined in a subset of widgets without escape-is essential.

Arrow Key Navigation

Arrow keys often serve to navigate within or between compound widgets, such as list boxes, menus, tree views, and grids. Implementations should align with user expectations and platform conventions:

- Up and Down arrows move focus vertically between items.

- Left and Right arrows navigate horizontally or expand/collapse nodes in hierarchical controls.

Correct handling includes updating both visual selection states and the logical focus to maintain coherency.

Focus Wrapping and Boundary Handling

When reaching the last widget in a focus chain, pressing Tab typically wraps focus to the first widget; Shift+Tab wraps focus backward. Some contexts discourage automatic wrapping (such as modal dialogues) to prevent user confusion. The navigation policy must be context-aware, preserving expected behavior within each frame of interaction.

Visual Cues to Indicate Focus

Visual focus indicators provide critical feedback to users about which widget is active. These cues must be unambiguous, visible under varied display conditions, and not solely reliant on color to support users with vision deficiencies.

Common visual indicators include:

- Highlighted widget borders or shadows.

- Distinct background or text color changes.

- Underlines or outlines that contrast with surrounding content.

Following established design guidelines such as the Web Content Accessibility Guidelines (WCAG) ensures sufficient contrast ratios and perceptibility. Systems should allow customization of focus indicators to cater to user preferences and special needs, such as high-contrast themes.

Input Focus Policies and Behavioral Considerations

Input focus policies govern when and how widgets acquire or relinquish focus. Comprehensive systems incorporate:

- *Focus Follows Mouse* policies, where hovering over a widget can activate focus without clicks.

- *Click to Focus* policies, which require explicit click to set focus.

- *Programmatic Focus*, enabling applications to assign focus dynamically based on workflow logic or accessibility needs.

Each policy has trade-offs concerning user expectations, discoverability, and accidental focus shifts. Systems can expose configuration options or heuristics that adapt to context, such as touch input versus desktop environment.

Accessibility APIs and Assistive Technology Integration

Accessibility Application Programming Interfaces (APIs) connect the UI framework to assistive technologies (AT) like screen readers, Braille displays, voice input, and eye-tracking devices. These APIs provide a semantic map of interface elements, their states, relationships, and user interactions.

Core Accessibility Interface Concepts

- **Roles:** Each widget is assigned an accessibility role (e.g., button, checkbox, slider) to communicate its function.

- **States:** Properties such as focused, disabled, selected, or expanded are exposed.

- **Name and Description:** Human-readable labels and descriptions give meaningful context.

- **Hierarchy:** The parent-child relationships model the UI containment.

- **Actions:** Supported user actions like click, scroll, or activate.

These elements enable AT to generate accurate spoken or tactile feedback and interpret user commands correctly.

Platform-Specific Accessibility APIs

Accessibility frameworks vary by operating system and environment:

- Microsoft Active Accessibility (MSAA) and UI Automation for Windows.

- Apple Accessibility API and VoiceOver for macOS and iOS.

- AT-SPI for Linux and Unix-like platforms.

- ARIA (Accessible Rich Internet Applications) for web-based interfaces.

Modern UI toolkits abstract these differences by implementing a common accessibility layer that translates internal widget models into platform-specific representations.

Enabling Accessible User Flows

To accommodate users relying on assistive technologies, UI frameworks must expose complete and accurate accessibility metadata and preserve logical navigation sequences. Key practices include:

- Synchronizing focus management with accessibility focus, ensuring that focus events trigger corresponding accessibility notifications.

- Avoiding hidden interactive elements without accessibility roles or labels.

- Maintaining live regions and dynamic content updates through appropriate events or change notifications for AT.

- Supporting accessible names by ensuring that all interactive elements have labels or descriptions available programmatically.

- Implementing keyboard shortcuts and accelerators consistently with accessibility context.

Considerations for Complex Widgets and Custom Controls

Custom controls and composite widgets introduce complexity in managing internal focus and accessibility. Effective strategies involve:

- Defining internal focus scopes where components within a composite widget manage local navigation independently from the global focus chain.

- Mapping keyboard navigation to logical item boundaries in complex structures, such as tables with row and cell focus modes.

- Providing custom accessibility roles and state explanations to reflect composite widget semantics correctly.

- Implementing ARIA live regions or analogous mechanisms to announce dynamic state changes.

Developers must ensure that such controls remain operable and understandable through keyboard and assistive technologies without requiring pointer interaction.

Summary of Best Practices

The orchestration of focus, navigation, and accessibility demands meticulous design and implementation to deliver equitable user experiences. Core principles include:

- Ensuring exclusive and well-defined keyboard focus with consistent visual indication.

- Structuring navigable widget sequences that respect logical and visual ordering.

- Adhering to established input focus policies suited to the application context.

- Integrating with accessibility APIs to expose comprehensive semantic information.

- Verifying operability without pointer interaction and enabling full AT compatibility.

By maintaining rigorous control over these elements, UI frameworks can support seamless, inclusive user flows across diverse user profiles and interaction modalities.

Chapter 4

Graphics, Drawing, and Custom Rendering

Step behind the scenes of FLTK's visual engine and unlock the tools to create visually striking, high-performance interfaces. This chapter navigates the powerful realm of FLTK's drawing primitives, advanced graphics integration, and custom rendering pipelines. Whether charting data, building dashboards, or animating controls, you'll learn to wield both built-in and OpenGL-powered techniques, elevating your applications to new heights of visual expressiveness.

4.1. FLTK Graphics Context and Primitives

The Fast Light Toolkit (FLTK) provides a foundational graphics context designed for efficient rendering of 2D graphics within its windowing framework. Central to FLTK's rendering model are its core primitives-lines, shapes, text, and images-which offer the necessary building blocks for custom graphical user interface components and dynamic visualizations. Understanding FLTK's graphics context requires familiarity with its drawing model, coordinate systems, and the event-driven lifecycle governing paint operations.

Graphics Context and Drawing Model

FLTK's graphics context abstracts the underlying platform-specific drawing mechanisms into a unified interface accessible via member functions of the base widget class `Fl_Widget`. Application code seldom interacts directly with low-level device contexts; instead, drawing commands are issued during designated paint events via methods in `Fl_Widget` or related classes such as `Fl_Window` and `Fl_Drawable`.

The fundamental drawing model is immediate mode: each paint event triggers a redraw of the widget's visible area, with no retained graphical state across frames. Consequently, application code must re-issue all drawing commands for a widget's appearance every time a paint event occurs. This stateless paradigm simplifies cross-platform rendering but places the onus on the developer to correctly manage repaint logic and avoid visual artifacts or flickering.

Rendering commands target the widget's current clipping region, which restricts drawing to visible portions and optimizes rendering performance. FLTK automatically sets the clipping region to the widget's bounds before invoking its `draw()` method, ensuring that drawing outside these bounds is not displayed.

Coordinate Systems

FLTK employs a two-dimensional Cartesian coordinate system for all drawing operations. Coordinates are integer-based, corresponding to pixel locations, with the origin $(0, 0)$ positioned at the top-left corner of the widget's drawing area. The x-axis increases towards the right, and the y-axis increases downwards, consistent with conventional GUI coordinate systems.

Because coordinates represent device pixels, primitives drawn at non-integer positions are subject to implicit integer rounding by FLTK, generally resulting in crisp, well-aligned rendering on raster displays. For widgets scaled with higher-DPI settings or transformed environments, applications must manually adjust coordinates or provide higher-resolution assets to maintain visual fidelity.

The coordinate system is local to each widget's drawing area. For composite widgets or nested drawing, coordinate transformations must be managed by the application, typically by offsetting drawing commands relative to the widget's geometry. FLTK itself does not provide an extensive matrix transformation API akin to modern graphics toolkits; it relies on simple translation via coordinate offsets.

Core Drawing Primitives

The core FLTK graphics API offers a concise set of drawing primitives, encapsulated mainly by `Fl_Widget`'s protected members. These primitives include:

- **Lines and Polylines**: The function `fl_line(int x1, int y1, int x2, int y2)` draws a straight line segment between two points. For connected sequences of line segments, `fl_curve()` or multiple `fl_line()` calls can be used. Line thickness and color are controlled through FLTK's color and line style settings prior to drawing.

- **Rectangles and Boxes**: Rectangular areas are drawn with `fl_rect(int x, int y, int w, int h)` for outline rectangles, and `fl_rectf(int x, int y, int w, int h)` for filled rectangles. FLTK supports various frame styles through the `Fl_Box` enum, allowing for consistent borders and beveled edges across widgets.

- **Circles and Ellipses**: `fl_arc(int x, int y, int w, int h, int angle1, int angle2)` draws an elliptical arc within the specified bounding rectangle from `angle1` to `angle2` degrees. A full ellipse is obtained by specifying 0 to 360 degrees. Filled ellipses can be created by combining `fl_begin_polygon()`, `fl_vertex()`, and `fl_end_polygon()` calls to trace the ellipse outline and fill it.

- **Polygons**: Polygonal shapes are constructed using `fl_begin_polygon()`, a sequence of `fl_vertex(int x, int y)`, and completion with `fl_end_polygon()`. This provides an efficient way to fill arbitrary convex or concave shapes.

- **Text**: Text rendering is performed by `fl_draw(const char* text, int x, int y, int w=0, int h=0, Fl_Align alignment=FL_ALIGN_LEFT)`. The baseline of the text aligns with the (x, y) coordinate. FLTK supports font selection, size adjustment, and color settings through `fl_font()` and `fl_color()`.

- **Images**: Rendering bitmaps or images leverages the `Fl_Image` hierarchy. The polymorphic `Fl_Image::draw(int x, int y, int w=0, int h=0)` method paints the image at the specified coordinates, optionally scaling it to the given width and height. Image formats supported include `Fl_Bitmap`, `Fl_Jpeg`, `Fl_Png`, and others, facilitating flexible graphical content.

- **Pixel Operations**: FLTK supports direct pixel manipulation using `fl_set_pixel(int x, int y, Fl_Color c)` and pixel reading with `fl_get_pixel(int x, int y)`. These low-level operations allow for fine-grained control, although their performance is limited compared to batch drawing primitives.

Paint Event Lifecycle

110

Painting in FLTK is event-driven and tightly integrated into its widget and window system. When a portion of a widget requires updating-due to exposure, resizing, or explicit redraw requests-FLTK schedules a paint event and calls the widget's draw() method. This method encapsulates all drawing commands needed to render the widget's appearance.

The typical paint sequence proceeds as follows:

1. **Invalidation and Event Scheduling**: User code or FLTK internals mark rectangular regions as needing redrawing using Fl_Widget::damage() or Fl_Window::redraw(). FLTK consolidates these damage areas to optimize repainting.

2. **Preparation**: Prior to invoking draw(), FLTK establishes the drawing context, including clipping regions and current color and font states. It ensures the graphics state is initialized consistently for the widget.

3. **Drawing Commands**: The widget's overridden draw() method issues rendering calls using the core primitives. Drawing must be idempotent, producing consistent visual results on each invocation.

4. **Completion**: Upon return from draw(), FLTK flushes the drawing commands to the display buffer, presenting the updated visuals on the screen.

Because paint events may be triggered asynchronously and at any time, widget implementations must avoid side effects or state changes within draw(). All resource loading, state updates, or computation should occur separately, ensuring that drawing operations remain fast and free of external dependencies.

Color and Line Styles

Colors in FLTK are represented by an integer Fl_Color, encodable as RGB values or predefined symbolic constants such as FL_BLACK,

FL_WHITE, and FL_RED. Calling fl_color(Fl_Color c) sets the current drawing color globally for subsequent primitives.

Line and fill styles are controlled independently. Line thickness can be adjusted with fl_line_width(int w). Line patterns (solid, dashed, dotted) are configured with fl_dashes(const char* dashes) by providing dash patterns as a string of bytes describing lengths of on/off segments. The default solid lines are specified by passing nullptr to fl_dashes().

Text Rendering Details

FLTK's text primitive supports minimal layout capabilities but provides key properties necessary for GUI text drawing. Font selection is done using fl_font(Fl_Font f, int size) to set both the font face and size before text is drawn. Typical fonts include system defaults and standard variants such as FL_HELVETICA, FL_COURIER, and FL_TIMES.

Text alignment options, controlled via the Fl_Align enum, allow left, center, right, top, bottom, or baseline alignment relative to the specified coordinates. The drawing primitive respects clipping and color settings established prior to rendering.

Multiline text is achieved by invoking the fl_draw() multiple times or utilizing the Fl_Text_Display class for complex editing and selection capabilities, although these are beyond the scope of the primitive drawing commands.

Image Handling and Rendering

Images in FLTK follow an object-oriented design encapsulated by subclasses of Fl_Image. Images can be created from files (e.g., JPEG, PNG), embedded bitmaps, or generated programmatically. These image objects manage their own memory and platform-specific cache of rendering resources.

Drawing an image consists of calling its draw(int x, int y) method, which places the image at the specified widget-relative coordinate. Optional parameters allow scaling if the source and destination dimensions differ. FLTK handles transparency and masking internally using alpha channels or color keying methods depending on the image type.

Because image rendering interacts with the underlying platform's graphics APIs, performance varies by image format and system capabilities. Developers should prefer the appropriate image class for their use case and leverage caching where possible.

```cpp
void MyWidget::draw() {
    // Clear background
    fl_color(FL_WHITE);
    fl_rectf(0, 0, w(), h());

    // Draw a red rectangle
    fl_color(FL_RED);
    fl_rect(10, 10, w() - 20, h() - 20);

    // Draw a blue diagonal line
    fl_color(FL_BLUE);
    fl_line(10, 10, w() - 10, h() - 10);

    // Draw centered text
    fl_color(FL_BLACK);
    fl_font(FL_HELVETICA, 14);
    fl_draw("Sample Text", w()/2 - 40, h()/2);

    // Draw a filled circle using polygon approximation
    fl_color(FL_GREEN);
    fl_begin_polygon();
    for (int i = 0; i < 360; i += 10) {
        int x = w()/2 + 50 * cos(i * M_PI / 180.0);
        int y = h()/2 + 50 * sin(i * M_PI / 180.0);
        fl_vertex(x, y);
    }
    fl_end_polygon();
}
```

```
[Output: The widget appears with a white background,
a red rectangle inset by 10 pixels on all sides,
a blue diagonal line crossing from top-left to bottom-right,
centrally positioned black text "Sample Text",
and a filled green circle centered within the widget.]
```

Performance and Best Practices

Efficient custom painting in FLTK demands minimizing expensive drawing calls and avoiding unnecessary complexity within `draw()`. Drawing operations should be limited to affected regions, adhering to the current clipping bounds. Complex shapes and repeated graphics can be cached into `Fl_Pixmap` or `Fl_Image` objects to accelerate redraws.

Because FLTK does not provide hardware-accelerated rendering by default, leveraging the smallest necessary region for repainting and reducing overdraw improves both visual responsiveness and CPU usage. Managing offscreen buffers or double buffering is typically handled by FLTK's windowing system but can be manually implemented for advanced scenarios.

The FLTK graphics context offers a direct and effective model for widget rendering through platform-agnostic primitives. The immediate mode drawing model, centered around the `draw()` method, promotes clarity and predictability in rendering logic, while the coordinate system, color management, and paint lifecycle dictate the structure and flow of graphical updates. A thorough grasp of FLTK's primitives-lines, shapes, text, and image rendering-enables precise customization of widget appearances and interactive graphics within the cross-platform FLTK environment.

4.2. Bitmap, Vector, and SVG Integration

Graphical user interface applications frequently rely on the effective integration of diverse visual content to present information and enhance user interactivity. Within the FLTK (Fast Light Toolkit) framework, incorporating external visual assets such as bitmap images, vector graphics, and Scalable Vector Graphics (SVG) demands attention to loading mechanisms, rendering strategies, and runtime manipulations compatible with FLTK's event-driven and widget-based architecture.

Bitmap images, comprising rasterized pixel data formats such as BMP, PNG, JPEG, and GIF, constitute the most common form of graphical content embedded in GUI components. FLTK provides built-in support for reading bitmap formats primarily via the Fl_Image class hierarchy, with subclasses including Fl_Bitmap, Fl_Jpeg_Image, Fl_Png_Image, and Fl_Gif_Image to handle respective formats.

The loading procedure typically involves instantiating the appropriate image class with the file path or raw image buffer. For instance, PNG images are loaded via Fl_Png_Image, which decodes the file and maintains the pixel buffer internally. Rendering bitmap images is achieved by attaching the image object to an FLTK widget or by directly invoking draw() methods within custom widget drawing contexts.

```
Fl_Png_Image* png_img = new Fl_Png_Image("icon.png");
widget->image(png_img);
widget->redraw();
```

Runtime manipulation of bitmap images in FLTK is constrained due to the library's lightweight nature. Direct pixel buffer access is limited; however, image transformations such as scaling and cropping can be performed through the Fl_Image interface which provides methods like copy() and crop(). For advanced image processing (e.g., color adjustments or alpha blending), integration with external libraries such as OpenCV or FreeImage is advisable, followed by converting processed output back into FLTK-compatible image objects for GUI representation.

The pixel format in bitmaps is an important consideration. FLTK expects images in 32-bit ARGB format (8 bits per channel with an alpha channel for transparency). When loading images with different channel orders or depths, appropriate conversion is necessary before rendering to avoid color inaccuracies and artifacts.

Unlike bitmaps, vector graphics use mathematical primitives such as points, lines, curves, and polygons to represent images in a resolution-independent manner. These graphics are essential for user interfaces requiring infinite scalability, crisp rendering at arbitrary zoom levels, or dynamic graphic manipulation.

FLTK's native support for vector graphics is limited. It provides basic primitives through its drawing API, such as `fl_line()`, `fl_arc()`, `fl_polygon()`, and `fl_rect()`, which enable the construction of vector shapes within custom widget `draw()` methods. These primitives allow the implementation of complex vector renderings entirely in code.

```
void draw() override {
  fl_color(FL_BLUE);
  fl_line(x1, y1, x2, y2);
  fl_arc(x, y, w, h, 0, 360);
  fl_polygon(points, num_points);
}
```

For rich vector content designed externally, encapsulating vector data directly in FLTK is inconvenient. To bridge this gap, two approaches are prominent:

- **Conversion to Bitmap:** Vector graphics can be rasterized into high-resolution bitmaps before loading into FLTK widgets. This is effective for static content but forfeits scalability benefits.

- **External Vector Rendering Engines:** Libraries such as Cairo or Anti-Grain Geometry (AGG) provide advanced vector rendering capabilities. By directing their output onto FLTK widget draw contexts (via native window handles or shared buffers), these libraries enable rendering of complex vector designs, including anti-aliased curves and gradients.

Coordination between FLTK's coordinate system and that of the external renderer is essential, including transformations to align device pixel ratios, DPI considerations, and widget resizing.

Scalable Vector Graphics (SVG) is an XML-based vector image for-

116

mat widely used for web and GUI applications due to its text-based structure, scalability, and support for complex vector shapes, gradients, and filters. Embedding SVGs in FLTK extends the toolkit's graphic versatility notably.

Since FLTK does not provide native SVG parsing or rendering, integration is achieved by leveraging third-party libraries specifically designed for SVG:

- **NanoSVG:** A lightweight, single-header SVG parser and rasterizer written in C. It can decode SVG into simple path data and rasterize into bitmaps.

- **lunasvg:** A comprehensive C++ library for SVG parsing and rendering with support for advanced SVG features.

- **Cairo with librsvg:** A powerful combination where librsvg parses the SVG, and Cairo handles rendering. This yields high-quality output with extensive SVG support.

The general workflow involves loading an SVG document, parsing its XML structure, and then rendering it into a format suitable for FLTK display. Two common techniques are:

Rasterization-Based SVG Integration

SVG files are converted to bitmap images at runtime or pre-rendered externally. Rasterization parameters control the resolution and quality, after which the resulting raster image is loaded into an FLTK-compatible image class (e.g., Fl_Rgb_Image or Fl_Bitmap).

Example using NanoSVG for rasterization:

```
NSVGimage* svg = nsvgParseFromFile("icon.svg", "px", 96);
unsigned char* imgData = rasterizeSVG(svg, width, height);
Fl_RGB_Image* fl_img = new Fl_RGB_Image(imgData, width, height,
    4);
widget->image(fl_img);
```

This approach demands management of conversion resolution to maintain adequate quality and performance. Upscaling leads to increased memory usage and potential slowdown, while downscaling sacrifices detail.

Vector Path Rendering into FLTK Draw Calls

An alternative is extracting path and shape data from the SVG format and issuing corresponding FLTK drawing commands within widget paint methods. This requires traversing the SVG's XML tree, interpreting path definitions (e.g., M, L, C commands), transforming coordinates, and using FLTK's primitive drawing functions to render the vector structure.

This method preserves sharpness during scaling but can be challenging for complex SVGs with filters, masks, and gradients. Partial support may be implemented focusing on essential geometric objects to balance complexity and performance.

Once visual assets-bitmap, vector, or SVG-are integrated into FLTK widgets, specific runtime manipulations are often required:

- **Positioning and Scaling:** FLTK uses coordinate systems based on widget geometry. Images can be repositioned or scaled by adjusting the target drawing rectangle in the draw() method or using built-in image manipulation functions (Fl_Image::draw() allows specifying coordinates and scaling factors).

- **Transparency and Alpha Blending:** Bitmap images with alpha channels (e.g., PNG) are supported in FLTK by default. For vector and SVG-derived graphics rendered through external engines or custom draw calls, maintaining alpha compositing requires careful management of drawing layers and blending modes.

- **Animation:** For dynamic visuals, incremental redrawing strategies with timed events or FLTK's Fl::add_timeout()

mechanisms facilitate frame-wise updates, allowing transformations such as translation or morphing of visual elements.

- **Color and Style Adjustments:** FLTK's drawing primitives support color setting and line styles, which can be employed to alter vector graphics dynamically. Bitmap recoloring or filtering necessitates pixel-level operations external to FLTK.

Efficient integration of external visual content mandates balancing fidelity, responsiveness, and memory usage:

- **Lazy Loading and Caching:** Images should be loaded and decoded only once and reused to prevent runtime delays. For SVGs, pre-parsing and converting to optimized raster or vector structures improve render performance.

- **Resolution Independence:** Vector graphics and SVGs intrinsically offer resolution independence, beneficial for high-DPI displays. Whenever possible, leveraging vector-based approaches over bitmap rasterization ensures consistent quality.

- **Resource Cleanup:** FLTK images and externally allocated graphic buffers must be deallocated properly to avoid memory leaks. Using smart pointers or RAII idioms in C++ accelerates safe resource management.

- **Toolkit Compatibility:** When embedding external graphic libraries, compliance with FLTK's event and drawing models is required. For instance, drawing should occur within widget `draw()` overrides, and any interaction must be synchronized with FLTK's main loop.

Asset Type	Recommended Method
Bitmap (PNG, JPEG, BMP)	Use FLTK's native Fl_Image classes for loading and rendering. Utilize external libraries for advanced processing if needed.
Vector Graphics	Employ FLTK draw primitives for simple shapes. For complex vector content, integrate with external rendering engines such as Cairo or AGG.
SVG	Prefer rasterization with NanoSVG or librsvg+Cairo for full-featured rendering; alternatively, parse SVG paths and render via FLTK primitives for lightweight, scalable drawing.

The comprehensive integration of bitmaps, vectors, and SVGs within FLTK empowers developers to construct visually rich and scalable user interfaces that leverage the strengths of each graphic format. Mastery of these techniques facilitates the production of adaptable and performant GUI applications across diverse platforms.

4.3. Buffered Drawing and Real-Time Animation

Efficient rendering and animation in interactive applications rely heavily on techniques designed to eliminate visual artifacts such as flicker and tearing, while maintaining smooth, real-time updates that enhance user engagement. Central to achieving flicker-free rendering is the employment of buffer strategies, particularly double and triple buffering, complemented by precise timing control and frame management mechanisms. These combined approaches enable the generation of consistent, high-fidelity visual output that is both computationally feasible and visually appealing.

Buffering Strategies for Flicker-Free Rendering

Flicker in animation results from the direct drawing of frames on the display surface while the image is being updated, causing partial updates to appear momentarily and produce perceptible instability. To mitigate this, rendering is performed off-screen in a memory buffer, and the fully rendered frame is then rapidly transferred to the display in a single operation, a technique known as double buffering.

Double buffering maintains two distinct buffers: a *front buffer*, representing the content currently visible on the screen, and a *back buffer*, where the next frame is rendered. Upon completion of rendering, the pointers or references to these buffers are swapped or the back buffer's content is copied to the front buffer, effectively presenting a complete frame without incremental updates being visible.

Triple buffering introduces an additional buffer, further decoupling the rendering and display processes. This third buffer serves as a standby buffer where the render engine can prepare a new frame while the previously rendered frame awaits display. This technique reduces latency and can help maintain steady frame rates especially when rendering times vary unpredictably.

Both double and triple buffering demand careful synchronization between rendering and display pipelines to prevent buffer access conflicts. Many graphical APIs and platforms provide native support for these buffering schemes, abstracting lower-level memory management while allowing explicit synchronization control.

Timing Control and Frame Management

Achieving smooth animations necessitates a deliberate strategy for timing control, primarily controlling the frame rate and synchronizing rendering updates with the display refresh cycle. Commonly, applications target a fixed frame rate, such as 60 frames per second (fps), corresponding to a frame duration of approximately 16.67 milliseconds.

Implementing a frame timer involves measuring elapsed time between successive frame updates and triggering renders when the desired frame period has elapsed. This timer facilitates frame skipping or interpolation adaptations, accommodating variations in computational load to preserve consistent output tempo.

In addition to fixed frame rates, variable frame time approaches adapt rendering schedules in response to device performance and workload fluctuations. By tracking the actual time elapsed, the animation state can be interpolated proportionally to ensure smooth transitions without abrupt jumps or pauses. This technique employs concepts like delta-time integration, where the duration between frames modifies animation parameters such as position and velocity.

Frame management also requires techniques to handle dropped frames, where a frame takes longer to render than the nominal frame duration. To avoid perceptible stuttering, the system may skip non-essential frames or reduce rendering complexity dynamically. An alternative approach buffers multiple frames ahead, allowing rendering to proceed optimistically while ensuring the display pipeline always has a ready frame to present.

Vertical synchronization (Vsync) is a hardware-driven mechanism that synchronizes buffer swaps with the display refresh to prevent tearing-visible artifacts where portions of multiple frames are presented simultaneously. Combining Vsync with buffer strategies ensures frames are swapped only during blanking intervals, eliminating partial frame updates on screen.

Rendering Pipeline for Real-Time Animation

At the core of real-time animation is a rendering pipeline organized into discrete stages: update, draw, and buffer swap. The *update* phase computes the new animation state based on inputs, physics simulations, or scripted behavior, often parameterized by the elapsed time since the last frame. The *draw* phase renders the current state into the off-screen buffer, including all primitives, textures, and effects required at that moment.

In double buffering, after the draw phase concludes, the buffer swap operation atomically presents the freshly rendered frame by making the back buffer the front buffer. This operation must be efficient and synchronized to avoid partial exposure of frame content.

Consider the following pseudocode outline of a simplified rendering loop employing double buffering and fixed timestep control:

```
const double FRAME_DURATION = 16.67; // milliseconds for 60 fps
double previousTime = getCurrentTime();
double accumulator = 0.0;

while (applicationRunning) {
    double currentTime = getCurrentTime();
    double frameTime = currentTime - previousTime;
    previousTime = currentTime;
    accumulator += frameTime;

    while (accumulator >= FRAME_DURATION) {
        updateScene(FRAME_DURATION / 1000.0);
        accumulator -= FRAME_DURATION;
    }

    renderSceneToBackBuffer();
    swapBuffers(); // Double buffer swap synchronized with Vsync
}
```

This method ensures consistent update intervals, while rendering is performed at variable rates depending on processing time and timing drift, maintaining temporal coherence.

Advanced Techniques for Smooth Visuals

Beyond fundamental buffering and timing, advanced techniques contribute to a perceptually smooth experience. Frame interpolation interpolates animation states between update ticks, reducing jitter when updates occur at lower rates than the display refresh frequency. This is particularly useful in physics-based or input-responsive animations, where discrete updates may not align perfectly with rendering frames.

Adaptive quality scaling dynamically adjusts rendering fidelity based on real-time performance metrics. For example, scene complexity, texture resolutions, or shader detail may be automated to reduce load and maintain target frame rates within user experience constraints.

Double or triple buffering combined with GPU-accelerated compositing also facilitates seamless integration of layered visual elements, reducing CPU overhead and enabling complex visual effects with minimal latency. Graphics APIs such as OpenGL, DirectX, and Vulkan provide mechanisms like framebuffer objects and command buffers for efficient off-screen rendering and compositing pipelines.

Considerations for User Engagement

Visual smoothness is a critical factor influencing user engagement, as perceptible frame drops or flicker degrade the immersive quality of interface interactions, games, and simulations. Psychological studies correlate frame rate consistency and latency reduction with improved user satisfaction and responsiveness.

To optimize engagement, minimizing input-to-display latency is paramount. Buffering strategies must balance between eliminating flicker and maintaining timely response to user inputs. Employing techniques such as partial buffer updates (dirty rectangles), predictive input sampling, and asynchronous input processing can further reduce perceived delays.

Additionally, incorporating frame pacing is beneficial-distributing frame render durations evenly to avoid clustering of long frames, which can cause brief but noticeable freezes. Profiling and analyzing frame timing data during development helps identify bottlenecks and optimize pipeline performance.

Integrating audio-visual synchronization also enhances the perception of smoothness. Coordinating animation frames with sound playback ensures coherent sensory feedback, improving immersion and overall experience quality.

Summary of Best Practices

Implementing flicker-free, real-time animation involves:

- Utilizing double or triple buffering to render frames off-screen, eliminating partial draw visibility.

- Synchronizing buffer swaps with display refresh cycles via Vsync to avoid tearing.

- Maintaining consistent frame rate through fixed timestep or adaptive timing mechanisms.

- Employing interpolation and adaptive quality techniques to handle variable workloads gracefully.

- Minimizing input-to-display latency by optimizing buffer management and update pipelines.

- Profiling and fine-tuning frame pacing to prevent stutters and maintain fluid visual flow.

Adherence to these principles enables the creation of visually robust, responsive animation systems essential for modern interactive applications demanding high user engagement and seamless graphics performance.

4.4. OpenGL Integration within FLTK

Embedding OpenGL contexts within FLTK widgets enables advanced custom rendering capabilities by leveraging hardware-accelerated graphics in a cross-platform, lightweight GUI framework. FLTK's flexible widget architecture, combined with OpenGL's powerful rendering pipeline, facilitates complex visualizations and interactive 3D graphics directly integrated into standard application interfaces. Achieving robust integration requires precise management of OpenGL contexts bound to FLTK widget lifecycles, effective synchronization between FLTK's event handling system and OpenGL's drawing commands, and appropriate subclassing of FLTK widgets to customize rendering behavior.

The foundation of OpenGL integration in FLTK lies in subclassing the Fl_Gl_Window class, a specialized widget designed to support OpenGL rendering. Unlike standard FLTK widgets which rely primarily on software-based drawing routines, Fl_Gl_Window encapsulates an internal OpenGL rendering context, managing buffer swaps and context activation.

Creating a custom OpenGL widget involves deriving from Fl_Gl_Window and overriding critical virtual methods: draw() for rendering content and optionally handle(int event) for specialized event processing. The draw() method is automatically triggered in FLTK's event loop when the widget needs refresh or exposure. Overriding draw() ensures that OpenGL commands execute between a valid context setup and buffer swap, confining all rendering logic to a safe, well-defined location.

```cpp
class MyGLWidget : public Fl_Gl_Window {
public:
    MyGLWidget(int X, int Y, int W, int H, const char* L=0)
        : Fl_Gl_Window(X, Y, W, H, L) {
        // Widget initialization and OpenGL state setup
    }

    void draw() override {
        if (!valid()) {
            // Setup viewport and projection matrices here
            glViewport(0, 0, w(), h());
            glMatrixMode(GL_PROJECTION);
            glLoadIdentity();
            gluPerspective(45.0, (float)w() / h(), 1.0, 1000.0);
            glMatrixMode(GL_MODELVIEW);
            glLoadIdentity();
            // Additional OpenGL state initialization
            glEnable(GL_DEPTH_TEST);
        }

        // Clear the color and depth buffer
        glClear(GL_COLOR_BUFFER_BIT | GL_DEPTH_BUFFER_BIT);

        // Render scene content
        glLoadIdentity();
        glTranslatef(0.0f, 0.0f, -5.0f);
        glRotatef(30.0f, 1.0f, 0.0f, 0.0f);

        // Sample drawing: a colored triangle
        glBegin(GL_TRIANGLES);
```

```
        glColor3f(1.0f, 0.0f, 0.0f);
        glVertex3f(-1.0f, -1.0f, 0.0f);
        glColor3f(0.0f, 1.0f, 0.0f);
        glVertex3f(1.0f, -1.0f, 0.0f);
        glColor3f(0.0f, 0.0f, 1.0f);
        glVertex3f(0.0f, 1.0f, 0.0f);
      glEnd();

      // FLTK automatically swaps the buffer after draw()
    returns
    }
};
```

The valid() method is a key component of the Fl_Gl_Window interface; it indicates whether the underlying OpenGL context needs reinitialization-typically on the first draw or after resizing. This conditional allows costly operations, such as viewport adjustment, projection updates, or shader compilation, to be done only when necessary, thereby improving rendering efficiency. OpenGL state setup here is fundamental to establishing a consistent rendering environment.

FLTK internally manages OpenGL context creation and activation, binding it to Fl_Gl_Window instances. However, developers must understand the implicit context activation and validity to align OpenGL resource management correctly.

A crucial feature is that the OpenGL context is made current before every draw() invocation and is released afterward. This means OpenGL calls can be safely made during draw(), but attempting OpenGL operations in other widget functions or external threads without context activation risks errors or undefined behavior.

Resource loading operations, such as texture or buffer object generation, should ideally be deferred until the context is valid. Attempting to perform OpenGL resource initialization prior to context creation can fail silently or cause application crashes. Overriding valid() or leveraging FLTK's Fl_Gl_Window::valid() flag ensures proper synchronization of resource acquisition with context readiness.

Seamless interaction between FLTK's event-driven model and OpenGL's rendering pipeline requires careful event synchronization and redrawing strategies. Widgets integrating OpenGL must respond to FLTK input events by overriding the handle(int event) method. Common event types involve keyboard, mouse, and window resizing messages.

```
int MyGLWidget::handle(int event) {
    switch(event) {
        case FL_PUSH:   // Mouse button pressed
            // Capture initial mouse position or state
            return 1;   // Indicate event handled

        case FL_DRAG:   // Mouse dragged
            // Update rotation or view parameters based on mouse
    movement
            redraw();   // Request redraw to update rendering
            return 1;

        case FL_RELEASE:
            // Handle mouse button release
            return 1;

        case FL_KEYDOWN:
            if (Fl::event_key() == FL_Left) {
                // Modify rotation angle or camera position
                redraw();
                return 1;
            }
            return 0;

        default:
            return Fl_Gl_Window::handle(event);
    }
}
```

The redraw() call queues a widget repaint event within FLTK's event loop without forcing immediate execution. This deferred redraw mechanism enables batching multiple event updates before committing to rendering, improving responsiveness and reducing redundant OpenGL calls.

Additionally, handling window resize events is critical to maintain correct aspect ratios and viewport settings. FLTK sends an FL_RESIZE event when the widget changes dimensions, which can be captured in handle() or implicitly checked via the valid()

flag to adjust OpenGL projection matrices accordingly. Because
draw() executes after resizing, updating projection parameters
there ensures the viewport matches current widget size:

```
glViewport(0, 0, width(), height())
```

The combination of event-driven input processing and periodically triggered redraw cycles constitutes an efficient rendering loop
tightly integrated within FLTK's main loop. Unlike free-running
OpenGL contexts, this event-based approach conserves CPU and
GPU resources.

For applications requiring multiple OpenGL contexts or sharing
resources between contexts (e.g., textures, buffer objects), FLTK
provides control via the Fl_Gl_Window::context() method and
context attribute configurations at construction.

Managing multiple contexts can involve creating several
Fl_Gl_Window instances, each with its own context, or sharing
resources through platform-specific extensions such as WGL
(Windows), GLX (Linux/X11), or CGL (macOS). FLTK supports
specifying context attributes such as double buffering, color depth,
and stencil buffer availability through the mode() method or via
constructor parameters.

Proper synchronization when accessing shared resources between
contexts entails explicit binding and fence synchronization in modern OpenGL, necessitating advanced knowledge of OpenGL extensions and FLTK's native context handles accessible through
context().

Examples of such advanced usage include:

- Offscreen rendering in a hidden Fl_Gl_Window invoking
  framebuffer objects (FBOs).

- Compositing multiple OpenGL outputs into a complex GUI

layout.

- Implementing custom context switching for dynamic rendering pipelines.

OpenGL integration with FLTK requires mindful practices to sustain frame rates and maintain responsive interfaces:

1. **Minimize expensive OpenGL state changes** within draw(). Cache state where possible and avoid redundant matrix resets or shader recompilation on each draw call.

2. **Leverage FLTK's event system** to control redraw frequency-calling redraw() only when visual changes occur prevents unnecessary GPU load.

3. **Use double buffering and depth testing** to ensure flicker-free and correct depth rendering. These are standard enabled flags via mode() or context attributes.

4. **Properly handle widget resizing**: update OpenGL viewport and projection immediately to prevent visually distorted renderings.

5. **Defer OpenGL resource loading** to the point where context validity is assured (usually inside draw() when valid() is false). This avoids invalid contexts during application startup.

6. **Threading restrictions**: OpenGL contexts bound to FLTK windows are not inherently thread-safe. All OpenGL calls must happen on the main thread where FLTK's event loop runs unless explicit platform-level context sharing and synchronization are used.

7. **Profile and debug** using OpenGL tools (e.g., gDEBugger, RenderDoc) alongside FLTK's diagnostics for detecting leaks, context failures, or inefficient render loops.

Although FLTK's Fl_Gl_Window affords straightforward OpenGL context embedding, modern graphics applications increasingly adopt programmable pipelines with GLSL shaders, Vertex Array Objects (VAOs), and Framebuffer Objects (FBOs). Such practices are fully supported within the context of Fl_Gl_Window as long as the OpenGL context version requested supports the desired features, which can be specified using platform-specific hints before window creation.

Shader compilation, buffer object initialization, and texture loading should be encapsulated within the scope of context validity. Uploading data to GPU memory is best performed only once or when resources change, with rendering commands referencing preinitialized buffers and shader programs within draw().

An example shader initialization pattern:

```
void init_shaders() {
    vertex_shader = glCreateShader(GL_VERTEX_SHADER);
    const char* vertex_source = "...";
    glShaderSource(vertex_shader, 1, &vertex_source, nullptr);
    glCompileShader(vertex_shader);
    // Check compile errors...

    fragment_shader = glCreateShader(GL_FRAGMENT_SHADER);
    const char* fragment_source = "...";
    glShaderSource(fragment_shader, 1, &fragment_source, nullptr)
    ;
    glCompileShader(fragment_shader);
    // Check compile errors...

    shader_program = glCreateProgram();
    glAttachShader(shader_program, vertex_shader);
    glAttachShader(shader_program, fragment_shader);
    glLinkProgram(shader_program);
    // Check link errors...
}
```

This initialization would occur when valid() first returns false, ensuring the proper OpenGL context is current.

The key to robust OpenGL integration in FLTK includes:

- Deriving from Fl_Gl_Window and implementing the draw()

131

method for rendering.

- Utilizing `valid()` to control OpenGL state initialization and resource setup.

- Overriding `handle(int)` to synchronize FLTK events with rendering updates and user interaction.

- Managing OpenGL context lifecycle implicitly via FLTK's backend while accounting for resource initialization timing.

- Efficiently coordinating redraw calls with user input and avoiding costly operations on every frame.

- Extending capabilities by writing and managing modern OpenGL shaders and buffer objects within the context.

The elegance of combining FLTK's minimalistic yet powerful GUI toolkit with the rendering flexibility of OpenGL lies in the clean separation of event-driven GUI management and direct, high-performance hardware rendering, delivered through a well-structured widget subclassing and context management strategy.

This approach yields interactive applications capable of sophisticated 3D visualization, simulation, and graphics processing without sacrificing the lightweight portable nature intrinsic to FLTK.

4.5. Image Processing and Post-Processing Effects

Pixel-level image manipulation forms the foundation for numerous complex visual effects and transformations essential in computer graphics, computer vision, and digital photography. Implementing efficient image processing routines requires a deep understanding of pixel data organization, mathematical transformations, filter design, and hardware capabilities. This section elaborates on core techniques for pixel manipulation, examines typical post-processing effects, and addresses performance considerations by comparing CPU- and GPU-centric approaches.

At its core, an image can be viewed as a two-dimensional array of pixels, each with component values representing color intensities in various color spaces (e.g., RGB, HSV, or grayscale). Pixel-level transformations typically involve mapping input pixels to output pixels through spatial transformations or intensity modifications. A fundamental image transformation is affine mapping, which preserves points, straight lines, and planes. Affine transformations include translation, scaling, rotation, and shearing, often represented by a 3×3 homogeneous coordinate matrix $\mathbf{A}$:

$$\mathbf{A} = \begin{bmatrix} a_{11} & a_{12} & t_x \\ a_{21} & a_{22} & t_y \\ 0 & 0 & 1 \end{bmatrix}$$

The transformed coordinate $\mathbf{x}' = (x', y', 1)^T$ is obtained from the source coordinate $\mathbf{x} = (x, y, 1)^T$ via $\mathbf{x}' = \mathbf{A}\mathbf{x}$. Applying inverse mapping ensures that all output pixels are assigned appropriate input pixel values by sampling the original image at non-integer locations using interpolation methods such as nearest neighbor, bilinear, or bicubic interpolation. Choosing the right interpolation method balances computational cost and visual quality.

Filtering operations alter pixel intensities to enhance or extract features and play a central role in noise reduction, edge detection, and image sharpening. Linear spatial filtering convolves an image I with a kernel K:

$$I'(x, y) = \sum_{i=-m}^{m} \sum_{j=-n}^{n} K(i, j) \cdot I(x - i, y - j)$$

where $(2m+1) \times (2n+1)$ is the kernel size. Common kernels include Gaussian blur for smoothing, Laplacian for edge enhancement,

133

and Sobel operators for edge detection in horizontal and vertical directions. Gaussian kernels approximate the two-dimensional Gaussian function:

$$G(x, y) = \frac{1}{2\pi\sigma^2} e^{-\frac{x^2+y^2}{2\sigma^2}}$$

where σ controls the blur radius. The separability property of Gaussian kernels allows decomposition into two one-dimensional convolutions applied sequentially along rows and columns, reducing computational complexity from $O(k^2)$ to $O(2k)$ per pixel, where k is kernel width.

Non-linear filters such as median filters offer robust noise removal for salt-and-pepper noise by replacing each pixel with the median intensity in a neighborhood. Unlike linear filters, median filtering preserves edges better but is computationally more expensive.

Post-processing effects integrate pixel manipulation strategies to create compelling visuals in real-time rendering and image enhancement pipelines. Bloom, tone mapping, depth of field, motion blur, and color grading rely on multiple passes over image data, often with specialized filtering stages. Bloom simulates light bleeding from bright areas by applying a thresholded Gaussian blur to bright pixels and additive blending to the original image. Tone mapping compresses high dynamic range values into viewable low dynamic range displays by applying perceptual and device-specific operators. Common tone mapping functions include Reinhard and filmic curves which dynamically map luminance values to maintain detail in highlights and shadows.

Depth of field effects simulate camera lens characteristics by blurring regions outside the focal plane. A popular method segments the image into layers of varying blur radii based on depth buffers and applies spatial filtering weighted by the circle of confusion. Motion blur aggregates pixel contributions from multiple temporal samples or employs velocity buffers to guide directional blur

134

kernels. Color grading adjusts the chromatic distribution and luminance to achieve desired stylistic looks, frequently represented by three-dimensional lookup tables (3D LUTs) mapping input RGB values to output corrected colors.

Performance optimization is paramount when implementing image processing routines, especially for real-time applications such as video games and interactive visualization. CPU-based approaches offer flexibility and ease of debugging but often struggle with throughput when processing high-resolution images or complex kernels. Key CPU optimization techniques include:

- **Memory access patterns:** Organizing pixel data linearly to improve cache locality minimizes memory latency.

- **Loop unrolling and SIMD:** Exploiting Single Instruction Multiple Data (SIMD) extensions (e.g., SSE, AVX) enables parallel processing of multiple pixels per instruction cycle.

- **Multithreading:** Utilizing multi-core CPUs with thread pools or task parallel libraries partitions image data across cores to harness concurrency.

GPU-based implementations leverage massive parallelism and dedicated memory bandwidth to dramatically accelerate pixel manipulations. Fragment shaders operate on millions of pixels in parallel, naturally mapping to image processing tasks. Modern graphics APIs such as Vulkan, OpenGL, and Direct3D facilitate programmable pipelines where custom shaders compute transformations and filters on the GPU. Tessellation and compute shaders extend flexibility for complex algorithms outside standard rasterization. GPU implementations pose unique challenges:

- **Memory bandwidth and latency:** Optimizing texture fetch patterns by exploiting locality and leveraging shared memory reduces bottlenecks.

135

- **Precision constraints:** Fixed-point or half-precision floating-point formats may introduce quantization errors affecting visual fidelity.

- **Branch divergence:** Control flow instructions that lead to different execution paths per thread reduce throughput; algorithms must minimize conditionals or restructure processing.

A hybrid approach frequently yields an advantageous balance between CPU and GPU capabilities. Preprocessing steps-such as loading, decoding, or CPU-side filtering for small kernels-and postprocessing steps requiring global image statistics or multiple image passes can reside on the CPU. In contrast, pixel-shader intensive tasks like convolutions with large kernels, tone mapping, and bloom effects benefit from GPU acceleration. Data transfer overhead between CPU and GPU imposes a design constraint, where minimizing back-and-forth memory copies is critical.

The following example illustrates a basic CPU-side implementation of a Gaussian blur filter using a separable kernel, demonstrating essential kernel creation and the two-pass convolution paradigm:

```cpp
#include <vector>
#include <cmath>

using Image = std::vector<std::vector<float>>; // Grayscale image

std::vector<float> createGaussianKernel(int radius, float sigma)
    {
    int size = 2 * radius + 1;
    std::vector<float> kernel(size);
    float sum = 0.0f;
    float invTwoSigmaSq = 1.0f / (2.0f * sigma * sigma);

    for(int i = -radius; i <= radius; ++i) {
        float val = std::exp(-i * i * invTwoSigmaSq);
        kernel[i + radius] = val;
        sum += val;
    }

    for(float &v : kernel) {
```

```cpp
        v /= sum;
    }

    return kernel;
}

Image convolveHorizontal(const Image &input, const std::vector<
    float> &kernel, int radius) {
    int width = input[0].size();
    int height = input.size();
    Image output(height, std::vector<float>(width, 0.0f));

    for(int y = 0; y < height; ++y) {
        for(int x = 0; x < width; ++x) {
            float acc = 0.0f;
            for(int k = -radius; k <= radius; ++k) {
                int sampleX = std::min(std::max(x + k, 0), width
    - 1);
                acc += input[y][sampleX] * kernel[k + radius];
            }
            output[y][x] = acc;
        }
    }
    return output;
}

Image convolveVertical(const Image &input, const std::vector<
    float> &kernel, int radius) {
    int width = input[0].size();
    int height = input.size();
    Image output(height, std::vector<float>(width, 0.0f));

    for(int y = 0; y < height; ++y) {
        for(int x = 0; x < width; ++x) {
            float acc = 0.0f;
            for(int k = -radius; k <= radius; ++k) {
                int sampleY = std::min(std::max(y + k, 0), height
    - 1);
                acc += input[sampleY][x] * kernel[k + radius];
            }
            output[y][x] = acc;
        }
    }
    return output;
}

Image gaussianBlur(const Image &input, int radius, float sigma) {
    auto kernel = createGaussianKernel(radius, sigma);
    Image temp = convolveHorizontal(input, kernel, radius);
    Image output = convolveVertical(temp, kernel, radius);
    return output;
}
```

This CPU-based implementation is straightforward but limited in throughput for large images. GPUs expedite such convolutions using fragment shaders, where kernels can be hardcoded or sampled from textures, and memory fetches are optimized using hardware interpolation and caching.

Adopting higher-level compute frameworks such as CUDA or OpenCL enables explicit control over parallelization on heterogeneous systems but increases development complexity. These frameworks allow custom kernel definitions, shared memory usage, and synchronization to optimize filtering and transformation pipelines efficiently.

Fine-tuning algorithmic parameters based on input image sizes, expected output quality, and deadline constraints further guides whether a CPU, GPU, or hybrid implementation suffices. For instance, real-time applications demand low-latency pipeline stages where GPU acceleration of convolution and post-processing is indispensable. Conversely, offline high-quality rendering or batch image processing may afford CPU-based or multi-threaded strategies emphasizing numerical precision and stability.

Understanding image data layout and formats is critical for both CPU and GPU implementations. On CPUs, planar or interleaved formats affect cache coherence and SIMD vectorization efficiency, while on GPUs texture types and formats influence sampling precision and filtering capabilities. Conversion and normalization steps between color spaces and component ranges consume additional cycles and should be minimized in the processing loop.

Mastering pixel-level processing requires an integrated approach that balances mathematical rigor, algorithmic efficiency, and hardware exploitation. Transformations, filtering, and post-processing effects constitute successive layers that reshape image content with controlled alterations. Achieving optimal performance involves careful kernel design, interpolation strategy selection, memory access optimization, and appropriate use of parallel architectures.

These principles form the basis for high-quality, real-time capable image processing systems.

4.6. Performance Profiling in Rendering

In high-performance rendering, understanding the computational cost and execution characteristics of the rendering pipeline is essential for optimization. Profiling provides quantitative insights into bottlenecks and resource utilization, enabling developers to make informed decisions about where and how to improve efficiency within custom rendering workflows.

Profiling in rendering involves detailed measurement of execution times at various stages, memory bandwidth usage, shader performance, and GPU-CPU synchronization overheads. The goal is to isolate critical path segments that limit frame rate or increase latency. Key metrics include frame time, draw call counts, shader invocation costs, and memory transactions.

Frame time-the duration between frame starts-is a primary performance indicator. Maintaining a frame time below the refresh period of the display (e.g., 16.67 ms for 60 Hz) is fundamental to smooth interactivity. Spikes and inconsistencies in frame timing reveal underlying inefficiencies or synchronization stalls.

Rendering workloads may be bounded by various hardware resources: GPU compute, memory bandwidth, CPU processing, or driver overhead. Bottleneck identification proceeds through isolating these constraints using both quantitative measurements and architectural understanding.

- **CPU vs. GPU Bound:** Profiling tools can report CPU and GPU times separately. When GPU time exceeds CPU time significantly, the workload is GPU-bound, suggesting optimization efforts focus on shader complexity, overdraw reduction, or memory optimizations. Conversely, a CPU-dominant profile indicates driver overhead, command buffer generation inefficiencies, or excessive state changes.

- **Command Submission and API Overhead:** High numbers of draw calls and state changes increase CPU cost. Reducing draw calls through batching, instancing, or occlusion culling can alleviate CPU load. Some APIs and drivers incorporate costly validation or synchronization steps which can manifest as CPU stalls.

- **Memory Bandwidth Limitations:** Profiling memory utilization using vendor-specific counters (e.g., NVIDIA Nsight or AMD Radeon GPU Profiler) reveals whether bandwidth is saturated. Excessive texture fetches, framebuffer readbacks, or buffer reads can cause memory bottlenecks affecting both performance and power consumption.

- **Shader Execution Efficiency:** Shader profiling identifies instructions and resource usage per invocation. High arithmetic intensity, branch divergence, or texture fetch latency degrade performance. Shader compilers may provide static analysis; dynamic profiling uncovers cache misses and memory latency.

A combination of CPU and GPU profiling tools is essential for comprehensive insight:

- **RenderDoc:** An open-source frame debugger and profiler ideal for capturing GPU workloads, analyzing draw calls, and inspecting framebuffer content. It supports detailed traversal of frame commands and shader inspection.

- **NVIDIA Nsight Graphics:** Provides GPU hardware-level profiling, including warp occupancy, memory throughput, and detailed timeline views relating CPU and GPU activity. It supports Vulkan, OpenGL, DirectX, and CUDA.

- **AMD Radeon GPU Profiler (RGP):** Offers low-level hardware counters for AMD GPUs, covering wavefront efficiency, memory accesses, and cache performance.

- **Intel Graphics Performance Analyzers (GPA):** Focuses on integrated GPUs and CPU-GPU interactions, useful for power-efficient platforms.

- **Platform-specific CPU profilers:** Such as Visual Studio Profiler or Linux perf, useful for detecting CPU-bound bottlenecks related to command generation, resource loading, or synchronization.

- **API layer validation and profiling:** Tools like Vulkan's validation layers and DirectX debug runtimes can highlight inefficient API usage and synchronization errors affecting performance.

Each tool serves to measure complementary aspects of rendering performance. Integrating these insights produces a holistic understanding of the rendering workload.

Analyzing frame timing patterns aids in distinguishing between consistent bottlenecks and transient stalls. Frame timing metrics can be visualized as histograms or line graphs illustrating frame duration variance. Tools with GPU and CPU timeline views reveal the pipeline stages active during each frame:

- **CPU-GPU parallelism:** Ideally, GPU work proceeds concurrently with CPU preparation of subsequent frames. When timelines indicate GPU finish waiting on CPU tasks, or vice versa, it suggests synchronization inefficiencies or pipeline stalls.

- **Pipeline stall causes:** Render passes requiring frame-buffer reads, complex memory barriers, or dynamic shader recompilations introduce latency. Profilers can highlight such stalls by detecting idle periods on GPU queues.

141

- **Latency Reduction Techniques:** Introducing frame pacing algorithms, asynchronous resource streaming, and double or triple buffering help smooth frame times and reduce input-to-display latency.

Accurate frame timing analysis is especially critical in virtual reality and interactive simulations, where variability in frame delivery causes perceptible judder and motion sickness.

Profiling results inform many effective optimizations:

Render Pass and Draw Call Minimization: Reducing the number of state changes and render passes minimizes CPU overhead and allows better GPU command prefetching. Employ techniques such as:

- Instanced rendering to handle many similar objects with fewer draw calls.

- Persistent command buffers to amortize driver overhead across frames.

- Deferred shading and tile-based rendering architectures to reduce framebuffer bandwidth.

Shader Code Optimization: Using profile-driven feedback, optimize shader algorithms by:

- Reducing unnecessary operations and complex control flow.

- Exploiting GPU-specific intrinsic functions for common math operations.

- Minimizing texture fetches and using compressed or lower precision formats when feasible.

- Balancing the use of precomputed data versus dynamic calculations.

Memory Access and Bandwidth Optimization: Given memory bandwidth constraints, optimize by:

- Aligning vertex and uniform buffers for cache-friendly access patterns.

- Employing texture atlases and efficient sampling strategies to reduce fetches.

- Using asynchronous resource loading to prevent stalls.

Pipeline and Synchronization Management: Efficient command submission and synchronization are critical:

- Leverage multi-threaded command buffer generation where API supports.

- Avoid unnecessary pipeline flushes and barriers.

- Utilize fine-grained synchronization rather than global critical sections.

Continuous profiling integrated into development cycles ensures early detection of performance regressions. Automated regression tests with performance targets and regression thresholds facilitate maintaining optimal frame rates. Capturing representative workload samples under realistic input scenarios reveals meaningful bottlenecks beyond synthetic tests.

Detailed profiling data should be correlated with visual debugging tools that verify rendering correctness and quality trade-offs inherent in performance optimizations. Adjustments to quality settings, level of detail (LOD), and resolution scaling can be actuated dynamically at runtime based on profiling feedback, balancing performance and visual fidelity.

A typical high-performance rendering frame may be decomposed as follows:

$$\text{Total Frame Time} = T_{\text{CPU}} + T_{\text{GPU}} + T_{\text{Sync}} + T_{\text{Wait}}$$

where

- T_{CPU}: Command generation, culling, and resource management.

- T_{GPU}: Shader execution, rasterization, blending.

- T_{Sync}: Driver and API synchronization overhead.

- T_{Wait}: Idle periods due to imbalances or stalls.

Measuring and minimizing each component contributes to overall frame rate improvement.

Timestamp queries embedded in command buffers provide fine-grained GPU timing data. A simple Vulkan query usage pattern is:

```
vkCmdWriteTimestamp(commandBuffer,
    VK_PIPELINE_STAGE_BOTTOM_OF_PIPE_BIT, queryPool,
    startQueryIndex);
// ... rendering commands ...
vkCmdWriteTimestamp(commandBuffer,
    VK_PIPELINE_STAGE_BOTTOM_OF_PIPE_BIT, queryPool,
    endQueryIndex);
```

After command buffer execution, collected timestamps yield GPU duration per stage:

```
uint64_t timestamps[2];
vkGetQueryPoolResults(device, queryPool, startQueryIndex, 2,
                      sizeof(timestamps), timestamps,
                      sizeof(uint64_t),
                      VK_QUERY_RESULT_64_BIT |
    VK_QUERY_RESULT_WAIT_BIT);

double gpuTime = (timestamps[1] - timestamps[0]) *
    timestampPeriod; // in nanoseconds
```

This approach allows isolating costly passes or draws, facilitating targeted optimization.

Profiling thus serves as an indispensable methodology in custom rendering workflows, guiding developers toward maximal efficiency and responsive, resource-aware graphics applications.

146

Chapter 5

Data Binding, MVC, and Reactive Programming Patterns

Transform how your FLTK applications manage complexity and state by harnessing proven design patterns and responsive programming techniques. This chapter unpacks the structures that keep interfaces clean, maintainable, and effortlessly synchronized with underlying data. From classic MVC to modern reactive flows, you'll discover practical strategies to construct flexible, testable, and scalable GUIs that react seamlessly to user and data changes.

5.1. Model/View/Controller in FLTK

The Model/View/Controller (MVC) architectural pattern is essential to structuring complex graphical user interface (GUI) applications with clear separation of concerns, promoting maintainability, scalability, and testability. The Fast Light Toolkit (FLTK), a lightweight cross-platform C++ GUI library, does not enforce MVC explicitly but provides a flexible foundation on which MVC paradigms can be rigorously implemented. This section addresses the adaptation of MVC within FLTK applications, emphasizing design principles that yield modular, reusable, and maintainable codebases.

Separation of Concerns

At the core of MVC is the partitioning of application logic into three distinct components:

- **Model**: Encapsulates the domain data and business logic. It is responsible for managing the underlying state irrespective of the user interface.

- **View**: Presents the data to the user by rendering the model visually. It maintains a visual representation and forwards user interactions for processing.

- **Controller**: Handles user input, converts it into model updates or view changes, and mediates between model and view.

In an FLTK context, the `Fl_Widget` subclasses naturally fulfill the role of the View by managing graphical rendering and event response mechanisms. However, FLTK widgets often combine input handling and rendering in a single class, which necessitates deliberate architectural choices to decouple model and controller responsibilities.

148

Model Implementation

The Model should be kept free of any GUI dependencies. Typically, the model is implemented as Plain Old C++ Objects (POCO) that encapsulate application state and domain logic. For example, consider a model representing a text document, with a data structure storing its content and methods for editing:

```cpp
class TextDocument {
  std::string content_;
public:
  const std::string& content() const { return content_; }
  void insert(size_t pos, const std::string& text) {
    content_.insert(pos, text);
    notifyObservers();
  }
  void erase(size_t pos, size_t count) {
    content_.erase(pos, count);
    notifyObservers();
  }

  using Observer = std::function<void()>;
  void addObserver(Observer obs) { observers_.push_back(std::move
    (obs)); }
private:
  std::vector<Observer> observers_;
  void notifyObservers() {
    for (auto& obs : observers_) obs();
  }
};
```

This design leverages the Observer pattern, enabling views and controllers to be notified of model updates without tight coupling. The model thus remains autonomous, unaware of the user interface or input mechanisms.

View Design in FLTK

Views in FLTK derive from Fl_Widget or related classes and are responsible solely for displaying the model state and forwarding interaction events. They query the model for data when redrawing and defer any state mutation actions to the controller or model interface.

A view tailored for the TextDocument model might extend

149

Fl_Widget and subscribe to model changes:

```cpp
class TextView : public Fl_Widget {
  TextDocument& model_;
public:
  TextView(int X, int Y, int W, int H, TextDocument& model)
    : Fl_Widget(X, Y, W, H), model_(model) {
    model_.addObserver([this]() { this->redraw(); });
  }
protected:
  void draw() override {
    fl_color(FL_WHITE);
    fl_rectf(x(), y(), w(), h());
    fl_color(FL_BLACK);
    fl_draw(model_.content().c_str(), x() + 5, y() + 20);
  }
};
```

The view maintains no internal state representing the document beyond holding a reference to the model. It reacts to model change notifications by redrawing itself, ensuring its representation remains consistent with the underlying data.

Controller Implementation

The Controller in FLTK acts as the event handler for input devices (keyboard, mouse) and translates these events into model manipulations. Its separation from the view is crucial to maintain MVC integrity. Controllers may be implemented as separate classes that listen to widget callbacks or may be embedded within specialized handler objects associated with widgets.

Consider a simple controller class handling text editing input:

```cpp
class TextController {
  TextDocument& model_;
  TextView& view_;
  size_t cursorPosition_ = 0;
public:
  TextController(TextDocument& model, TextView& view)
    : model_(model), view_(view) {
    view_.callback(TextController::staticCallback, this);
  }

  static void staticCallback(Fl_Widget* w, void* data) {
    static_cast<TextController*>(data)->handleEvent(w);
  }
```

```
void handleEvent(Fl_Widget* w) {
  Fl_Keyboard_State keyboard;
  Fl::get_keyboard_state(keyboard);
  int key = Fl::event_key();
  if (Fl::event() == FL_KEYBOARD) {
    if (key == FL_Delete && cursorPosition_ < model_.content().
size()) {
      model_.erase(cursorPosition_, 1);
    } else if (key == FL_Left && cursorPosition_ > 0) {
      --cursorPosition_;
    } else if (key == FL_Right && cursorPosition_ < model_.
content().size()) {
      ++cursorPosition_;
    } else if (Fl::event_text()[0] >= 32) {
      model_.insert(cursorPosition_, std::string(1, Fl::
event_text()[0]));
      ++cursorPosition_;
    }
    view_.redraw();
  }
}
};
```

This controller listens for key events, updating the model accordingly. Note that the specific position handling and boundary checks ensure robust modifications. The linkage between controller and view happens through the view's callback registration, enabling isolation of event interpretation logic from visual rendering.

Communications and Event Propagation

A pivotal part of MVC in FLTK is the event flow and update mechanism implemented via observer callbacks and widget event callbacks. By managing model updates through an observer pattern, multiple views can remain synchronized without explicit dependencies. These callbacks should be lightweight to maintain UI responsiveness.

Moreover, controllers can handle multiple views or models to implement composite interfaces. Separation is reinforced by ensuring controllers do not directly modify view state aside from invoking redraw or update methods.

Techniques for Maintainability and Reuse

To foster maintainability and reuse, FLTK MVC implementations benefit from consistent design patterns:

- **Interface Abstraction**: Defining interfaces for models and controllers alleviates compile-time dependencies and facilitates unit testing.

- **Signal/Slot or Observer Abstractions**: Employing observer pattern utilities (e.g., `std::function` and `std::vector` callbacks) instead of direct calls prevents tight coupling.

- **Decoupling Event Handling**: Centralizing input event translation within controllers enables multiple views to leverage common input logic and simplifies changing input policies.

- **Model-First Updates**: All state changes should flow through the model to preserve a single source of truth, simplifying reasoning about application behavior.

- **Minimal Widget Subclassing**: Restricting customizations of `Fl_Widget` subclasses mainly to visual aspects reduces complexity and avoids embedding business logic in views.

As an illustration, consider a reusable controller interface for data editing:

```
class ITextController {
public:
  virtual ~ITextController() = default;
  virtual void handleKey(int key, const char* text) = 0;
  virtual void handleCursorMovement(int direction) = 0;
};
```

This abstraction allows swapping different controller implementations without touching view or model code, enabling flexible user interaction schemes.

152

Example Integration

The interplay between components forms a graph of command and notification paths:

- The `Controller` receives input via FLTK event callbacks.

- The `Controller` calls mutators on the `Model` to change data.

- The `Model` notifies registered observers, which include `Views`.

- The `Views` invoke their redraw methods, querying fresh `Model` data.

Such a design ensures that the user interface is responsive to dynamic data changes, while each component remains focused on its responsibility. The loose coupling achieved reduces side effects and simplifies debugging.

Adopting MVC in FLTK requires careful architectural discipline since the toolkit itself is agnostic to this pattern. The explicit separation of model, view, and controller leverages FLTK's lightweight widget system while reinforcing software engineering best practices. Employing observer-based communication and isolating input handling in dedicated controllers results in flexible applications that are easier to extend and maintain. This approach maximizes the strengths of FLTK for performance and portability while delivering a robust and modular GUI application framework.

5.2. Bidirectional Data Binding Techniques

Bidirectional data binding establishes a synchronized link between application data models and user interface widgets, ensuring changes in either are mutually reflected. This technique is foundational in interactive systems where state coherence and real-time responsiveness are critical. Achieving robust bidirectional synchronization involves carefully orchestrated strategies concerning change detection, propagation, and update management while conscientiously avoiding adverse effects such as infinite update loops.

At the core of bidirectional binding is the concept of *change notification*. A well-structured observer pattern or event subscription mechanism monitors modifications in both the data model and the UI element. When a user edits a widget's displayed value, the binding system listens for an event or callback signaling this alteration. Conversely, programmatic changes in the model trigger corresponding notifications that initiate widget updates. The design of these notification systems must guarantee minimal latency and consistency to preserve the interactive experience.

Typically, bidirectional binding utilizes a pair of *value accessors* bridging model and widget. The model accessor reads and writes the application's internal data representation, while the widget accessor interfaces with the UI control's state. Synchronization proceeds through intermediary update functions: when a user action modifies the widget, the new value is propagated to the model, and when the model state changes, the widget is updated accordingly. This can be summarized as two distinct propagation channels-model-to-widget and widget-to-model.

A fundamental challenge lies in the possibility of *infinite update loops*. Such loops occur when a change originating in one component triggers an update in the other, which then triggers a reciprocal update back, creating a cycle. For example, updating a textbox's content programmatically fires the widget's change event, which then attempts to write to the model, causing another model change event, and so forth. To prevent this, binding frameworks implement various forms of *update cycle prevention*.

One common approach is to introduce *change origin tracking*. Before propagating a change, the binding system records the source of the update and suppresses subsequent updates that originate from the same source within the same transaction or event cycle. This can be implemented using flags or context tokens that indicate whether an update is in progress, effectively preventing reentrant calls. Pseudocode illustrating this logic resembles the following:

```
bool isUpdating = false;

function onWidgetChange(newValue):
    if not isUpdating:
        isUpdating = true
        model.setValue(newValue)
        isUpdating = false

function onModelChange(newValue):
    if not isUpdating:
        isUpdating = true
        widget.setValue(newValue)
        isUpdating = false
```

In more sophisticated implementations, *transactional update groupings* and *deferred notifications* are used. These batch multiple changes to avoid redundant or conflicting updates and guarantee atomic state transitions.

Another technique to avoid infinite loops involves *value equality checks* before propagation. Before pushing an updated value from one side to the other, the binding system compares the current target value with the new source value. Only if the two differ meaningfully does it proceed. This prevents redundant updates when values are semantically the same but events are repeatedly fired due to platform or framework quirks.

Handling *asynchronous updates* introduces additional complexity into bidirectional binding. Widgets or models may change independently due to asynchronous operations, external input, or delegated computations. Binding systems often integrate queueing or scheduling mechanisms to serialize updates and enforce order consistency, preventing race conditions.

Data type conversions between model and widget pose further

challenges. Models often cache data in formats optimized for business logic-numbers, complex objects, or domain-specific representations-whereas widgets require textual strings, ranges, or UI-specific types. *Value converters* or *adapter layers* transform data bidirectionally. These converters encapsulate validation, formatting, and normalization logic so that the binding operates on semantically correct values. For instance, a currency amount stored as a float in the model may be converted to a localized string for display and parsed back when edited.

Integrating validation into bidirectional binding is essential for maintaining data integrity without obstructing user input. Input widgets demand feedback mechanisms that do not prematurely reject transiently invalid states (e.g., half-typed numerals). A common pattern separates *presentation state* from *model state* by allowing the widget to temporarily hold invalid or intermediate values, only committing validated values to the model. The binding system employs asynchronous or event-driven validation callbacks, enabling graceful handling of error states and notifications.

Consider the following exemplar Python-like pseudo-implementation demonstrating the management of bidirectional updates with change origin tracking and value checking:

```
class BidirectionalBinding:
    def __init__(self, model, widget, converter=lambda x: x):
        self.model = model
        self.widget = widget
        self.converter = converter
        self.is_updating = False
        self.model.on_change(self.on_model_change)
        self.widget.on_change(self.on_widget_change)
        self.widget.set_value(self.converter(self.model.get_value
())))

    def on_model_change(self, new_value):
        if self.is_updating:
            return
        widget_value = self.converter(new_value)
        if widget_value != self.widget.get_value():
            self.is_updating = True
            try:
                self.widget.set_value(widget_value)
```

```
        finally:
            self.is_updating = False

def on_widget_change(self, new_value):
    if self.is_updating:
        return
    model_value = self.converter(new_value)
    if model_value != self.model.get_value():
        self.is_updating = True
        try:
            self.model.set_value(model_value)
        finally:
            self.is_updating = False
```

In this pattern, the is_updating flag guards against cycle reentry, while value comparisons prevent unnecessary updates.

Furthermore, the synchronization between model and widget may require *debouncing* or *throttling* to manage rapid or high-frequency changes, such as those induced by user input via sliders or text fields. Debouncing batches rapid sequences of events, sending only the final value, reducing processing overhead and visual flicker. Throttling limits update frequency, maintaining responsiveness in resource-intensive contexts.

Additional risk factors include *order-of-operations* issues when multiple bindings or dependencies interact, potentially causing transient inconsistencies or glitches. Employing a central *binding coordinator* or *message bus* promotes orderly propagation and cycle detection in complex graphs of bindings.

In declarative UI frameworks, bidirectional binding is often specified tersely, with automatic change detection and update resolution handled by the underlying runtime. However, understanding and explicitly implementing the mechanisms ensures tailored control in performance-critical or domain-specialized applications.

Sound bidirectional data binding architecture hinges on:

- Robust change notification systems that track source identity.

157

- Careful prevention of infinite loops via state flags and equality checks.

- Support for asynchronous and deferred updates.

- Seamless data conversion and validation integration.

- Performance optimizations through debouncing and throttling.

- Coordination for complex dependency networks.

Each of these elements must be thoughtfully integrated to realize efficient, maintainable, and user-friendly interfaces exhibiting continuous model-widget coherence.

5.3. Observer and Signal-Slot Mechanisms

Event notification is a fundamental aspect of interactive and reactive software systems, enabling the decoupling of components and promoting modular architectures. Two prevalent patterns for event notification are the Observer pattern and the signal-slot mechanism. Both architectures facilitate communication between a subject (or emitter) and its dependents (observers or slots), allowing an event producer to notify multiple consumers of state changes or triggered conditions without tight coupling. These patterns are intrinsic to designing responsive user interfaces, modeling dynamic data sets, and implementing extensible frameworks.

Observer Pattern Implementation

The Observer pattern formalizes the dependency between a subject and its observers. The subject maintains a collection of observer references and notifies them of relevant state changes. Observers implement a callback interface or listener protocol, which the subject invokes upon specific events. This design allows any number of observers to register or deregister dynamically, thus supporting flexible broadcast and reception of notifications.

A canonical implementation employs abstract interfaces defining the contract between subjects and observers. Consider an example applied to a model-view architecture:

```cpp
class IObserver {
public:
    virtual ~IObserver() = default;
    virtual void update() = 0;
};

class Subject {
public:
    void attach(IObserver* observer) {
        observers_.insert(observer);
    }

    void detach(IObserver* observer) {
        observers_.erase(observer);
    }

protected:
    void notify() {
        for (auto observer : observers_) {
            observer->update();
        }
    }

private:
    std::unordered_set<IObserver*> observers_;
};
```

In this design, the subject encapsulates the state and exposes methods to manage its observer list. When its internal state changes, it invokes `notify()`, which sequentially calls `update()` on each registered observer. Observers implement `update()` to react appropriately. The use of raw pointers suggests careful lifecycle management to avoid dangling pointers; in modern C++, employing `std::weak_ptr` and `std::shared_ptr` semantics can better manage object ownership.

Decoupling through Observer Interfaces Observers need not know about the subject's internals beyond the callback signa-

159

ture. This segregation promotes low coupling and high cohesion: subjects focus on state maintenance and notification dispatching, while observers concentrate on response logic. This facilitates independent evolution, unit testing, and reuse.

Notification Granularity The basic observer pattern notifies all observers of any change, without specifying what exactly changed. For complex applications, this may be insufficient. Extending the update interface to accept specific event data or change descriptors refines control over event propagation:

```
class IObserver {
public:
    virtual ~IObserver() = default;
    virtual void update(const std::string& eventType, const void*
      eventData) = 0;
};
```

This enables observers to filter events and minimize unnecessary updates, increasing efficiency.

Signal-Slot Architecture

The signal-slot pattern generalizes the observer concept by formalizing event declarations (signals) and multiple handlers (slots). A signal is an emitted event with a specific signature, and slots are callbacks connected to signals. Unlike a simple callback interface, signals and slots provide type-safe, multi-cast wiring with automatic management of connections.

This architecture is prevalent in frameworks such as Qt, where signals and slots form the backbone of widget communication and model-view interaction.

Signal Emission and Slot Invocation Signals are objects that maintain lists of connected slots-callable functions or methods conforming to the signal's signature. When a signal emits, it invokes all connected slots sequentially or concurrently.

A minimalist C++14 implementation example:

```
#include <functional>
```

```
#include <vector>

template<typename... Args>
class Signal {
public:
    using SlotType = std::function<void(Args...)>;

    void connect(SlotType slot) {
        slots_.push_back(std::move(slot));
    }

    void emit(Args... args) {
        for (auto& slot : slots_) {
            slot(args...);
        }
    }

private:
    std::vector<SlotType> slots_;
};
```

This pattern supports any function, lambda, or member function as a slot, providing broad flexibility. It also allows adding and removing slots dynamically.

Decoupling and Type Safety Signal-slot mechanisms further decouple components over the observer pattern through explicit event signatures. The subject defines signals with specific parameter lists, meaning slots must conform precisely to these types, preventing mismatched notifications at compile-time rather than runtime.

Integration with Object Lifetimes Advanced implementations track the lifetimes of objects owning slots and automatically disconnect signals when the slots become invalid, avoiding dangling invocations. This automatic resource management is central to reducing errors in reactive systems.

Practical Usage in Widget and Model Interactions

Widgets (UI components) and data models frequently need to broadcast and react to fine-grained state changes. Signal-slot and observer mechanisms provide crisp and maintainable solutions to propagate these changes efficiently.

Model Notifications A model exposing a detailed set of signals can notify views of specific data updates, such as insertion, deletion, or modification of rows, rather than broadcasting generic "data changed" events. This enables views to update only parts of their rendering, improving performance and responsiveness.

For example:

```
class Model : public Subject {
public:
    void insertRow(int rowIndex) {
        // Update internal data...
        notifyRowInserted(rowIndex);
    }

    Signal<int> rowInserted;

private:
    void notifyRowInserted(int rowIndex) {
        rowInserted.emit(rowIndex);
    }
};
```

Views connect corresponding slots to the `rowInserted` signal and update only the affected region.

Widget Reactions to Model Signals UI widgets listen to model signals and execute their repaint or data retrieval operations on specific notifications. This keeps user interfaces in sync with underlying data without tight coupling or redundant refreshes.

Multi-Module Interaction In application architectures involving many heterogeneous modules-models, views, controllers, and services-the observer and signal-slot patterns enable a modular, event-driven ecosystem. Modules only maintain references or connections to well-defined interfaces (observers or signals), avoiding inter-module dependencies on internal implementation details.

Comparative Analysis

The observer pattern primarily offers a pull-based approach-observers query the subject for updated state upon notification-whereas signal-slot mechanisms implement a push-based model, delivering event data directly to slots. The push model tends to yield better encapsulation and clarity, especially when event data is complex.

Signal-slot mechanisms often incorporate additional features such as scoped connections, queued connections for thread-safety, and prioritization of slots-capabilities that enhance robustness in large-scale applications but come with increased complexity.

Common Challenges and Mitigations

Memory and Lifetime Management A persistent issue in event notification systems is ensuring that observers or slots remain valid when invoked. Strategies such as weak references, scoped connections, and careful ownership design mitigate dangling pointers and leaks.

Performance Considerations Frequent notifications with numerous observers or slots can degrade performance. Efficient container usage, event coalescing, and rate limiting are typical optimization techniques.

Debugging and Maintenance Tracing signal-slot connections or observer relationships in large systems can be challenging. Tools that visualize connections or provide diagnostic hooks simplify maintenance.

Summary of Key Advantages

- **Loose Coupling**: Producers and consumers communicate without direct dependencies, permitting independent development and testing.

- **Extensibility**: New observers or slots can be added without modifying subjects or signal emitters.

- **Modularity**: Clear separation of concerns is maintained, facilitating code understanding and reuse.

- **Fine-Grained Control**: Event-specific notifications allow precise and efficient updates.

- **Type Safety**: Signal-slot designs enforce consistent interfaces and signatures.

These patterns collectively form the backbone of reactive programming in modern software systems, contributing to scalable, maintainable, and performant applications.

5.4. State Persistence and Undo/Redo Frameworks

Robust management of application state is critical for delivering responsive and user-friendly software, especially within graphical user interface toolkits such as the Fast Light Toolkit (FLTK). Maintaining persistent state, combined with comprehensive undo/redo capabilities, greatly enhances the user experience by allowing seamless recovery from errors and flexible interaction workflows. This section explores key principles and practical implementation strategies for structuring these components within FLTK applications.

State persistence involves saving the current state of an application or a document so that it can be restored later, either after a program restart, a crash, or user action. The complexity of persistence mechanisms varies with the nature of the application data and user interaction model. Principally, state data comprises user input, widget configurations, selection models, and document content.

Two predominant approaches exist for state persistence: snapshot serialization and incremental state updates. Snapshot serialization captures the entire state at a specific moment, typically serializing complex objects into streams or files (e.g., JSON, XML, or binary formats). This approach simplifies restoration by loading the precise state snapshot but may be expensive for large or frequently changing states. Incremental updates, conversely, record individual state transitions, akin to a log of changes. This approach facilitates fine-grained undo/redo by replaying or reversing changes but requires an efficient change-tracking infrastructure.

In FLTK, state persistence should leverage its inherent widget data access patterns. Most widgets provide getter and setter methods for their internal state. A disciplined approach to persistence involves extracting widget state through these interfaces and composing a serializable representation. Standard C++ serialization libraries (such as Boost.Serialization or custom serializers) are often employed. For example, a complex dialog's state might be converted into a structured map of key-value pairs reflecting widget identities and their values.

Undo and redo functionalities fundamentally rely on the Command design pattern. Each user action that modifies application state is encapsulated within a command object that knows how to perform and undo the operation. A command object typically implements two core methods: execute() and undo(), allowing the operation to be reversibly applied.

```
class Command {
public:
    virtual ~Command() = default;
    virtual void execute() = 0;
    virtual void undo() = 0;
};
```

Commands are pushed onto an undo stack upon execution. When the user requests an undo, the command at the top of this stack is reverted by invoking its undo() method and then pushed onto a redo stack. Redo operations move commands back from the redo stack to the undo stack after re-execution.

As commands encapsulate discrete state mutations, their implementations require careful design to ensure consistency and completeness. For example, editing a text buffer demands capturing not only the inserted or removed text but also cursor positions and other relevant metadata. For complex operations, a hierarchical or composite command pattern can aggregate multiple related commands, preserving transactional integrity.

Effective command history management is essential to balance functional completeness against resource consumption. The size of undo and redo stacks must be bounded to prevent unbounded memory growth, especially when commands encapsulate large data.

A common strategy involves limiting the number of stored commands or the total memory footprint. When capacity is reached, older commands at the bottom of the undo stack are discarded. Partial state snapshotting can optimize memory by storing deltas rather than full state copies.

Garbage collecting redo histories upon new user actions maintains logical consistency; issuing new commands invalidates the redo stack since previous rerun operations no longer apply. Furthermore, commands should be designed to release or recycle resources upon removal from the history.

The integration of persistence and undo/redo requires harmonizing FLTK's event-driven model with the command pattern and serialization mechanisms. Typical FLTK applications respond to widget callbacks, translating user interactions into state modifications via commands.

The core integration steps follow:

1. **Encapsulate State Changes as Commands:** User actions triggering state changes-such as button clicks, data entry, and menu commands-are encapsulated within command subclasses. For instance, modifying a file name in a text in-

put widget would correspond to a `RenameCommand` storing old and new names.

2. **Command Execution and Stack Maintenance:** Commands are executed via a centralized manager that handles undo and redo stacks. The command manager interfaces with FLTK menu items or shortcut keys binding undo (e.g., `Ctrl+Z`) and redo (e.g., `Ctrl+Y`) operations, ensuring immediate visual feedback.

3. **Widget State Synchronization:** After command execution or undo, widgets must synchronize their displayed state to reflect the current application model. This can be accomplished by invoking setter methods or triggering widget redraws. FLTK's efficient expose and redraw mechanisms support this reactive update model.

4. **Persistent Storage of State and History:** Upon saving or closing the application, the current full state can be serialized. Additionally, undo history may be serialized to provide session continuity; however, this should be weighed against storage overhead and complexity. On application startup, state deserialization restores the user environment.

Consider a simplified example of undo/redo integration with an FLTK `Fl_Text_Editor` widget. The command records the text content before and after the user edit, facilitating reversal.

```
class TextModificationCommand : public Command {
    Fl_Text_Editor* editor_;
    std::string oldText_;
    std::string newText_;
public:
    TextModificationCommand(Fl_Text_Editor* editor,
                            const std::string& oldText,
                            const std::string& newText)
        : editor_(editor), oldText_(oldText), newText_(newText)
    {}

    void execute() override {
        editor_->buffer()->text(newText_.c_str());
    }
```

```
        void undo() override {
            editor_->buffer()->text(oldText_.c_str());
        }
};
```

Command execution modifies the text widget's buffer directly. An external controller observes text changes, constructs the command with old and new text snapshots, executes it, and pushes it onto the undo stack.

Beyond the Command pattern, two advanced approaches enhance persistence and undo/redo functionality:

Memento Pattern. The memento pattern captures and externalizes an object's internal state without violating encapsulation, storing it in a separate memento object. This approach simplifies complex state saves and restores but can be memory intensive for large objects. Implementing mementos in FLTK involves capturing widget state copies, often requiring wrapper classes that serialize internal widget parameters.

Event Sourcing. This technique records all changes as a sequence of immutable events rather than storing states or snapshots. The application reconstructs current state by replaying events from a log. Event sourcing naturally supports undo when combined with inverse events or compensations but demands sophisticated event modeling and persistence infrastructure. In FLTK, capturing low-level user interactions and translating them into meaningful events is non-trivial but can produce highly flexible state management.

FLTK is primarily single-threaded with respect to GUI operations; hence persistence and undo/redo handlers must coordinate carefully when involving background threads (e.g., for auto-saving or remote synchronization). Command execution should occur within FLTK's main event loop to avoid widget race conditions. Any asynchronous persistence logic must serialize access to shared state and command stacks via mutexes or FLTK's Fl::lock()

mechanisms if multithreading is enabled.

Optimizing undo/redo frameworks in FLTK applications requires minimizing command execution overhead and memory use. Incremental text commands (e.g., character insertions and deletions) can be represented efficiently by grouping multiple edits into composite commands, reducing command stack size. Lazy serialization defers writing state to disk until idle periods, preventing UI blocking. Employing efficient data structures-such as ring buffers for command stacks-can guarantee stable performance even with large undo histories.

- Use the Command pattern to encapsulate all user-modifiable operations, ensuring clear boundaries for undo/redo.

- Design commands to be lightweight and capture all necessary data for full undo without external dependencies.

- Implement a centralized command manager to serialize operations, maintain undo/redo stacks, and provide user interfaces for state navigation.

- Leverage FLTK widget getter/setter methods for state extraction during persistence and for synchronizing visual state after command execution.

- Bound command history size and implement garbage collection to maintain predictable resource utilization.

- Integrate state persistence with command management to allow session restoration and continuous user workflows.

- Consider advanced patterns such as Memento and Event Sourcing for sophisticated applications requiring extensible undo/redo and recovery strategies.

- Ensure all state modifications and persistence operations respect FLTK's single-threaded GUI requirements to maintain synchronization and prevent race conditions.

Adhering to these principles enables FLTK-based applications to deliver resilient and user-friendly editing experiences, with undo and redo seamlessly integrated into an effective state management framework.

5.5. Reactive Patterns and Change Propagation

Reactive programming embodies a paradigm centered on data flows and the propagation of change, enabling systems to automatically react to alterations in underlying data sources. Within graphical user interfaces created using FLTK (Fast Light Toolkit), reactive patterns facilitate dynamic, adaptive behaviors through declarative data dependencies rather than imperative event handling. Such patterns minimize boilerplate and enhance maintainability by allowing UI components to synchronize automatically with the evolving state of the application.

Central to reactive programming is the concept of *observables*, which represent values that can change over time. Observables maintain a set of observers-subscribers registered to receive notifications when the observable's value changes. This relationship forms an *observer chain*, through which change propagates from data sources to dependent computations or UI elements. In the context of FLTK, widgets can subscribe to these observables, thereby updating their presentation in response to model changes without explicit callback wiring.

The observer pattern underlying reactive flows can be formalized by defining a data source O with a state $s \in S$, and a collection of observers $\{o_i\}$ each associated with a callback function $f_i : S \to$ void. When s changes to s', the source notifies all observers:

$$\forall i, \quad f_i(s').$$

Consequently, reactive user interfaces transform into networks of interconnected observables and observers, where each UI element reacts automatically to relevant state updates, facilitating a declarative style of programming.

This reactive cadence aligns naturally with functions in FLTK such as callbacks connected to widgets. However, classical FLTK callbacks are inherently imperative and one-to-one: each callback executes as a response to a single event, demanding explicit update logic. Reactive patterns transcend this by treating widget state and data as reactive variables. Consider abstractions that wrap mutable values alongside notification mechanisms. These abstractions enable composing complex UI behavior declaratively.

```
template <typename T>
class Observable {
  T value;
  std::vector<std::function<void(const T&)>> observers;

public:
  Observable(T init) : value(init) {}

  void set(const T& newValue) {
    if (value != newValue) {
      value = newValue;
      notify();
    }
  }

  T get() const { return value; }

  void subscribe(std::function<void(const T&)> observer) {
    observers.push_back(observer);
  }

private:
  void notify() {
    for (auto& obs : observers) obs(value);
  }
};
```

Here, the template class `Observable` encapsulates a mutable value with the capability for observers to register via `subscribe()`. The method `set()` mutates the value and triggers all observers, facilitating automatic update propagation. GUI elements, such as sliders or text displays, can bind to `Observable` instances to reflect and

171

mutate application state consistently.

Linking several observables creates *reactive data flows*. For instance, one can define computed observables whose values depend on others, establishing a chain that recalculates outputs upon input changes. Defining a derived observable involves subscribing to one or more source observables and updating accordingly:

```cpp
template <typename T, typename U>
class ComputedObservable {
  U value;
  std::function<U(const T&)> computeFunc;
  Observable<T>& source;
  std::vector<std::function<void(const U&)>> observers;

public:
  ComputedObservable(Observable<T>& src, std::function<U(const T
    &)> func)
    : source(src), computeFunc(func), value(func(src.get())) {
    source.subscribe([this](const T& newVal) {
      U newValue = computeFunc(newVal);
      if (newValue != value) {
        value = newValue;
        notify();
      }
    });
  }

  U get() const { return value; }

  void subscribe(std::function<void(const U&)> observer) {
    observers.push_back(observer);
  }

private:
  void notify() {
    for (auto& obs : observers) obs(value);
  }
};
```

This ComputedObservable listens to a source observable, applies a transformation, and propagates changes downstream. Within FLTK, this seamlessly integrates with widget updates-such as adjusting label texts per slider positions or updating graphs dynamically upon parameter modification.

Building a UI with these patterns supports automatic consistency:

when the application data changes, all derived UI components reflecting that data update without explicit imperative state synchronization. For example, consider an FLTK slider controlling a numeric parameter wrapped inside an `Observable<double>`, and a label displaying its value through a `ComputedObservable<double, std::string>` that transforms the numeric value into formatted text:

```
Observable<double> sliderValue(0.0);
ComputedObservable<double, std::string> formattedText(
  sliderValue,
  [](const double& val) {
    std::ostringstream oss;
    oss.precision(2);
    oss << std::fixed << "Value: " << val;
    return oss.str();
  }
);

Fl_Slider* slider = new Fl_Slider(10, 10, 200, 20, "Adjust");
Fl_Box* label = new Fl_Box(10, 40, 200, 20);

slider->callback([](Fl_Widget* w, void* data) {
  auto val = static_cast<Observable<double>*>(data);
  Fl_Slider* s = static_cast<Fl_Slider*>(w);
  val->set(s->value());
}, &sliderValue);

formattedText.subscribe([label](const std::string& text) {
  label->label(text.c_str());
  label->redraw();
});
```

This code snippet exhibits automatic propagation from slider input to label text without direct coupling: the slider modifies the observable, which triggers the computed observable to recalculate the string representation, which then updates the label.

Reactive chains can be composed arbitrarily: multiple observables, computations, and widgets combine to form complex dependency graphs. Asynchrony may be introduced by integrating reactive updates with FLTK's event loop via timers or idle callbacks, enabling reactive data to update from external sources or background computations while ensuring thread safety through synchronization primitives.

Change propagation under reactive patterns must also address challenges such as cycle detection, guaranteeing termination during dependency updates. In well-structured UIs, these cycles are avoided by design, but reactive frameworks often implement mechanisms like topological sorting or version stamping to prevent infinite update loops.

Memory management is equally vital as observer lifetimes must be carefully managed to avoid dangling pointers or leaks. Employing smart pointers or weak references is a standard approach to decouple observable observership from object lifetimes, allowing widgets or other observers to safely unsubscribe upon destruction.

Key elements imperative for applying reactive patterns in FLTK include:

- Encapsulate mutable application data in observable containers with change notification.

- Derive dependent observables through pure functions over source observables, establishing data flow graphs.

- Bind FLTK widget properties-such as labels, slider values, and visibility-to observables to reflect application state reactively.

- Use subscription callbacks to propagate changes and trigger FLTK's redraw operations for the affected widgets.

- Manage observer lifetimes and update sequencing to ensure correctness and avoid cyclic dependencies.

Reactive programming complements FLTK's callback-based model by providing a higher-level abstraction for managing UI state and responses declaratively. This approach reduces boilerplate and error-prone manual synchronization, leading to more robust, easily modifiable applications. Reactive flows blur the distinction between model and view updates, fostering tight coherence between application data and its graphical presentation through continuous, automatic change propagation.

Consequently, adopting reactive patterns manifests in FLTK as a seamless interplay of observable data sources, observer-driven UI updates, and computed derivations-an architecture that establishes responsive, resilient user interfaces capable of adapting fluidly to evolving inputs and conditions.

5.6. Testing MVC and Data Flow Integration

Achieving reliable and maintainable applications using the Model-View-Controller (MVC) architecture necessitates meticulous testing of both individual components and their interactions, particularly the intricate model-view interaction and data binding mechanisms. These tests ensure the integrity of data flow, synchronicity between application state and user interface, and resilience against future codebase modifications.

Unit Testing of Models and Views

Unit testing in an MVC context primarily targets the isolated behavior of each component. Models encapsulate business logic and data management, and thus tests validate domain rules, data transformations, validation routines, and state transitions without dependence on UI elements. Mocking dependencies such as databases or external services allows deterministic and fast execution of model tests.

Views, responsible for rendering and user input handling, present a unique challenge in isolation, as they inherently rely on GUI frameworks and runtime environments. Testing views at the unit level typically involves verifying that the correct rendering instructions are generated given a particular model state. This can be approached by decoupling rendering logic from UI frameworks into testable functions or by employing shallow rendering techniques that confirm output structure without full component instantiation.

Integration Testing of Model-View Synchronization

Integration tests extend beyond component boundaries to verify the correctness of data flow and event propagation between models and views. Key target areas include:

- **Data Binding Integrity**: Confirming that changes to model data automatically trigger appropriate view updates, and that user inputs correctly modify the underlying model state.

- **Event Propagation**: Ensuring that events such as user actions, model notifications, and controller commands propagate properly through the system hierarchy.

- **State Consistency**: Validating that the UI consistently and accurately reflects the current state of the model after various sequences of operations.

Test scenarios can simulate user interactions and verify resulting model states and view outputs, or alternatively, manipulate the model and assert correctness of the visual response. Such dual-direction verification fosters confidence in the robustness of two-way data binding constructs and observer patterns widely employed in sophisticated MVC frameworks.

Testing Approaches for Data Binding Logic

Data binding, which synchronizes state between models and views, is crucial for responsive and intuitive UI behavior. Testing strategies include:

- **Observer and Listener Mocks**: Utilize test doubles that simulate observers or listeners to verify that model events fire consistently and that bound views react appropriately.

- **Change Notification Verification**: Instrument the model to confirm that property changes trigger all expected notifications, detecting missed updates or superfluous event emissions.

- **Automated UI Test Emulation**: Deploy headless rendering environments or test harnesses that simulate UI updates and input bindings to validate continuous data synchronization.

Balancing coverage with test execution speed is vital; excessive reliance on full UI rendering can yield brittle and slow tests. Instead, testing the binding logic through modular binding engines or middleware layers, where data transformation rules and event dispatching are isolated, proves more scalable.

Best Practices for Robust and Refactorable Test Suites

The complexity inherent in extensive GUI architectures mandates disciplined testing practices to enable safe, confident refactoring:

- **Isolate Side Effects**: Ensuring that tests do not rely on external services or global state facilitates repeatability and accurate failure attribution.

- **Employ Dependency Injection**: This design principle allows swapping real components for mocks or stubs during testing, simplifying control over interactions and system behavior.

- **Adopt Interface-Driven Development**: Coding against interfaces rather than concrete implementations decouples components, enabling more targeted and reliable tests.

- **Automate Regression Testing**: Continuous integration pipelines should run comprehensive unit and integration test suites to catch regressions early, particularly around data binding and event-driven updates.

- **Use Descriptive Assertions**: Tests that clearly express expected behavior improve maintainability and ease diagnosis of failure causes.

- **Prioritize Testing Critical Paths**: Focus initial testing efforts on core data flows and user interactions, progressively covering edge cases and ancillary features.

Illustration: Unit Testing Model-View Binding Using Observer Pattern

Consider an MVC implementation where the model exposes observable properties, and the view subscribes to these notifications to update its visual state. The following pseudocode outlines a testing pattern validating the notification mechanism:

```
class ObservableModel:
    def __init__(self):
        self._data = None
        self._listeners = []

    def add_listener(self, listener):
        self._listeners.append(listener)

    @property
    def data(self):
        return self._data

    @data.setter
    def data(self, value):
        self._data = value
        for listener in self._listeners:
            listener.update(value)

class ViewMock:
    def __init__(self):
        self.updated_values = []

    def update(self, value):
        self.updated_values.append(value)

def test_model_notifies_view_on_data_change():
    model = ObservableModel()
```

```
view = ViewMock()
model.add_listener(view)

model.data = 42

assert view.updated_values == [42], "View did not receive
 update notification"
```

This test captures the fundamental contract: whenever the model's data changes, subscribed views are notified with the new value. By abstracting the listener with a mock object, it isolates the notification behavior from concrete UI rendering, thus enabling efficient and reliable unit testing.

Framework Support and Tooling

Modern testing frameworks provide robust support to address the challenges in MVC testing. Features such as spies, mocks, and stubs automate the creation of test doubles, while declarative data binding test utilities simplify observability verification. Frameworks like QtTest (for Qt), Jasmine or Jest (for JavaScript MV* frameworks), and JUnit coupled with Mockito or PowerMock (for Java desktop/Web applications) offer specialized capabilities for model-view interaction tests.

Test harnesses supporting headless UI environments allow integration testing of view updates triggered by model changes without requiring a full graphical environment, improving test run times and CI/CD pipeline throughput.

Mitigating Flakiness and Ensuring Determinism

Event-driven and asynchronous interactions are prevalent in MVC architectures, increasing the risk of non-deterministic test failures. Confining asynchronous operations within test-controlled contexts, utilizing synchronization primitives, and comprehensive mocking of timers or event dispatchers can greatly reduce flakiness. Additionally, deterministic seeding of random generators and consistent test data further stabilize outcomes.

Quantitative Metrics and Coverage Considerations

In addition to qualitative test design, quantitative metrics provide insights into coverage adequacy. Instrumentation to log model-view event flows, code coverage analysis focusing on binding logic, and mutation testing targeting data propagation statements offer objective measures. Regular evaluation of these metrics enhances test suite effectiveness and identifies latent weaknesses ahead of regression exposure.

Achieving comprehensive testing of MVC model-view integration therefore requires a careful alignment of testing methods, infrastructure, and development practices, fostering codebases that are robust, adaptable, and maintainable in the face of evolving requirements and technological shifts.

Chapter 6

System Integration and Platform Services

Bridge the world of your FLTK application with the diverse ecosystem of modern operating systems. This chapter uncovers the techniques and patterns for tapping into native services, external devices, and essential platform features. Learn how to connect, extend, and secure your FLTK projects—transforming standalone GUIs into versatile, fully integrated solutions.

6.1. Interfacing with Native Platform APIs

The immediate strength of FLTK (Fast Light Toolkit) lies in its portability and minimalism when creating cross-platform graphical user interfaces. However, real-world applications frequently demand integration with native platform-specific functionality to optimize behavior, access specialized services, or provide advanced user experiences not directly supported by FLTK's abstraction. Interfacing with native operating system (OS) APIs from within an FLTK environment requires deliberate design strategies, particularly to maintain safe abstractions, leverage foreign function interfaces (FFIs), and preserve portability despite platform-specific extensions.

Motivations and Challenges

While FLTK abstracts windowing, input events, font rendering, and graphics drawing uniformly, many OS environments offer unique capabilities and optimizations accessible only via native APIs. Examples include leveraging Direct2D on Windows for high-performance 2D rendering, macOS's native text services and accessibility APIs, Linux's advanced clipboard mechanisms, or integrating with system notifications and security subsystems. Extracting benefits from these capabilities necessitates invoking native APIs safely and cleanly from FLTK applications, demanding an expressive yet robust interface layer.

The primary challenges include:

- **Safety**: Native APIs often expose low-level constructs and require meticulous management of memory, pointers, threading, and object lifetimes, which, if mishandled, cause instability or security vulnerabilities.

- **Portability**: Introducing native calls risks fragmenting codebases. Maintaining platform agnosticism requires isolating platform-specific code and providing fallback behaviors.

- **Complexity**: Language and runtime mismatches when calling native libraries, especially across different programming languages or binary interfaces, necessitate careful design of foreign function interfaces (FFIs).

Architectural Patterns for Native API Integration

A principled approach to interfacing entails layered architectural patterns, encapsulation, and disciplined use of abstraction boundaries.

Abstraction Layers

A common design is to define interface classes or modules representing the desired functionality while deferring implementation to platform-specific subclasses or code paths. For instance, a class `NativeNotification` might declare methods for triggering notifications, with implementations in `NativeNotificationWin32`, `NativeNotificationMac`, and `NativeNotificationX11` subclasses encapsulating platform APIs such as `IToastNotificationManagerStatics`, `NSUserNotificationCenter`, and `libnotify`, respectively.

This isolates platform dependencies while allowing the core FLTK code to utilize a uniform API.

Conditional Compilation and Runtime Detection

Using preprocessor directives (e.g., `#ifdef _WIN32`, `#ifdef __APPLE__`) restricts native API usage to appropriate builds. Combined with runtime platform detection, this enables fallback to FLTK-native capabilities or generic implementations on unsupported platforms without code duplication.

Foreign Function Interfaces (FFIs)

FFIs mediate interactions between the FLTK application's environment (commonly C++ or other languages) and the native OS API, typically expressed in C or platform-specific languages. Effective FFIs must handle calling conventions, data marshaling, error reporting, and callback mechanisms.

Techniques for Safe and Portable Foreign Function Calls

Extern "C" and Dynamic Loading

Native APIs often provide C-style interfaces or COM (Component Object Model) on Windows. Employing `extern "C"` linkage in

C++ minimizes name mangling issues when calling native functions. For dynamic libraries (DLLs, shared objects), explicit runtime linking via LoadLibrary (Windows) or dlopen (POSIX) enables optional loading, enhancing portability by deferring binding to runtime.

Example of dynamic loading for MessageBox on Windows:

```
// Dynamically load user32.dll and resolve MessageBoxW
HMODULE user32 = LoadLibraryW(L"user32.dll");
if (user32) {
    typedef int (WINAPI *MessageBoxFunc)(HWND, LPCWSTR, LPCWSTR,
    UINT);
    auto MessageBoxWPtr = (MessageBoxFunc)GetProcAddress(user32,
    "MessageBoxW");
    if (MessageBoxWPtr) {
        MessageBoxWPtr(NULL, L"Test message", L"Title", MB_OK);
    }
    FreeLibrary(user32);
}
```

This approach guards against absence of the API or running on incompatible platforms.

Data Marshaling and Type Safety

Native APIs often expect binary structures (e.g., POINT, RECT) or UTF-16 encoded strings (Windows) whereas FLTK and C++ natively employ UTF-8 or standard data types. Careful conversion and marshaling are obligatory, avoiding unsafe casts:

- Convert FLTK Fl_String or std::string to platform-appropriate encodings using MultiByteToWideChar on Windows or ICU libraries.

- Use RAII wrappers to manage native resources, e.g., smart handles to release COM interfaces or global memory.

- Validate structure packing and alignment matching that expected by native APIs.

Exception Safety and Error Handling

Most native APIs return error codes rather than throwing exceptions. Wrapping these return values in `std::optional` or `std::expected` types (C++23) permits fluent and expressive error propagation. Exception boundaries must not propagate through native function boundaries without specific guarantees.

Handling Platform-Specific Extensions Without Compromising Portability

Extending FLTK interfaces with native capabilities must be carefully scoped:

Explicit Extension Interfaces

Platform-specific features should live outside the core FLTK API. For example, defining optional interfaces (e.g., `class IFlyoutMenu`) implemented only on Windows or macOS avoids contaminating portable API surfaces.

Capability Queries

Providing methods for runtime queries of feature availability allows adaptive functionality:

```
if (NativeAPI::IsFeatureSupported(NativeFeature::TouchInjection))
    {
    NativeAPI::EnableTouchInjection();
} else {
    // fallback to standard FLTK mouse input
}
```

Such conditional logic ensures backward compatibility and graceful degradation.

Bridging Callbacks and Events

Native platforms frequently employ asynchronous callbacks or message loops distinct from FLTK's event handling. Safely integrating these requires:

- Posting native event notifications into the FLTK event queue, typically via thread-safe signals or custom event types.

- Synchronizing thread affinity when native APIs invoke callbacks on background threads but FLTK GUI operations must occur on the main thread.

- Utilizing platform synchronization primitives (mutexes, condition variables) to coordinate state safely.

Case Study: Windows COM Integration with FLTK

Windows COM interfaces exemplify advanced native APIs necessitating careful handling within FLTK.

Initialization and COM Apartments

COM requires initialization per thread, typically via `CoInitializeEx`. FLTK applications often run a main GUI thread and several background threads; thus each must explicitly initialize COM to interact with COM objects.

```
HRESULT hr = CoInitializeEx(NULL, COINIT_APARTMENTTHREADED);
if (FAILED(hr)) {
    // Handle initialization failure
}
```

Referencing COM Objects

Using `Microsoft::WRL::ComPtr` or `CComPtr` (ATL) smart pointers manages lifetime and reference counting of COM objects, thereby preventing leaks.

Using Native Controls

ActiveX or DirectX components can be embedded inside FLTK windows by retrieving native window handles from FLTK widgets and initializing COM controls on those parent windows, bridging between FLTK's cross-platform windowing and detailed Windows UX.

Ensuring Maintainability in Native API Integration

Rigorous documentation, modular design, and test coverage are needed to maintain clarity as platform-specific code evolves.

Cross-platform continuous integration systems must validate compilation on all targeted platforms, flagging regressions in native interface handling early.

Abstractions should expose minimal and stable interfaces to the higher application layers; volatile platform details belong exclusively to isolated implementation files.

Summary of Best Practices

- **Encapsulate** native API calls behind well-defined interfaces to isolate complexity and ease testing.

- **Use dynamic loading** and runtime detection to maintain graceful degradation across platforms.

- **Handle data conversions** explicitly, respecting character encodings and binary layouts.

- **Adopt RAII** and smart pointers or handles to prevent resource leaks.

- **Integrate event loops** and callbacks carefully to maintain thread safety and responsiveness.

- **Separate platform-specific extensions** cleanly, avoiding contaminating the FLTK core with platform-dependent code.

The discussed strategies facilitate powerful integration of native platform APIs within FLTK applications, balancing the desire for rich platform-tailored features against the essential requirement for cross-platform consistency and reliability.

6.2. Printing, Clipboard, and Shell Integration

Modern desktop applications frequently require interaction with fundamental operating system services such as printing documents, manipulating clipboard content, and running shell commands. Efficient and consistent integration with these services across multiple platforms is paramount to delivering a smooth user experience without compromising portability or maintainability. This section examines the essential technical details and recommended patterns for handling system printing, clipboard operations, and shell command execution in a cross-platform context.

System Printing

Printing remains a core desktop function, yet it involves considerable complexity due to the divergence in platform-specific APIs and print architectures. Abstracting printing logic to achieve a uniform interface is the foundation of reliable cross-platform print support.

Most desktop environments implement document printing through a print spooler managed by the operating system; however, the interfaces range from Windows GDI-based APIs, macOS's Core Printing system, to the UNIX/Linux Common UNIX Printing System (CUPS). Key commonalities include the need to describe print jobs through device contexts or print settings, dialogs for user-driven printer selection and configuration, and document rendering either as native drawing commands or as print-ready formats such as PDF.

A widely adopted design pattern encapsulates the printing flow within an abstraction layer exposing:

- **Print Job Configuration**: Querying available printers,

188

specifying number of copies, page ranges, and print orientation.

- **Print Preview**: Rendering document content to an off-screen buffer or intermediate format to facilitate preview before actual printing.

- **Print Rendering Interface**: An abstraction over platform-specific drawing APIs or mechanisms to render the content.

- **Print Dialog Integration**: Presenting native print dialogs to end users, leveraging platform APIs to maintain consistent user experience.

For example, on Windows, the use of `StartDoc`, `StartPage`, and `EndPage` GDI functions coordinates print jobs, whereas on macOS, `NSPrintOperation` and `NSPrintInfo` provide the necessary facilities. On Linux with CUPS, the application typically generates PostScript or PDF output which is then sent to the print queue using `lp` or `lpr` command-line utilities or the CUPS API.

An effective strategy involves rendering document content to an intermediate device-independent format such as PDF, which is portable and supported by all platforms' printing subsystems. Such an approach allows the application to offload actual printing responsibility to the operating system's native PDF print pipeline, simplifying code paths and yielding consistent quality.

Example pseudocode outlining a cross-platform print invocation might appear as follows:

```
PrintSettings settings = PrintService::getDefaultSettings();
if (PrintService::showPrintDialog(settings)) {
    DocumentRenderer renderer = DocumentRenderer(document);
    PrinterInterface printer = PrintService::getPrinter(settings)
    ;
    printer.printDocument(renderer, settings);
}
```

Here, `PrintService` abstracts platform-specific printer enumeration and dialog invocation, `PrintSettings` encapsulates user-specified parameters, and `DocumentRenderer` is responsible for producing printable content irrespective of the platform.

Clipboard Operations

Clipboard integration enables applications to exchange data seamlessly with other programs, providing cut, copy, and paste functionality fundamental to user interactivity. Clipboard operations often must handle multiple data formats to maximize compatibility, such as plain text, rich text, images, and proprietary data types.

The architecture of clipboard handling follows a typical producer–consumer model: an application places data on the clipboard (the producer), and other applications or the same one retrieve data from it (the consumer). A robust approach to clipboard management abstracts:

- **Platform Clipboard Access APIs**: Windows provides the `OpenClipboard`, `EmptyClipboard`, and `SetClipboardData` functions; macOS uses NSPasteboard; Linux desktop environments often rely on X11 selections or Wayland protocols.

- **Data Format Negotiation**: Applications should attempt to place multiple representations on the clipboard (e.g., both plain text and HTML) and query for supported formats on paste operations.

- **Synchronization and Ownership**: Clipboard content ownership varies by platform, and applications must manage this carefully to avoid data loss or race conditions.

A cross-platform clipboard interface typically implements methods to:

- Set clipboard content for standard types (text, images) and optionally custom formats.

- Retrieve data from the clipboard, selecting the most preferred format supported.

- Detect changes to clipboard content asynchronously or through polling mechanisms if supported.

For greater portability, it is advisable to implement clipboard functionality using a facade pattern that encapsulates platform-specific details while exposing a uniform API. For instance, the following pseudocode outlines a high-level clipboard interaction:

```
Clipboard clipboard = Clipboard::getInstance();
clipboard.setText("Example clipboard text");

if (clipboard.hasFormat(DataFormat::Text)) {
    std::string text = clipboard.getText();
    processText(text);
}
```

Applications must anticipate clipboard content variability and implement graceful fallback logic. For example, when requesting formatted HTML may not be available, falling back to plain text ensures continuity.

Shell Command Execution

Executing system shell commands from an application facilitates automation, integration with existing tools, and access to services beyond the application's direct API. Despite inherent security and platform dependencies, controlled shell execution remains vital in many advanced desktop scenarios, such as invoking file managers, external scripts, or administrative tools.

The core challenges in shell command execution revolve around:

- **Cross-Platform Command Invocation**: Windows typically uses CreateProcess or ShellExecute, while POSIX-compliant systems rely on fork and exec functions or higher-level popen for easier interaction.

- **Command Argument Quoting and Sanitization**:

Properly escaping shell metacharacters or whitespace is critical to prevent injection vulnerabilities and execution errors.

- **Process Control and Output Capture**: Applications often need to wait for process completion, retrieve standard output/error streams, and handle exit codes.

- **Unicode and Encoding Considerations**: Command-line arguments and outputs must be encoded consistently to support internationalization.

A platform-neutral API for shell integration typically exposes functions to synchronously or asynchronously execute shell commands, optionally retrieving output and error streams. This abstraction should internally implement platform-specific methods for spawning processes, ensuring that command-line construction correctly handles argument quoting according to each operating system's shell syntax.

The following C++-style pseudocode exemplifies a safe pattern for executing shell commands and capturing output:

```
ShellResult result = ShellExecutor::runCommand("mytool --option
    \"some value\"");

if (result.success) {
    std::string output = result.stdoutData;
    processOutput(output);
} else {
    logError(result.errorMessage);
}
```

In this model, `ShellExecutor` encapsulates platform-specific APIs (`CreateProcess` on Windows, `popen` or `posix_spawn` on UNIX-like systems). It automatically manages argument escaping, stream redirection, and timeout handling.

Security is paramount: all user input passed to shell commands must be validated and sanitized to prevent injection attacks. Wherever possible, direct API calls should replace shell invocation to minimize exposure.

Unified Cross-Platform Integration Patterns

Integrating printing, clipboard, and shell services under unified abstraction layers promotes clean architecture and eases cross-platform development. Recommended design considerations include:

- **Facade Pattern**: Define high-level interfaces that internalize platform variations, exposing consistent APIs for client code.

- **Strategy Pattern**: Implement platform-specific strategies allowing dynamic binding of service implementations depending on runtime environment.

- **Asynchronous Operation Support**: Provide non-blocking variants for potentially long-running operations (e.g., print dialogs, shell command executions) to maintain responsive UI.

- **Resource and State Management**: Carefully manage system resources such as clipboard ownership handles, print device contexts, or process handles to avoid leaks and race conditions.

- **Error Handling and Diagnostics**: Normalize error reporting across platforms, capturing detailed diagnostic information to facilitate troubleshooting.

Additionally, employing formats and protocols with wide native support (PDF for printing, Unicode UTF-8 for clipboard and shell) enhances portability and integration fidelity.

By leveraging these service integrations with disciplined abstraction and attention to platform semantics, applications achieve seamless access to essential desktop capabilities, allowing developers to focus on domain-specific logic rather than OS intricacies.

6.3. Networking and IPC within FLTK Apps

Incorporating networking and interprocess communication (IPC) capabilities into FLTK applications substantially enhances their functionality by enabling distributed architectures, inter-application cooperation, and dynamic data exchange. While FLTK primarily provides GUI elements and event handling, effective integration with networking and IPC mechanisms requires combining FLTK's event loop with external asynchronous or synchronous communication APIs. This section examines the essential concepts and practical methods to embed socket-based networking, HTTP client functionality, local host messaging, and protocol design for app-to-app communication within FLTK apps.

FLTK itself does not natively provide networking primitives; thus, interaction with sockets and IPC channels often relies on native system APIs or portable libraries such as Boost.Asio, POSIX sockets, or platform-specific IPC mechanisms. Integrating these approaches within FLTK's single-threaded event-driven architecture demands careful synchronization to avoid blocking the GUI and maintain responsiveness.

Socket Programming Integration

Sockets enable low-level TCP/IP or UDP communication and form the backbone of network interactions in FLTK applications. The typical workflow involves creating a socket, binding or connecting it, and subsequently sending or receiving byte streams. For FLTK, non-blocking sockets or I/O multiplexing with `select()` or `poll()` system calls are crucial to prevent UI thread blocking.

The recommended pattern is to register the socket file descriptor with an FLTK-compatible file descriptor watcher, such as `Fl::add_fd()`, which monitors file descriptor readiness and triggers callbacks within the FLTK event loop. This design allows integration of asynchronous socket events with FLTK's GUI updates.

Below is an example snippet illustrating the setup of a non-blocking TCP socket monitored by FLTK:

```cpp
#include <FL/Fl.H>
#include <FL/Fl_Window.H>
#include <sys/socket.h>
#include <arpa/inet.h>
#include <fcntl.h>
#include <unistd.h>

int sockfd = -1;

void socket_callback(void*) {
    char buf[512];
    ssize_t n = recv(sockfd, buf, sizeof(buf), 0);
    if (n > 0) {
        // Process incoming data (e.g., update UI)
        Fl::awake(); // Trigger GUI updates safely
    } else if (n == 0) {
        // Connection closed
        Fl::remove_fd(sockfd);
        close(sockfd);
    }
}

void init_socket() {
    sockfd = socket(AF_INET, SOCK_STREAM, 0);
    fcntl(sockfd, F_SETFL, O_NONBLOCK);

    sockaddr_in addr{};
    addr.sin_family = AF_INET;
    addr.sin_port = htons(12345);
    inet_pton(AF_INET, "127.0.0.1", &addr.sin_addr);

    connect(sockfd, (sockaddr*)&addr, sizeof(addr));
    Fl::add_fd(sockfd, socket_callback, 0);
}
```

The Fl::add_fd() registers the socket for read readiness notifications, ensuring that socket_callback() is invoked on incoming data. Calling Fl::awake() within the callback prompts FLTK to process GUI events asynchronously, allowing safe updates to the interface.

HTTP Client Support

195

HTTP client functionality is often required for FLTK applications needing REST API access, web resource retrieval, or lightweight web-based interaction. Since FLTK lacks native support for HTTP, integrating third-party libraries such as libcurl, Boost.Beast, or cpp-httplib is a common approach.

Embedding HTTP requests in an FLTK app requires careful threading or asynchronous programming: synchronous blocking calls would freeze the UI, whereas background threads require thread-safe communication with FLTK's main thread for updating widgets.

An elegant technique uses worker threads to perform HTTP requests asynchronously while communicating completion results back to the UI thread through FLTK's Fl::awake() mechanism, which runs callbacks in the GUI context.

Example usage pattern:

```
#include <thread>
#include <curl/curl.h>
#include <FL/Fl.H>

// Callback called by libcurl to write received data
size_t write_data(void* ptr, size_t size, size_t nmemb, std::
    string* userdata) {
    userdata->append((char*)ptr, size * nmemb);
    return size * nmemb;
}

void do_http_request(const std::string& url, std::string*
    response) {
    CURL* curl = curl_easy_init();
    curl_easy_setopt(curl, CURLOPT_URL, url.c_str());
    curl_easy_setopt(curl, CURLOPT_WRITEFUNCTION, write_data);
    curl_easy_setopt(curl, CURLOPT_WRITEDATA, response);
    curl_easy_perform(curl);
    curl_easy_cleanup(curl);
}

void http_request_async(const std::string& url) {
    auto response = new std::string;
    std::thread([url, response]() {
        do_http_request(url, response);
        Fl::awake([](void* arg) {
            std::string* resp = static_cast<std::string*>(arg);
```

196

```
            // Update GUI here with *resp contents
            delete resp;
        }, response);
    }).detach();
}
```

This approach keeps the FLTK main loop responsive and safely synchronizes network callback results with the GUI update context. Such techniques extend to HTTP POST, authentication, and streaming via appropriate configuration of the underlying HTTP client library.

Local Host Messaging and IPC Mechanisms

Interprocess communication enables FLTK applications to cooperate with other local processes, facilitating tasks such as command relaying, status monitoring, or shared resource control.

Common IPC mechanisms include UNIX domain sockets, named pipes (FIFOs), shared memory, and higher-level message brokers. UNIX domain sockets mimic TCP sockets but connect processes on the same host via filesystem path addressing, offering lower latency and security through OS user permissions.

Named pipes provide unidirectional or bidirectional byte streams persisted as filesystem objects. Both UNIX domain sockets and named pipes can be monitored with FLTK's Fl::add_fd() framework similarly to network sockets.

Shared memory permits rapid data exchange without kernel overhead for each byte, but synchronization primitives like mutexes or semaphores are required to maintain data consistency. FLTK applications can combine OS-level shared memory APIs with FLTK timers or file descriptor watchers to process and display shared data updates.

Windows applications typically use named pipes or Windows Messages for IPC. The Windows message loop contrasts with FLTK's event loop, and so bridging requires mechanisms such as hidden

FLTK windows handling custom messages or asynchronous call-back models.

Protocols for Application-to-Application Communication

Choosing or designing a protocol for app-to-app communication balances complexity, extensibility, and performance. Protocols can be binary or text-based, synchronous or asynchronous, and may span multiple layers (application, transport).

Lightweight protocols utilizing JSON or XML over TCP or UNIX domain sockets are prevalent due to their human-readable format and ease of debugging. For fast, efficient binary communication, custom serialization approaches or protocols such as Protocol Buffers may be used.

A typical messaging protocol for FLTK apps will involve:

- A framing mechanism to delimit messages (e.g., length-prefixed, newline-terminated).

- Message identifiers or types to route commands and responses.

- A payload schema consistent across communicating processes.

For example, a JSON-based protocol over TCP might use newline-separated JSON objects. The app reads socket data until a newline, parses the JSON message, and dispatches handling routines accordingly.

```
// Pseudocode to parse newline-delimited JSON protocol data
void socket_callback(void*) {
    static std::string buffer;
    char tmp[512];
    ssize_t n = recv(sockfd, tmp, sizeof(tmp), 0);
    if (n <= 0) {
        // handle error or disconnect
        return;
```

```
    }
    buffer.append(tmp, n);
    size_t pos;
    while ((pos = buffer.find('\n')) != std::string::npos) {
        std::string line = buffer.substr(0, pos);
        buffer.erase(0, pos + 1);
        // parse JSON message from 'line'
        // handle message based on type and content
    }
}
```

When designing protocols, ensuring robustness against partial or malformed messages is essential, especially with streaming sockets. Furthermore, concurrency concerns and error reporting protocols improve resilience.

Threading and Event Dispatch Considerations

Because most networking and IPC facilities rely on blocking calls, integrating them with FLTK's single-threaded event loop often necessitates multithreading or non-blocking I/O with event-driven callbacks.

When employing threads, data shared between network code and the GUI must be synchronized carefully. FLTK is not thread-safe for GUI operations; all widget modifications must occur within the main thread. The standard solution is to use Fl::awake() to enqueue callbacks safely back to the FLTK main thread.

An alternative to threading is fully asynchronous I/O using non-blocking sockets combined with file descriptor watchers. This approach avoids synchronization overhead but can be complex, particularly with protocol stack implementations.

Summary of Best Practices

- Use Fl::add_fd() to monitor sockets, pipes, or IPC channels for readable or writable events, integrating communication seamlessly into FLTK's event loop.

- Keep networking operations asynchronous via background threads or non-blocking I/O to prevent freezing the GUI.

- Employ `Fl::awake()` when background threads must update FLTK widgets, ensuring thread-safe GUI operations.

- Prefer portable libraries (e.g., `libcurl`, Boost) for HTTP clients and socket abstraction to minimize platform-specific code.

- Design simple, robust message framing and parsing mechanisms to handle partial transmissions and malformed data.

- Leverage well-established IPC mechanisms fitting the platform and application domain (UNIX domain sockets, named pipes, shared memory, Windows Messages).

This strategy allows creation of responsive, network-aware FLTK applications capable of rich interprocess communication and integration with modern networked environments.

6.4. Timers, Background Tasks, and Idle Handlers

Efficient management of timers, background tasks, and idle handlers is critical for maintaining responsive graphical user interfaces (GUIs) when using the Fast Light Toolkit (FLTK). These mechanisms enable applications to execute periodic operations, offload computationally intensive work, and utilize idle CPU cycles without blocking the event loop or degrading user interaction responsiveness.

FLTK provides a simple yet effective timer mechanism to schedule functions to be called after a specific interval. Timers are commonly used for periodic updates, animations, or polling tasks. Timers in FLTK are implemented via the static method

Fl::add_timeout, which registers a callback function to be invoked after a specified delay (measured in seconds).

The critical attribute of FLTK timers is that callbacks are executed within the GUI thread context, integrated into the main event loop. This design guarantees that GUI drawing commands and event handling remain synchronized but also implies that timer callbacks should execute promptly to avoid freezing the interface.

A timer callback function signature must accept a single void* parameter, allowing user-defined data passing. The callback may re-register itself by calling Fl::repeat_timeout() if recurring execution is desired.

The following code snippet illustrates a simple timer for updating a widget once per second:

```
#include <FL/Fl.H>
#include <FL/Fl_Box.H>

void timer_callback(void* userdata) {
  Fl_Box* box = static_cast<Fl_Box*>(userdata);
  static int count = 0;
  ++count;
  box->label(("Timer count: " + std::to_string(count)).c_str());
  box->redraw();
  Fl::repeat_timeout(1.0, timer_callback, userdata);
}

int main() {
  Fl_Box box(100, 100, 200, 50, "Timer count: 0");
  box.show();
  Fl::add_timeout(1.0, timer_callback, &box);
  return Fl::run();
}
```

Timely execution of the callback depends on the main loop being active and unblocked. Long-running operations within a timer callback should be avoided to prevent interface lockups. For heavy processing, delegation to background threads is recommended.

Idle handlers provide a flexible mechanism to perform low-priority work during the GUI's idle time, i.e., when no events or timers need immediate attention. Registered with Fl::add_idle() or analogous functions, idle callbacks execute repeatedly whenever the event queue empties.

Idle callbacks receive no parameters and are expected to perform quick operations that can be chunked into small tasks to maintain interactivity. They are typically used for continuous, non-blocking background activities such as incremental computations, deferred updates, or maintenance routines.

To illustrate, the example below shows an idle handler that increments a progress counter and updates a widget:

```cpp
#include <FL/Fl.H>
#include <FL/Fl_Box.H>

Fl_Box* g_box = nullptr;
int g_progress = 0;

void idle_callback() {
  if(g_progress < 100) {
    ++g_progress;
    g_box->label(("Progress: " + std::to_string(g_progress) +
      "%").c_str());
    g_box->redraw();
  } else {
    Fl::remove_idle(idle_callback);
  }
}

int main() {
  Fl_Box box(100, 100, 200, 50, "Progress: 0%");
  g_box = &box;
  box.show();
  Fl::add_idle(idle_callback);
  return Fl::run();
}
```

Idle handlers are inherently cooperative; if they fail to yield or take excessive time, they can starve event handling and cause interface sluggishness.

FLTK's main loop and GUI operations must execute on the main thread. This restriction demands careful coordination when integrating background threads performing resource-intensive or blocking computations.

To decouple heavy tasks from the GUI thread, worker threads can run in parallel, signaling the main thread upon task completion or progress updates. Because FLTK widgets are not thread-safe, communication from worker threads to the GUI thread should occur via thread-safe mechanisms and result in requests for GUI updates or work scheduled on the main thread.

A canonical strategy involves:

- Launching long-running or blocking computations in separate `std::thread` instances or other threading APIs.

- Using synchronization primitives (mutexes, condition variables) to share computation results safely.

- Employing `Fl::awake()` to notify the main thread that data is ready, passing a pointer to update data or function objects.

- Implementing a static or singleton callback function registered with `Fl::awake` to safely update widgets on the GUI thread.

This approach enables the GUI to remain responsive, processing user input and screen redraws, while background threads proceed with computation.

An example demonstrating a background thread notifying the GUI via `Fl::awake()` is as follows:

```cpp
#include <FL/Fl.H>
#include <FL/Fl_Box.H>
#include <thread>
#include <atomic>
#include <chrono>

Fl_Box* g_box = nullptr;
std::atomic<int> g_result(0);

void update_gui(void*) {
    int value = g_result.load();
    g_box->label(("Result: " + std::to_string(value)).c_str());
    g_box->redraw();
```

```
}

void worker_thread_func() {
  // Simulate heavy calculation
  for(int i = 0; i <= 100; ++i) {
    std::this_thread::sleep_for(std::chrono::milliseconds(50));
    g_result.store(i);
    Fl::awake(update_gui, nullptr);
  }
}

int main() {
  Fl_Box box(100, 100, 200, 50, "Result: 0");
  g_box = &box;
  box.show();

  std::thread worker(worker_thread_func);
  worker.detach();

  return Fl::run();
}
```

Here, the worker thread updates an atomic variable and signals the main thread through Fl::awake. The main thread invokes update_gui, safely refreshing the display. Fl::awake guarantees thread-safe dispatch.

Optimally responsive FLTK applications often combine timers, idle handlers, and background threads, each playing distinct roles:

- **Timers** manage periodic, predictable updates tightly coupled to the GUI, such as animations or refreshes at fixed intervals.

- **Idle handlers** handle continuous small background work that can be executed incrementally without blocking or requiring precise scheduling.

- **Background threads** handle heavy, blocking, or non-GUI computations isolated from the event loop, communicating results asynchronously.

Separation of concerns and fine-grained control of task granularity prevent interface freezes and improve user experience. For example, a data acquisition application might:

- Use a background thread to read sensor data.

- Employ `Fl::awake()` to notify the main thread of new data.

- Trigger timer callbacks to update plots periodically.

- Use idle handlers for incremental calculations or housekeeping.

Maintaining application responsiveness requires observing the following principles:

- **Minimize work in callbacks:** Timer and idle callbacks should run quickly. Offload expensive computations to worker threads.

- **Thread safety:** FLTK widgets must be accessed only on the main thread. Use `Fl::awake()` or similar mechanisms for thread-safe updates.

- **Avoid long blocking operations:** Blocking the main loop delays event processing and redraws. Use asynchronous patterns instead.

- **Cleanup:** Remove timers and idle handlers properly when no longer needed to prevent runaway callbacks.

- **Synchronization:** Use atomic types or mutexes to protect shared data between the GUI and background threads.

The following table summarizes the core FLTK APIs related to timers, idle, and background task handling:

`Fl::add_timeout(double, callback, void*)`	Register a timer callback executed once after a given delay.
`Fl::repeat_timeout(double, callback, void*)`	Reschedule a timer for periodic execution.
`Fl::remove_timeout(callback, void*)`	Remove a registered timer callback.
`Fl::add_idle(callback)`	Add an idle handler called whenever the event loop has no immediate work.
`Fl::remove_idle(callback)`	Remove an idle handler.
`Fl::awake(callback, void*)`	Thread-safe mechanism for a background thread to signal the GUI thread and invoke a callback.
`Fl::run()`	Starts the FLTK event loop on the main thread.

Leveraging these in combination enables robust, fluid, and scalable FLTK applications that maintain interface reactivity even under significant processing loads.

6.5. Sensors, Devices, and Modern Peripherals

The seamless integration of hardware devices such as touchscreens, tablets, sensors, and various input peripherals into modern computing environments necessitates a comprehensive understanding of device detection, data acquisition, and adaptive user interface strategies. Each type of device introduces specific challenges and opportunities in terms of data flow, system interaction, and usability, influencing the design and implementation of robust hardware integration frameworks.

Device detection and enumeration are foundational steps in hardware integration. This process is critical for dynamically recognizing input peripherals as they become available or are removed without system reboots. Modern operating systems and hardware abstraction layers, such as the Linux kernel's udev or Windows Device Manager, rely on standardized protocols like USB, HID (Human Interface Device), and I2C buses to convey device identification data. Enumeration typically proceeds through a sequence of low-level hardware scans and retrieval of device descriptors, which encapsulate metadata such as vendor ID, product ID, device class, and version.

For embedded sensors and peripherals connected via serial interfaces, such as SPI or UART, detection might involve probing known bus addresses or issuing diagnostic commands. In all cases, maintaining an up-to-date device registry is essential for the operating system to manage resource allocation, driver loading, and communication pathways.

Touchscreens and tablets incorporate capacitive or resistive sensing technology to detect positional input, gestures, and sometimes pressure levels. The data acquisition pipeline begins with analog or digital signal capture from sensor arrays embedded beneath the input surface. These raw signals undergo preprocessing, including noise reduction and signal normalization, to generate accurate coordinate mappings.

Capacitive touch technology measures alterations in the electrical field caused by conductive objects such as fingers or styluses. The device firmware typically performs initial signal filtering and centroid computation for multi-touch points before relaying event data through standardized interfaces (e.g., HID over USB or Bluetooth). This event data includes touch coordinates, event types (touch down, move, lift), and additional parameters such as contact size or pressure.

Tablet devices often extend this functionality by including stylus device integration, which requires sampling pen-tip position, tilt, pressure sensitivity, and button states. Data acquisition includes handling proximity events where the stylus is detected before contacting the surface, enabling hover interactions. Timing considerations are paramount, as high sampling rates-often exceeding 100 Hz-ensure responsiveness and accurate rendering of input as continuous motion.

Sensors embedded in modern peripherals include accelerometers, gyroscopes, magnetometers, ambient light sensors, proximity detectors, and biometric units. Each sensor type produces data streams characterized by specific temporal and spatial properties. Integration strategies require configuring sensor registers for measurement modes, sampling rates, and resolution, often through protocols like I2C or SPI.

Real-time data acquisition necessitates efficient buffering strategies, interrupt handling, and timestamp synchronization to support downstream processing such as sensor fusion or event detection. For example, inertial measurement units (IMUs) combine accelerometer and gyroscope data to derive orientation and motion vectors, feeding adaptive interfaces or control systems.

Data integrity is maintained by incorporating calibration routines that correct systemic bias, scaling errors, and noise. Additionally, power management considerations influence operational modes, such as duty cycling sensors to minimize energy consumption without sacrificing data fidelity.

The proliferation of diverse input form factors requires user interfaces (UIs) to dynamically adjust to the capabilities and constraints of the detected devices. Adaptive UI design hinges on the concept of responsive interaction models that pivot according to input modality, screen size, and device orientation.

Touch-enabled devices necessitate larger target areas, gesture recognition support, and avoidance of hover-dependent interactions prevalent in pointer-based systems. Tablets and hybrid devices commonly employ context-aware UI element scaling and layout adjustments. For instance, when a stylus is detected, additional menus or drawing tools may become visible, enhancing productivity and precision.

Sensor data can also drive adaptive feedback mechanisms. Ambient light sensors enable automatic brightness adjustments, optimizing visibility and reducing power usage. Proximity detectors support context changes such as locking the screen upon device pocketing.

Event-driven architectures in user interface frameworks monitor hardware input states continuously, triggering UI updates without blocking non-interactive operations. Accessibility considerations factor heavily into adaptation strategies, ensuring that input from alternative devices (e.g., braille displays or eye-tracking sensors) integrates seamlessly.

Interfacing with sensors and peripherals typically involves layered communication stacks. Low-level device drivers abstract hardware specifics and expose a standardized interface for higher-level applications. For example, the HID protocol supports a wide range of input devices with minimal driver customization, whereas complex sensors or tablets may require vendor-specific drivers or middleware.

The use of middleware frameworks like Android's InputReader/InputDispatcher or Windows' Human Interface Infrastructure (HID) enables handling diverse input streams uniformly. These frameworks parse raw event data, coalesce multiple input sources, and deliver unified events to the application layer.

Implementing cross-platform compatibility benefits from adhering to open standards and leveraging HID report descriptors to describe device capabilities. Moreover, kernel-level event systems often employ ring buffers and mutex locks to coordinate concurrent data access and ensure thread-safe driver operation.

```
1. Detect tablet connection via USB using the vendor and product
   IDs.
2. Load the corresponding HID-compliant driver and confirm device
   capabilities.
3. Initialize data acquisition at the firmware level, enabling
   multi-touch and stylus input.
4. Continuously read input reports containing coordinates,
   pressure, and button states.
5. Translate raw device data into normalized screen coordinates
   considering resolution and orientation.
```

```
6. Dispatch events asynchronously to the input subsystem and
   application framework.
7. Adapt UI elements contextually recognizing stylus proximity
   and pressure sensitivity.
8. Calibrate input parameters regularly during use to maintain
   accuracy.
```

During operation, the sampling frequency must be sufficiently high (e.g., 125 Hz or above) to ensure smooth and responsive interaction. Data flow analysis may involve filtering raw input through moving average or Kalman filters to suppress jitter and enhance precision.

The integration landscape is evolving rapidly with the advent of flexible displays, haptic feedback devices, and context-aware peripherals incorporating embedded AI. New sensor modalities such as structured light scanners and time-of-flight cameras offer richer environmental interaction. Integration frameworks are increasingly leveraging machine learning models for gesture recognition and sensor fusion, further abstracting hardware complexity.

Standardization efforts, including the Universal Stylus Initiative (USI), aim to harmonize stylus interoperability across devices, reducing fragmentation. Concurrently, operating systems are enhancing their capabilities to support hot-plugging, power management, and security considerations for peripheral devices.

Incorporating low-latency, high-bandwidth communication protocols like USB4 and PCIe over Thunderbolt facilitates richer data transfer between devices and hosts, enabling advanced peripherals such as virtual reality controllers and multi-modal sensor arrays.

Reliable integration of sensors, touchscreens, tablets, and peripherals requires adherence to these foundational practices:

- Utilize standardized protocols and device descriptors for robust detection and compatibility.

- Implement efficient, low-latency data acquisition pipelines with appropriate filtering and calibration.

- Design adaptable user interfaces that respond to differing input modalities and device capabilities.

- Employ modular, well-maintained drivers and middleware layers to abstract hardware complexity.

- Maintain synchronization of sensor data streams with system time to support composite event processing.

- Prioritize power-efficient operation through dynamic sensor management and system event handling.

Such systemic rigor ensures hardware peripherals contribute positively to overall system responsiveness, usability, and reliability, forming a critical pillar of contemporary interactive computing architectures.

6.6. Security, Sandboxing, and Permissions

The design and deployment of FLTK applications that interact with system resources necessitate a comprehensive security architecture to mitigate risks to user data and system integrity. The intrinsic simplicity and cross-platform nature of FLTK offer both opportunities and challenges in securing applications. This section details the principles and best practices for limiting application privileges, managing permission requests, and employing sandboxing techniques to ensure robust security in FLTK environments.

FLTK (Fast Light Toolkit) is primarily a GUI framework with minimal dependencies, which inherently reduces the attack surface by decreasing external interactions beyond the graphical layer. However, when FLTK applications extend functionality to access system resources such as file systems, network interfaces, or hardware devices, the security model must be explicitly considered.

The architecture should assume that any operation involving external resources has potential vectors for privilege escalation, data leakage, or unauthorized access.

The fundamental principle is least privilege: an FLTK application should operate with the minimum permissions necessary for its intended functionality. This aligns with established security models across modern operating systems and frameworks, requiring developers to isolate resource-sensitive operations from the user interface code whenever feasible. Such separation aids in applying sandboxing or privilege reduction techniques to critical components without impairing basic user interaction.

Limiting privileges involves constraining the capabilities of an FLTK application to reduce the impact of bugs, compromises, or malicious exploitations. The methods for privilege limitation depend on the target platform but share common strategic approaches:

- **User-Level Permissions:** Applications should run under non-administrative user accounts, avoiding elevated rights unless explicitly required for specific tasks. On Unix-like systems, this is a default security layer, whereas Windows applications may need manifest modifications or access control lists (ACLs) configured to enforce standard user rights.

- **Fine-Grained Access Control:** When file system or device access is necessary, precise path restrictions and minimal access scopes should be specified. For instance, applications should request read-write permissions only to designated application data directories rather than the entire file system. This may be reinforced by configuring operating system-level sandbox profiles or container-based policies.

- **Capability Tokens and Scoped Access:** On platforms supporting capability-based security (e.g., macOS with its sandbox or Windows with AppContainers), developers

212

should leverage these tokens to scope resource access to the granular level stipulated by FLTK application requirements. This involves declarative provisioning of access rights in application bundles or manifest files.

Many modern operating systems enforce runtime permission models where user consent is required before an application can access sensitive resources such as location data, camera, microphone, or contacts. Although FLTK itself does not provide built-in abstractions for permission requests, integrating with native platform APIs to manage these requests is essential.

- **Platform API Integration:** FLTK applications must invoke native system dialogs and callbacks to request permissions synchronously or asynchronously before accessing protected resources. This typically involves writing conditional platform-specific code paths that interoperate with OS-level frameworks, such as Cocoa on macOS, Windows Runtime (WinRT) APIs on Windows, or the Permissions API on Linux desktop environments.

- **Graceful Degradation:** Applications should implement fallback mechanisms for denied permissions, such as disabling feature sets gracefully or notifying the user of functional limitations without causing crashes or undefined behavior. Proper error handling ensures robustness in constrained permission contexts.

- **Explicit Declaration:** For some platforms, permissions must be declared statically in metadata files (e.g., Info.plist on macOS/iOS or manifest.json on Windows Store apps) before runtime requests can function correctly. This requires careful auditing of required permissions to avoid over-privileging and consequent security risks or application rejections during store validations.

Sandboxing is the encapsulation of application execution within a restricted environment with controlled access to system resources and user data. It effectively contains the consequences of application compromises and prevents malicious or erroneous code from impacting the broader system.

- **OS-Level Sandboxing:** Modern operating systems provide sandboxing infrastructures tailored for graphical applications. For instance, macOS App Sandboxing enforces strict entitlements limiting file system access, network connections, and interprocess communication. Windows App-Containers and Linux containers (such as Flatpak or Snap) offer analogous hardening mechanisms.

  Deploying FLTK applications within these environments requires:

  - Packaging the application in the appropriate format with sandbox profiles specifying allowed interactions.

  - Adapting application architecture to comply with sandbox restrictions, typically by offloading privileged operations to helper services residing outside the sandbox or by requesting temporary elevated privileges explicitly allowed by the system.

- **Process Isolation:** Another sandboxing strategy is logical separation of concerns within the application itself. By dividing the application into multiple processes-isolating UI code from resource-intensive or sensitive operations-compromise restrictions can be enforced by the operating system. Communication between processes uses secure, audited IPC mechanisms.

- **Virtualization and Containers:** In scenarios where strict isolation and reproducibility are critical, developing and deploying FLTK applications in virtual machines or containerized environments enhances security. Containers can limit the system calls, network access, and visible file systems accessible to the application, reducing the attack surface further.

Protecting user data in FLTK applications encompasses secure collection, storage, transmission, and destruction:

- **Data Minimization:** Only essential data required for application functionality should be collected and persisted. Avoid caching sensitive information unnecessarily, and whenever possible, encrypt data at rest using platform-native cryptographic services or external libraries.

- **Secure Inter-Process Communication:** If the application uses multiple processes or interfaces with external components, ensure all communication channels are encrypted and authenticated. Utilize OS-provided secure IPC primitives or established cryptographic protocols (e.g., TLS) in custom implementations.

- **Input Validation and Sanitization:** Since FLTK applications often process external data (including files or network inputs), rigorous validation routines are critical to defend against injection, buffer overflows, or malformed data exploitation. This directly affects both the UI components and backend data handling layers.

- **Logging and Audit Trails:** Implement controlled logging mechanisms that exclude sensitive information or redact it appropriately. Audit trails that track access to restricted functions assist in forensic analysis and incident response without compromising user privacy.

When FLTK applications access system resources, architecting safe integration involves anticipatory design decisions and cross-layer controls:

- **Encapsulation of Resource Access:** Abstract system resource access into well-defined modules with explicit APIs. This separation facilitates easier auditing, testing, and application of security policies independently from the UI code.

- **Principle of Defense in Depth:** Layer multiple security controls around resource access points, including access control lists, encryption, runtime checks, and user authentication where applicable. Any single control failure should be compensated by others.

- **Regular Security Reviews and Updates:** Continuously assess the impact of changes in system APIs or OS security policies on the application's security posture. Maintain up-to-date dependencies and address newly discovered vulnerabilities in libraries interfacing with the system.

- **User Consent and Transparency:** Design clear and comprehensible user interfaces communicating permission requests and data usage. Providing transparency builds user trust and complies with privacy regulations.

A practical example involves restricting file access through a controlled file dialog with explicit read/write paths and limited permissions:

```
#include <FL/Fl_Native_File_Chooser.H>

bool open_secure_file_dialog(std::string& filepath) {
    Fl_Native_File_Chooser chooser;
    chooser.title("Open Data File");
    chooser.type(Fl_Native_File_Chooser::BROWSE_FILE);
    chooser.filter("Data Files\t*.dat\n");

    // Restrict access to user's Documents folder
    const char* user_doc = getenv("HOME");
    if(user_doc) {
      chooser.directory(std::string(user_doc).append("/Documents
    ").c_str());
    } else {
      // Fallback to current directory
      chooser.directory(".");
    }
```

```
if (chooser.show() == 0) {
    filepath = chooser.filename();
    // Additional check: ensure file is within allowed folder
    if(filepath.find("Documents") != std::string::npos) {
        return true;
    }
}
return false;
}
```

This code snippet demonstrates combining user-guided file selection with environmental safeguards to reduce privilege scope. Complementary OS sandbox policies should reinforce these programmatic checks to prevent circumvention.

Robust security for FLTK applications interfacing with system resources requires an integrated discipline encompassing least privilege principles, permission management, sandbox enforcement, and secure programming practices. Adoption of platform-specific features and continuous security assessments align FLTK deployments with modern standards, enabling user confidence and regulatory compliance. Security is an ongoing process ingrained in design, development, deployment, and maintenance phases, critical to preserving the integrity and privacy goals of FLTK applications.

Chapter 7

Build Automation, Tooling, and Deployment Strategies

From source code to users' desktops, this chapter guides you through the full lifecycle of building and shipping FLTK applications. Discover the techniques that underpin smooth, repeatable builds, efficient testing, and hassle-free deployment on every major platform. Whether you deploy internally or to millions, master the art of automating, packaging, and distributing professional-grade software with confidence.

7.1. CMake and Advanced Build Systems

The Fast Light Toolkit (FLTK) leverages CMake as its principal build system, offering a robust, extensible, and cross-platform environment suited to managing complex build processes. Unlike traditional Makefiles or platform-specific project files, CMake abstracts many idiosyncrasies of varying compilation environments, allowing developers to maintain a unified project configuration that can be easily adapted for Windows, macOS, Linux, and other operating systems. Understanding CMake's capabilities in the context of FLTK involves appreciating project setup, the nuances of cross-platform configuration, the definition and use of custom build targets, and the seamless integration of external dependencies and code generation tools.

Project Setup with CMake in FLTK

At the core of FLTK's build system lies a well-structured CMakeLists.txt hierarchy. The top-level CMake script defines fundamental variables such as project name, version, and minimum required CMake version using:

```
cmake_minimum_required(VERSION 3.12)
project(FLTK VERSION 1.4.0 LANGUAGES C CXX)
```

Project-wide configurations specify compiler standards (commonly C++11 or later), global include directories, and compiler flags that accommodate FLTK's multi-platform goals. For instance, enforcing a C++ standard is achieved via:

```
set(CMAKE_CXX_STANDARD 11)
set(CMAKE_CXX_STANDARD_REQUIRED ON)
set(CMAKE_CXX_EXTENSIONS OFF)
```

FLTK's modular design benefits from CMake's support for multiple subdirectories, each hosting its own CMakeLists.txt. This modular approach isolates components such as core widgets, utilities, and platform-specific implementations. The add_subdirectory() command propagates configuration and builds component libraries or executables separately, which are ultimately linked into the main FLTK library or example projects.

Cross-Platform Configuration and Portability

One of CMake's distinguishing strengths is its native support for cross-platform builds. FLTK takes advantage of this by defining platform-specific options and source files conditionally. The use of if() and elseif() constructs enables the inclusion or exclusion of platform-dependent code, compiler options, and libraries.

For Windows, CMake automatically detects compilers such as MSVC (Microsoft Visual C++) or MinGW and sets appropriate flags. For example:

```
if(WIN32)
  set(PLATFORM_SRC src/win32/fltk_win32.cpp)
  add_compile_options(/DWIN32_LEAN_AND_MEAN)
elseif(APPLE)
  set(PLATFORM_SRC src/macos/fltk_mac.cpp)
  set(CMAKE_OSX_ARCHITECTURES "x86_64;arm64")
else()
  set(PLATFORM_SRC src/linux/fltk_linux.cpp)
endif()
```

Furthermore, CMake's find_package() mechanism locates system libraries and external dependencies in a way that is tailored to each operating system's conventions. This is particularly crucial for graphical dependencies such as X11 on Linux, Cocoa frameworks on macOS, and Win32 libraries on Windows.

The abstraction extends to compiler toolchains and linker flags. CMake's generator expressions and variables (e.g., ${CMAKE_CXX_COMPILER}, ${CMAKE_INSTALL_PREFIX}) allow build scripts to adapt dynamically, enabling developers to create build trees that target multiple platforms without manual intervention.

Custom Build Targets and Build System Extensibility

Custom build targets enhance FLTK's build system by encapsulating auxiliary tasks beyond simple compilation and linking. These include generating documentation, running code analysis tools, packaging, and executing post-build scripts.

A typical custom target declaration utilizes the

`add_custom_target()` command, specifying commands or dependencies explicitly. For instance, generating documentation with Doxygen can be integrated as:

```
find_package(Doxygen QUIET)
if(DOXYGEN_FOUND)
  add_custom_target(doc
    COMMAND ${DOXYGEN_EXECUTABLE} ${CMAKE_CURRENT_SOURCE_DIR}/
    Doxyfile
    WORKING_DIRECTORY ${CMAKE_CURRENT_BINARY_DIR}
    COMMENT "Generating API documentation with Doxygen"
    VERBATIM)
endif()
```

Such targets can be made dependencies of the main build target or executed independently. They improve automation and maintain coherence between generated assets and compiled code.

Another common use case is the definition of `add_custom_command()` to process files pre-build, such as converting interface description files or running code generators. This integration ensures that generated sources are seamlessly incorporated into the compilation pipeline.

Integration with Code Generation Tools

FLTK's extensibility often demands integration with external code generation utilities, for example, protocol buffers, interface builders, or custom parsers. CMake facilitates this by adequately defining custom commands that invoke these tools, ensuring generated code is correctly linked in the build.

Consider a scenario where an IDL (Interface Definition Language) file must be parsed and transformed into C++ source and header files. CMake's approach involves:

```
add_custom_command(
  OUTPUT generated_protocol.cpp generated_protocol.h
  COMMAND idl_compiler ARGS ${CMAKE_CURRENT_SOURCE_DIR}/protocol.
    idl
         -o ${CMAKE_CURRENT_BINARY_DIR}/generated_protocol.cpp
  DEPENDS ${CMAKE_CURRENT_SOURCE_DIR}/protocol.idl
  COMMENT "Generating protocol source and header from IDL"
  VERBATIM
```

```
)
add_custom_target(generate_protocol_files DEPENDS
    generated_protocol.cpp generated_protocol.h)
```

The build system subsequently incorporates these generated files into libraries or executables by listing them as sources. This approach guarantees that changes in interface definitions correctly propagate through rebuilds without manual intervention.

Management of External Dependencies

The robustness of FLTK's build system is further demonstrated by the careful handling of external dependencies. Using modern CMake's find_package() and FetchContent modules, dependencies are either searched for in the system or fetched and built as part of the build tree.

For libraries present on the development system, find_package() attempts to locate suitable installs according to standard or customized search paths:

```
find_package(Threads REQUIRED)
find_package(X11 REQUIRED)
```

The located libraries provide imported targets, which FLTK uses to correctly set link options and include directories, fostering a decoupled and modular build description.

For dependencies not guaranteed to exist on the host system, FetchContent enables automatic downloading and inclusion:

```
include(FetchContent)
FetchContent_Declare(
  imgui
  GIT_REPOSITORY https://github.com/ocornut/imgui.git
  GIT_TAG v1.89.0
)
FetchContent_MakeAvailable(imgui)
```

This declarative style reduces setup complexity and guarantees consistency across different build environments.

The adoption of CMake within FLTK reflects the toolkit's requirements for a versatile, maintainable, and extendable build infrastructure. By employing modern CMake features-such as modularized project files, platform-aware configurations, custom targets, code generation hooks, and dependency management-FLTK achieves a scalable build system that proficiently adapts to evolving development environments and workflows. The resulting architecture simplifies collaboration, enhances reproducibility, and streamlines continuous integration pipelines essential for modern software delivery.

7.2. Static and Dynamic Linking

Linking constitutes a fundamental phase in software build processes, responsible for combining various compiled object files and libraries into a single executable or library. The two principal linking methodologies, *static* and *dynamic linking*, offer distinct mechanisms for integrating program dependencies, each manifesting unique implications on binary size, dependency management, performance, and portability.

Static linking produces a standalone binary by embedding all library routines directly into the executable at compile time. This approach consolidates dependencies into a single file, removing external runtime requirements for linked libraries. The resulting executable embodies all necessary code, facilitating deployment simplicity and deterministic runtime behavior. One intrinsic consequence of static linking is an increase in binary size, proportional to the quantity of linked library code utilized. For example, linking a large utility library statically can significantly inflate the executable due to inclusion of entire object modules, even those with unused functions owing to coarse granularity in library partitioning.

Conversely, dynamic linking defers the resolution of external symbols to runtime, loading shared libraries into memory only when the executable is invoked. Shared object files or dynamic-link libraries (DLLs) contain reusable code that multiple executables can reference, enabling memory and disk space savings through code sharing. Dynamic linking confers advantages when multiple applications depend on common libraries, permitting centralized updates and reducing redundant code storage. However, this paradigm introduces additional complexity in managing library versioning and compatibility. The phenomenon commonly known as *dependency hell* arises when conflicts occur between different versions of a shared library required by various applications on the same system.

Dependency management under static linking is inherently straightforward. Once compiled into the executable, all necessary code is fixed; there is no requirement for external library presence at runtime. This stability simplifies deployment in constrained or unmanaged environments and mitigates risks associated with shared library mismatches or missing dependencies. Nevertheless, updates to static libraries necessitate recompilation and relinking of all dependent binaries to incorporate the changes, which can be impractical in large-scale or distributed software ecosystems.

Dynamic linking facilitates modular software design by enabling independent library updates without rebuilding the executable. This modularity can improve security by allowing patches to shared libraries to propagate immediately to dependent applications. However, ensuring *binary compatibility* between shared library versions and applications imposes stringent constraints on API evolution. Inconsistent or incompatible updates risk runtime failures, segmentation faults, or subtle undefined behaviors. Tools such as symbol versioning and SONAMEs in Unix-like systems, or side-by-side assemblies and manifests in Windows, partially mitigate these risks but do not eliminate the inherent challenges in maintaining a stable Application Binary Interface (ABI).

Binary size optimization remains a crucial consideration in selecting between static and dynamic linking strategies. Static linking amalgamates all referenced code, presenting opportunities and challenges in minimizing bloat. Advanced linkers employ *dead code elimination* (garbage collection of unused symbols) and *function-level linking* to remove extraneous routines, but the effectiveness heavily depends on the granularity of object modules and compiler optimizations like LTO (Link Time Optimization). Dynamic linking, by enabling multiple executables to share a single copy of library code in memory, presents overall system-wide memory savings but does not reduce the individual executable's size substantially since dynamic libraries themselves occupy disk space independent of the executables.

Consider the trade-offs from a performance perspective. Statically linked programs tend to exhibit faster startup times, as symbol resolution and relocation are completed at compile time. The absence of dynamic loader overhead at runtime can contribute to improved execution predictability, which is critical in real-time or embedded systems. Conversely, dynamically linked programs might incur negligible runtime overhead during library loading and address relocations, though modern operating systems optimize such processes substantially. Additionally, dynamic linking enables shared memory utilization across processes, reducing the total memory footprint when multiple applications concurrently use the same shared libraries.

Cross-platform build consistency heightens in importance given divergent operating systems' conventions for library formats, naming, and loading mechanisms. Static libraries typically have platform-specific file extensions (e.g., .lib on Windows, .a on Unix-like systems) and toolchain requirements. Dynamic libraries display even greater variability: Windows employs .dll files with import libraries, whereas Linux and macOS utilize .so and .dylib files, respectively, each coupled with distinct dynamic loader semantics.

Ensuring reproducible and consistent builds across platforms requires careful control over linking parameters and robust dependency tracking. Build systems must accommodate differences in library search paths, environment variables (e.g., LD_LIBRARY_PATH on Linux), and tooling conventions. Static linking can simplify cross-platform deployment by producing self-contained binaries, albeit at the cost of larger files and less runtime flexibility. Dynamic linking mandates meticulous version synchronization and often leverages containerization or package managers to harmonize the runtime environment.

Practical considerations also guide linking strategy decisions in large-scale software projects. High-performance computing and embedded applications frequently prefer static linking to maximize determinism and minimize external dependencies. Desktop and server applications leaning heavily on plugin architectures or frequent library updates often favor dynamic linking to facilitate extensibility and maintenance.

A concise example illustrates the differences in build commands for linking a simple executable against the math library (libm):

```
# Static linking (Unix-like systems):
gcc -o calc calc.o /usr/lib/libm.a

# Dynamic linking (default on Unix-like systems):
gcc -o calc calc.o -lm
```

Here, static linking explicitly references the static archive libm.a, embedding the math library code. Dynamic linking, indicated by the -lm flag without specifying a static archive, instructs the linker to resolve symbols against the shared library libm.so at runtime.

Understanding the nuances of symbol resolution reveals additional distinctions. Static linking binds symbols at link time, producing a binary with no unresolved symbols. Dynamic linking allows *symbol interposition*, where runtime symbol resolution can override definitions, enabling mechanisms like function interposing or runtime patching. While offering versatility, this ability complicates debugging and security audits.

In summary, the choice between static and dynamic linking embodies a complex balance among binary size constraints, deployment environment characteristics, performance requisites, and maintenance strategies. Deep comprehension of both methodologies' underlying mechanisms and implications enables informed decisions tailored to specific application domains. Optimization efforts must consider the interplay between static code inclusion, dynamic dependency management, and build reproducibility to achieve robust, efficient, and maintainable software systems.

7.3. Continuous Integration for FLTK Projects

Continuous Integration (CI) pipelines for FLTK (Fast Light Toolkit) projects present a unique combination of challenges and opportunities arising from the GUI-centric nature of the toolkit, its cross-platform dependencies, and the imperative for thorough testing of visual components. Establishing a robust CI/CD pipeline tailored for FLTK requires an orchestrated approach to automated building, testing, code quality assurance, and artifact management, all aligned with the idiosyncrasies of C++ and FLTK's dependencies.

Automated Builds

FLTK projects typically compile with a C++ toolchain, relying on build systems like Make, CMake, or custom scripts. The automation of builds within CI services such as GitHub Actions, GitLab CI, or Jenkins hinges upon configuring environments that reproduce local build conditions across multiple platforms.

Key considerations for automated FLTK builds include:

- **Environment Setup**: Pre-installation or caching of dependencies including the FLTK library and the compiler

228

toolchain (e.g., GCC, Clang on Linux/macOS; MSVC on Windows). Many CI providers offer prebuilt runners with multiple toolchains or container support to systematically manage these dependencies.

- **Cross-Platform Compilation**: FLTK's multi-platform compatibility necessitates configuring build jobs per OS. For example, on Linux and macOS, a typical build may invoke cmake followed by make, whereas Windows builds may require configuration through Visual Studio's MSBuild.

- **Build Caching Strategies**: Employing cache mechanisms to store compiled dependencies and intermediate files significantly reduces build times. CI services often provide cache key parameters that restore caches based on changes in configuration or source files.

A minimal example of a GitHub Actions workflow snippet for building an FLTK project with CMake on Ubuntu could be:

```
name: Build FLTK Project

on: [push, pull_request]

jobs:
  build:
    runs-on: ubuntu-latest
    steps:
    - uses: actions/checkout@v3

    - name: Install dependencies
      run: |
        sudo apt-get update
        sudo apt-get install -y libfltk1.3-dev build-essential
      cmake

    - name: Configure project
      run: cmake -S . -B build

    - name: Build project
      run: cmake --build build --config Release
```

Equivalent scripts for Windows and macOS trigger corresponding platform-specific build commands and dependency installation methods.

Testing Stages

Testing FLTK applications within CI pipelines extends beyond unit testing. While classic unit tests to verify core logic are fundamental, ensuring GUI correctness and integration consistency adds complexity.

- **Automated Unit Testing**: Utilizing frameworks such as Google Test or Catch2 integrates seamlessly with CMake test targets. Tests should be triggered post-build to verify core non-visual functionality.

- **GUI Testing and Validation**: FLTK provides GUI elements which are notoriously difficult to verify via headless CI runs. Approaches to GUI testing include:

- *Smoke Tests*: Launching the FLTK application in minimal modes and monitoring for crashes or initialization errors.

- *Screenshot Comparison*: Running the GUI application in virtual framebuffers (e.g., Xvfb on Linux) or headless modes to capture screen outputs and comparing against reference images using automated tools like ImageMagick or PerceptualDiff.

- *Scripted Interactions*: Employing tools such as xdotool on Linux to simulate user interaction sequences, verifying expected GUI behavior.

- **Continuous Integration of Tests**: Configuring CI jobs to run different classes of tests under isolated steps allows parallelism and better fault isolation. For instance, unit tests may run on all platforms, while GUI tests may be limited to Linux environments supporting virtual framebuffers.

An example command to run unit tests within CMake's test framework is:

```
cmake --build build --target test
```

For GUI smoke testing on Linux with Xvfb:

```
Xvfb :99 -screen 0 1024x768x24 &
export DISPLAY=:99
./build/my_fltk_application --test-mode
```

In this mode, the `--test-mode` flag can disable animations or external dependencies, focusing on validation.

Code Quality Enforcement

Maintaining code quality within FLTK projects dovetails with CI pipelines by enforcing static analysis, style conformance, and test coverage. This section details the integration of these controls for C++ FLTK codebases.

- **Static Analysis**: Tools such as `clang-tidy` and `cppcheck` identify semantic issues, memory misuse, and potential vulnerabilities before runtime. These can be embedded as separate CI steps using preconfigured tool commands.

- **Code Formatting**: Enforcing consistent styling reduces divergence and review overhead. Tools like `clang-format` can check formatting without applying changes by generating diffs. CI jobs rejected on formatting errors enforce discipline.

- **Test Coverage**: Coverage tools tailored for C++ (e.g., `gcov`, `lcov`, and `Codecov` integration) enable visualization of test coverage status and help focus additional test creation on under-tested code areas.

An example static analysis step in GitHub Actions leveraging `clang-tidy` may appear as follows:

```
- name: Run clang-tidy analysis
  run: |
    cmake -S . -B build -DCMAKE_EXPORT_COMPILE_COMMANDS=ON
    clang-tidy -p build src/*.cpp
```

For formatting checks with `clang-format`:

```
clang-format --dry-run --Werror src/*.cpp include/*.h
```

CI jobs fail if code does not comply, incentivizing pre-commit code formatting.

Artifact Distribution and Releasing

Automated artifact creation and distribution streamline FLTK software deployments, ensuring that releases are consistent, reproducible, and accessible to users.

- **Build Artifacts**: Executables, libraries, and documentation generated during builds must be collected as CI artifacts. Most CI services provide storage of build outputs and facilitate downloads or downstream job usage.

- **Packaging**: Platform-specific packaging tools can be incorporated to generate distributable installers or packages:

- *Linux*: deb or rpm packages via dpkg or rpmbuild.

- *Windows*: Creation of .msi, .exe installers (e.g., with NSIS or WiX Toolset).

- *macOS*: Signed app bundles or .dmg images.

- **Release Automation**: Tagging in version control systems like Git triggers automated release workflows. These workflows build and package the FLTK projects, then upload artifacts to platforms such as GitHub Releases, artifact registries, or custom FTP servers.

- **Containerization**: In some cases, distributing container images with FLTK applications (e.g., in X11 forwarding or VNC-accessible formats) provides a reproducible execution environment, especially for demo or test distributions.

A GitHub Actions release job example, uploading binaries on a new tag:

```
jobs:
  release:
    runs-on: ubuntu-latest
    if: startsWith(github.ref, 'refs/tags/')
    steps:
    - uses: actions/checkout@v3

    - name: Build project
      run: |
        sudo apt-get update
        sudo apt-get install -y libfltk1.3-dev cmake build-
      essential
        cmake -S . -B build
        cmake --build build --config Release

    - name: Upload Release Asset
      uses: softprops/action-gh-release@v1
      with:
        files: build/my_fltk_application
      env:
        GITHUB_TOKEN: ${{ secrets.GITHUB_TOKEN }}
```

This workflow ensures artifacts generated during build steps become downloadable assets attached to the GitHub release, ready for distribution.

Summary of Essential Practices for FLTK CI Pipelines

A well-designed CI/CD pipeline for FLTK projects integrates the following principles:

1. Multi-platform build and test environments reflecting user deployment targets, with caching to reduce build time.

2. Diverse testing strategies including unit tests, GUI smoke tests, and visually comparative regression testing under

headless modes.

3. Rigorous quality control through static analysis, coding style enforcement, and systematic measurement of test coverage.

4. Automated artifact packaging, release tagging, and distribution workflows ensuring consistent and readily available deliverables.

These components collectively accelerate development cycles, mitigate integration risks inherent in cross-platform GUI projects, and enhance maintainability and adoption readiness of FLTK software systems.

7.4. Packaging for Major Platforms

Effective software distribution requires carefully tailored packaging strategies for each major desktop operating system: Windows, Linux, and macOS. These strategies must address installer generation, bundling conventions, code signing, and tools that facilitate cross-platform packaging. The objective is to achieve reliable installation experiences, minimize compatibility issues, and maintain security guarantees across diverse user environments.

Windows remains the dominant platform for desktop applications, necessitating robust deployment mechanisms that integrate smoothly into the Windows ecosystem. The Windows packaging strategy often centers on producing an installer executable or a set of installation packages conforming to Windows Installer (MSI) specifications.

Installer Types

Two common installer types dominate Windows packaging:

- **MSI Installers:** MSI files leverage the Windows Installer service, providing transactional and standardized installation, repair, uninstall, and upgrade capabilities. MSI installers are well-suited for enterprise deployment and can be created using tools like WiX Toolset, Advanced Installer, or InstallShield. They allow precise control over installation sequences, registry entries, and component conditions.

- **Executable Installers:** Custom executable-based installers generated using frameworks such as NSIS (Nullsoft Scriptable Install System) or Inno Setup offer greater flexibility in user interaction design. These are often preferred for consumer applications requiring customized UI flows or bundled prerequisites.

Bundle Requirements

Windows applications often require bundling multiple components distinctively:

- Redistributables: Common runtimes such as Visual C++ Redistributables or .NET Framework versions must either be bundled or explicitly requested for installation.

- Dependencies: Shared libraries (DLLs) and supporting assets should be placed in standardized directories such as `Program Files` or application-specific subfolders, conforming to Windows filesystem conventions.

- Registry Entries: Installer scripts typically create registry keys for application settings, context menu integration, or file association.

Code Signing

Code signing is crucial for Windows to provide authentication and integrity verification, prevent tampering, and pass Microsoft Defender SmartScreen filters. Applications and installers are signed using Authenticode digital certificates issued by trusted Certificate Authorities (CAs). This requires:

- Obtaining an Extended Validation (EV) or Organization Validated (OV) certificate from providers like DigiCert or Sectigo.

- Using Microsoft's `signtool.exe` utility to digitally sign PE files (.exe, .dll).

- Timestamping signatures to ensure validity beyond certificate expiration.

Signed installers enhance user trust and reduce warnings during installation.

Linux distributions exhibit substantial heterogeneity in package formats, filesystem hierarchies, and dependency management approaches. Packaging strategies must accommodate these differences to maximize compatibility and minimize user friction.

Package Formats

Linux software is primarily distributed in native package formats associated with target distributions:

- **Debian packages (.deb):** Used by Debian and Ubuntu families, created with tools like `dpkg` and `debhelper`.

- **RPM packages (.rpm):** Utilized by Fedora, CentOS, openSUSE, and others, created using `rpmbuild`.

- **Others:** Distributions like Arch Linux use PKGBUILDs, while Gentoo relies on Portage ebuild scripts.

Authors often create multiple packages tailored to specific distributions or use universal packaging systems when possible.

Bundle and Filesystem Conventions

Linux distribution guidelines demand adherence to the Filesystem Hierarchy Standard (FHS):

236

- Executables typically reside in /usr/bin or /usr/local/bin.

- Libraries go into /usr/lib or architecture-specific variants.

- Configuration files are placed under /etc.

- Shared resources and documentation occupy /usr/share.

Proper package manifests must declare dependencies explicitly to enable automatic resolution through package managers.

Application Sandboxing and Universal Packages

Given the difficulty of supporting diverse Linux distributions, universal packaging formats have emerged:

- **AppImage:** A portable, self-mounting image containing application binaries and dependencies without installation. It runs directly without root privileges.

- **Snap:** Developed by Canonical, Snap packages are containerized, isolated with strict confinement, and integrate with the Snap store.

- **Flatpak:** Flatpak employs sandboxing, with runtimes providing shared dependencies. It is supported by many distributions and integrates desktop application portals.

These formats reduce dependency conflicts and simplify distribution but require consideration of runtime availability, system integration, and security models.

Signing and Verification

Package signing is integral to Linux security, enforcing trust by validating packages against known keys:

- Native package managers verify signatures against distribution-maintained GPG keys.

- Snap and Flatpak packages also support cryptographic signing, ensuring content integrity and trusted sources.

Developers must sign packages and upload them to trusted repositories or stores to enable seamless user installation.

macOS applications are typically distributed as application bundles (.app directories), disk images, or installation packages. The packaging approach must conform to Apple's conventions to provide the expected user experience and support distribution via Apple's ecosystem.

Application Bundles

An application bundle in macOS is a directory structure with a standardized layout recognized by the system as a single executable entity:

- The `Contents` directory contains `MacOS` (the executable), `Resources` (assets and localized files), and `Info.plist` (metadata).

- Bundles can be distributed as-is or further packaged for installation.

Bundles simplify application management by encapsulating all required components.

Installer Packages and Disk Images

Additional packaging methods include:

- **Installer Packages (.pkg):** Built using Apple's `pkgbuild` and `productbuild` tools, these allow complex installation workflows and system modifications. They can install to arbitrary filesystem locations and integrate with macOS Installer.

- **Disk Images (.dmg):** Used to present the application bundle in a convenient mountable volume, often with a custom background and instructions for dragging the app to the Applications folder. This form preserves the application bundle structure and simplifies distribution outside the App Store.

Code Signing and Notarization

Apple enforces signing and notarization as prerequisites for distribution, especially for Gatekeeper compliance:

- All applications and installer packages must be signed with an Apple Developer ID certificate obtained through the Apple Developer Program.

- The `codesign` utility digitally signs the app bundle, frameworks, and helper executables.

- Notarization involves submitting the signed app or installer to Apple's notarization service, which scans for malware and code issues. Successful notarization embeds a ticket enabling Gatekeeper to approve the app during installation.

- Notarization is mandatory for apps distributed outside the Mac App Store on recent macOS versions.

These processes increase user confidence and reduce security warnings.

Cross-platform development environments can reduce the complexity of building and distributing applications across Windows, Linux, and macOS by abstracting platform-specific packaging details.

Electron, Qt, and Java Packaging Tools

Frameworks such as Electron for JavaScript-based applications or Qt for C++ development include mechanisms to package applications into platform-appropriate bundles:

239

- Electron Builder automates production of MSI, NSIS installers on Windows; DMG images and PKG installers on macOS; and AppImage, Snap, or DEB packages on Linux.

- Qt Installer Framework supports creation of cross-platform installers and maintenance tools, reducing the need to manually manage platform peculiarities.

- Java applications can leverage tools such as jpackage (from JDK 14 onwards) to wrap JVM applications into native installers for all three platforms.

These tools help avoid duplication of effort and promote consistency across releases.

Containerization Approaches

While primarily server-oriented, container technologies like Docker are sometimes adapted for desktop application distribution in controlled environments. However, they usually lack seamless integration with native GUI experience and system services, limiting their general applicability for end-user desktop deployment.

Build Automation and Continuous Integration

Integrating packaging steps into automated build and continuous integration pipelines ensures reproducibility and timeliness of multi-platform releases. Tools like GitHub Actions, Azure Pipelines, and Jenkins support workflows producing binaries, signing them, and generating installers or packages for all target platforms, streamlining the overall process.

Packing applications for major desktop platforms requires balancing system conventions, security requirements, and user experience expectations. The choice of installer types, bundle formats, signing mechanisms, and packaging tools must reflect the target platform's ecosystem standards while considering distribution channels and end-user devices. Leveraging universal packaging formats or cross-platform frameworks can simplify the maintenance burden but must be weighed against limitations such as sandboxing policies and runtime dependencies. Ultimately, meticulous packaging strategy design accelerates adoption and stability of software deliveries in heterogeneous environments.

7.5. Distributing via App Stores and Open Source Channels

The distribution of FLTK (Fast Light Toolkit) applications encompasses diverse channels, prominently including major app stores and open source package repositories. Each distribution method imposes distinct technical requirements, submission workflows, and update management strategies. Adherence to these parameters ensures optimal application reach, user trust, and streamlined maintenance.

App stores serve as centralized platforms that enable developers to distribute applications to large user bases while providing mechanisms for payment processing, licensing, ratings, and updates. The principal app stores relevant to FLTK applications are the Apple App Store, Microsoft Store, and various Linux desktop environments' software centers.

Apple App Store (macOS/iOS)

Distributing FLTK applications on macOS via the Apple App Store imposes strict guidelines primarily centered on security, user privacy, and application sandboxing. While iOS support for traditional desktop toolkits such as FLTK is limited due to the mobile-oriented user interface framework of UIKit and SwiftUI, desktop macOS apps benefit significantly from app store deployment.

Key requirements include:

- *Code Signing and Notarization*: Applications must be signed with an Apple Developer ID certificate and notarized by Apple. This process entails submitting the app binary to the Apple notarization service, which performs a security scan to ensure absence of malware and meets system integrity standards.

- *Sandboxing*: Mandatory for all apps distributed through the Mac App Store, sandboxing restricts file system and inter-process interactions. Developers must leverage sandbox-entitled APIs and configure the sandbox profile accordingly. FLTK applications may need modifications to comply with sandbox constraints, especially for file I/O operations.

- *App Store Connect Submission*: Developers use Apple's App Store Connect portal to upload builds via Xcode or Transporter. Detailed metadata, screenshots, privacy disclosures, and pricing information are required.

Update delivery in the Mac App Store is managed via Apple's infrastructure, which automates version checks and enforces user consent for installation. Developers submit new builds following the same signing and notarization process; all updates undergo re-approval by Apple.

Microsoft Store (Windows)

The Microsoft Store provides a streamlined distribution method for Windows applications, with support for desktop apps packaged as MSIX or as Universal Windows Platform (UWP) apps. FLTK applications are typically wrapped as MSIX packages for store distribution.

Essential points include:

- *Packaging*: The MSIX format is preferred for its secure deployment, reliable updates, and clean uninstall capabilities.

The FLTK executable and all dependencies must be included and declared in the app manifest.

- *Code Signing*: A valid code signing certificate is mandatory to ensure application authenticity.

- *Submission and Certification*: Using the Partner Center portal, the developer uploads the MSIX package, provides descriptive metadata, and sets pricing or licensing. The app undergoes automated and manual certification, including functional, security, and content checks.

Update management on the Microsoft Store follows a similar pattern to Apple's: developers upload the new MSIX package version, and the store automatically distributes updates to users. Guaranteed backward compatibility and runtime stability require meticulous testing of new versions and their manifests.

Linux Software Centers and Infrastructure

Unlike macOS and Windows, Linux distributions utilize diverse packaging systems and software centers, such as Ubuntu Software Center, GNOME Software, and KDE Discover. FLTK applications are commonly distributed in packaging formats like DEB, RPM, Flatpak, or Snap:

- *Native Package Repositories*: Many Linux distributions provide official repositories or Personal Package Archives (PPAs). Submission typically requires:

- Packaging the application according to distribution-specific guidelines.

- Passing quality assurance checks and dependency audits.

- Engaging with maintainers or community stewards during review.

- *Universal Package Formats*: Flatpak and Snap offer distribution methods decoupled from base distributions, with sandboxing analogous to app stores:

  - Flatpak applications are bundled with runtime dependencies and uploaded to centralized repositories like Flathub.

  - Snap packages leverage confinement mechanisms for sandboxing, with publication through the Snap Store.

Update mechanisms in Linux software centers vary but usually involve package manager commands or automatic refresh services maintaining installed versions up-to-date from repositories.

Open source package managers establish repositories that facilitate distribution, discovery, and updating of software libraries and applications on various platforms. FLTK applications benefit from these channels by targeting developers and users preferring command-line package management or integration into custom environments.

Linux Package Management Systems

Linux systems use diverse package managers such as apt (Debian/Ubuntu), dnf/yum (Fedora/Red Hat), and pacman (Arch Linux). FLTK applications can be distributed as source packages or precompiled binaries.

Publishing involves:

- *Preparation of Packaging Files*: Including control files specifying dependencies, description, maintainer details, and build scripts.

- *Repository Submission*: Upload to official or third-party repositories, sometimes via upstream maintainers.

- *Version Control and Changelogs*: Maintainers must document changes rigorously to facilitate safe upgrades.

Users update these applications through standard package manager commands, with repositories providing signed metadata to ensure integrity.

Cross-Platform Package Managers (Conda, vcpkg, Homebrew)

Cross-platform managers simplify dependency resolution and installation across systems:

- *Conda*: Predominantly used in scientific computing but extensible for general binaries. Conda recipes define build instructions and dependencies for FLTK apps, enabling straightforward user install via `conda install`.

- *vcpkg*: Tailored for C++ dependencies and Windows environments but supports other platforms. Distribution involves maintaining ports with manifest files specifying source, patches, and build steps.

- *Homebrew*: The leading package manager for macOS (and Linux), requiring Formulae that describe how to fetch, build, and install the application. Submission occurs through pull requests to the Homebrew core repository or taps, with automated continuous integration testing.

Routine updates involve bumping version numbers, verifying build consistency with newer toolchains or dependencies, and submitting updated manifests or recipes for review.

Public Source Code Hosting and Distribution

Platforms such as GitHub, GitLab, and Bitbucket serve as both source code repositories and distribution channels. They offer:

- *Release Management*: Developers tag stable versions and attach precompiled binaries or source archives to releases.

- *Package Registries*: Integrated registries allow uploading compiled packages or container images, facilitating consumption via package managers or Docker.

- *Community Engagement*: Issues, pull requests, and discussions provide feedback channels for improving distribution processes.

Automation tools such as GitHub Actions or GitLab CI/CD pipelines can streamline packaging, signing, and publishing both to app stores and open source repositories.

Handling updates consistently and securely is critical for maintaining application lifecycle health, delivering new features, and addressing security vulnerabilities.

App Store Update Cycles

App stores impose review processes to validate updates, which may introduce release latency. Developers should:

- *Maintain Backwards Compatibility*: Avoid breaking changes to user data or preferences unless accompanied by migration strategies.

- *Monitor Review Feedback*: Promptly address compliance or technical issues flagged during automated/manual checks.

- *Leverage Beta Testing*: Platforms support staged rollouts or TestFlight/Test Programs to mitigate risk.

Open Source Channel Updates

Open source repositories and package managers rely heavily on automated tooling:

- *Continuous Integration and Testing*: Verify new versions build and pass tests across supported platforms prior to release.

- *Semantic Versioning*: Follow clear versioning to communicate compatibility and support incremental upgrades.

- *Automated Publishing*: Use scripts or CI pipelines to upload packages to relevant registries or mirrors after successful tests.

Due to the decentralized nature of open source ecosystems, developers and maintainers should document update instructions explicitly and notify users via mailing lists, forums, or communication platforms.

Distribution choice affects licensing modalities and compliance burdens:

- *Proprietary vs Open Source*: App stores often require explicit licensing declarations and may impose restrictions on usage or redistribution.

- *Dependency Licensing*: FLTK itself is LGPL, permitting linking in proprietary apps, but any bundled or linked libraries with conflicting licenses require careful management.

- *Metadata Accuracy*: License metadata in package manifests, app store listings, and repository descriptors must be consistent to avoid legal ambiguities.

Ensuring that the distribution channel's terms align with the application's licensing model prevents conflicts and potential removals.

- Tailor application packaging to the technical constraints and policies of each distribution channel.

- Automate build, signing, and testing pipelines to maintain consistency and reduce errors.

- Provide comprehensive and accurate metadata, including icons, descriptions, and licensing.

247

- Monitor deployment processes for user feedback and compliance issues.

- Maintain clear versioning schemes to facilitate reliable updates across channels.

In aggregate, these strategies ensure robust, wide-reaching, and maintainable distribution of FLTK applications spanning closed commercial ecosystems and open collaborative environments.

7.6. Diagnostics, Post-Deployment Monitoring, and Updates

Effective maintenance of software systems beyond deployment demands comprehensive diagnostics, continuous post-deployment monitoring, and efficient update mechanisms. These capabilities collectively ensure operational stability, enhance user experience, and facilitate timely responses to emergent issues. This section focuses on core tools and architectural patterns facilitating in-field observability, automated crash reporting, telemetry collection, and systematic delivery of updates.

In-Field Monitoring and Telemetry Collection

Robust in-field monitoring begins with the integration of telemetry systems designed to capture diverse operational signals and usage metrics in real time. Telemetry data spans multiple categories including performance counters (e.g., CPU, memory usage), application-level metrics (e.g., request latencies, error rates), and domain-specific events (e.g., transaction volumes, feature-specific interactions).

Instrumentation for telemetry must be minimally invasive to avoid perturbing application behavior while ensuring sufficient granularity to diagnose intricate faults. Emerging patterns emphasize *observable states* and *event tracing*, facilitating retrospective analysis and anomaly detection. Common strategies include:

- **Structured Logging**: Instead of plain-text logs, structured formats such as JSON enable powerful querying and correlation across distributed systems.

- **Distributed Tracing**: Assigning unique trace identifiers to requests propagated through microservices supports end-to-end latency analysis and pinpointing bottlenecks.

- **Metric Aggregation**: Utilizing tools like Prometheus enables time-series collection with flexible retention policies and alert rules.

Careful design of telemetry schemas standardizes data ingestion pipelines, allowing consistent interpretation across teams and tools. Additionally, metadata tagging such as environment, version, and tenant identifiers greatly aids targeted diagnostics.

Crash Reporting and Diagnostic Data Collection

Automated crash reporting is essential to detect runtime failures that evade local testing or pre-deployment verification processes. Tools tailored for crash capture generally perform the following:

- **Crash Dump Generation**: Collecting native stack traces, heap states, and execution contexts immediately upon fault occurrence.

- **Symbolication**: Translating raw memory addresses into human-readable function names and line numbers, crucial for debugging optimized or obfuscated binaries.

- **Contextual Data Attachment**: Associating logs, user actions, environment variables, and configuration snapshots to enrich diagnostic payloads.

Popular platforms provide SDKs integrated into client applications to facilitate automatic submission of crash reports to centralized dashboards. These reports support categorization by error frequency, impact severity, and regression identification. Efficient triage workflows combine automated clustering of similar failures and tooling for impact analysis.

To reduce noise, effective crash reporting pipelines implement sampling policies and heuristic filters, ensuring that signal-to-noise ratios remain high. Privacy considerations also mandate sensitive data anonymization or encryption prior to transmission.

Patterns for Post-Deployment Insight and Alerting

Sustaining operational health at scale requires actionable insights derived from aggregated telemetry and crash data. Several architectural patterns underpin these capabilities:

Centralized Observability Platforms ingest telemetry streams from distributed sources, offering raw data storage, real-time analytics, and visualization dashboards. Integration with machine learning-based anomaly detection algorithms automates early warning generation.

Alerting and Incident Management involve configured alert rules based on metric thresholds or abnormal error spikes to ensure rapid notification via multiple channels (email, SMS, incident response systems). Escalation policies and on-call rotations build operational resilience for critical systems.

Feedback Loops to Development continuously integrate diagnostic outputs directly into issue tracking and code review workflows. Evidence-backed error reproduction and performance regression data facilitate prioritized remediation aligned with business impact.

Integration of *feature flags* also enables controlled exposure of new capabilities or fixes, allowing selective rollback without full redeployment if anomalies surface in production.

Streamlined Update Delivery Mechanisms

Delivering application updates with minimal disruption involves a combination of deployment strategies and tooling designed for reliability and user transparency.

Blue-Green and Canary Deployments

- **Blue-Green Deployment** establishes two identical production environments (blue and green). New releases are deployed to the idle environment and, once verified, traffic is switched atomically. This eliminates downtime and allows instant rollback.

- **Canary Releases** gradually expose a subset of users to updated code, monitoring their behavior and system health before wider rollout. Automated gating based on monitoring metrics reduces risk of widespread issues.

Over-the-Air (OTA) Updates

For client applications, especially mobile and embedded systems, OTA updates enable remote patch delivery without physical access. Best practices include:

- **Differential Updates**: Transmit only changed parts of binaries, reducing bandwidth and update duration.

- **Atomic Update Transactions**: Ensure that updates either fully succeed or fail without leaving the application in an inconsistent state.

- **User Experience Considerations**: Provide transparent progress indications and options for update deferral or rollback.

Version Compatibility and Schema Evolution

Updates frequently involve changes to data schemas, communication protocols, or platform dependencies. Maintaining backward compatibility or employing gradual migration paths prevents client-server mismatches or data corruption. Techniques include:

- **Feature Flagging**: Decoupling release from feature activation to control adoption safely.

- **Schema Versioning**: Supporting multiple data formats concurrently with translation layers.

- **Graceful Degradation**: Designing clients to tolerate missing or new fields without failure.

Automated Update Pipelines and Continuous Delivery

Integration of automated testing, static analysis, and deployment automation pipelines enhances reliability and repeatability of updates. Monitoring feedback loops support continuous delivery cycles by validating successful rollout and triggering rollback on anomaly detection.

```
apiVersion: apps/v1
kind: Deployment
metadata:
  name: example-app
spec:
  replicas: 10
  selector:
    matchLabels:
      app: example-app
  template:
    metadata:
      labels:
        app: example-app
    spec:
      containers:
      - name: example-app
        image: example-app:v2   # Canary version
---
apiVersion: networking.k8s.io/v1
kind: Service
```

```
metadata:
  name: example-app-service
spec:
  selector:
    app: example-app
  ports:
  - protocol: TCP
    port: 80
    targetPort: 8080
```

```
# Monitoring output example during canary release:

[INFO] 2024-05-15T10:23:07Z - 50% of traffic routed to v1, 50% to v2.
[METRICS] v2 latency 200ms, error rate 0.2%, stable within thresholds.
[ALERT] None triggered.
```

Security and Privacy in Monitoring and Updates

Ensuring confidentiality and integrity in diagnostic data collection and update delivery is critical. Encryption of telemetry streams, secure authentication for update servers, and end-to-end signing of update packages prevent tampering and unauthorized access. Privacy regulations impose constraints on data collection scopes and retention policies, necessitating anonymization and explicit user consent mechanisms.

- **Comprehensive Instrumentation**: Achieve multidimensional coverage through structured logging, tracing, and metrics with consistent schemas.

- **Automated, Context-Rich Crash Reporting**: Capture deterministic diagnostic artifacts for thorough root cause analysis.

- **Centralized Observability with Proactive Alerting**: Enable rapid detection and mitigation of runtime issues.

- **Gradual, Controlled Deployment Strategies**: Minimize risk and downtime with blue-green, canary, and OTA update patterns.

- **Privacy-Aware, Secure Data Practices**: Adopt encryption and anonymization to safeguard operational data.

Embedding these practices into software engineering lifecycles transforms deployed applications into resilient, maintainable systems capable of adapting swiftly to evolving operational realities.

Chapter 8

Performance, Profiling, and Optimization

Push beyond functional correctness by engineering FLTK applications that are not only stable, but truly snappy and resource-efficient. This chapter dives deep into identifying bottlenecks, squeezing the most from CPU and memory, and perfecting render performance. Arm yourself with the strategies and tools necessary to benchmark, analyze, and optimize every layer of your software—whether you're targeting desktops, mobile, or embedded systems.

8.1. Memory Usage Analysis in FLTK

Memory management in FLTK (Fast Light Toolkit) applications is a crucial aspect of software development, particularly when targeting resource-constrained environments such as embedded systems, or ensuring responsiveness and stability in desktop applications. Profiling and analyzing the memory footprint enables developers to optimize resource allocation, detect leaks, and ensure predictable application behavior. Due to FLTK's minimalist design and direct control over widgets and their underlying resources, understanding memory consumption patterns requires a combination of precise tracking techniques and familiarity with both C++ memory models and FLTK internals.

Heap Profiling Tools and Techniques

Heap profiling involves monitoring dynamic memory allocations to identify hotspots, fragmentation, and leaks. In C++ applications based on FLTK, the primary memory consumers are widget objects, graphical buffers, image data, and any dynamic allocations performed by application logic.

Valgrind's Massif tool is a memory profiler that provides detailed snapshot information about heap usage over time. To use Massif effectively with an FLTK application, it is critical to configure the environment to minimize extraneous system allocations and to produce meaningful call stacks. Invoking Massif through the following command generates a detailed heap profile:

```
valgrind --tool=massif --massif-out-file=massif.out ./fltk_app
```

After execution, the `massif-visualizer` or the `ms_print` utility can be used to interpret the results. The output reveals peak heap usage moments, allocation sizes, and call stacks. Developers should focus on allocations related to FLTK's widget construction and image handling since these are often dominant contributors.

Heaptrack is another valuable tool for Linux environments, offering real-time tracking of heap allocations with minimal overhead. It records backtraces with every allocation, enabling precise source-level leakage detection:

```
heaptrack ./fltk_app
heaptrack_gui heaptrack.flk
```

Heaptrack's visualizations distinguish between retained heap allocations and temporary ones, helping isolate persistent memory growth patterns linked to erroneous object lifetimes.

For Windows development, tools such as Umdh (User-Mode Dump Heap) or the Visual Studio Diagnostic Tools provide heap snapshots and leak detection. When working cross-platform, integrating platform-specific profilers ensures comprehensive analysis.

Identifying Memory Leaks in FLTK Applications

Memory leaks in FLTK applications often originate from neglecting the deallocation of allocated widgets and associated resources. FLTK uses a lightweight parent-child ownership model, where widgets added to a group are managed collectively, but dynamically allocated objects outside this hierarchy require explicit memory management.

The default FLTK widget destructor implementations carefully release GUI resources; however, added custom allocations, such as images loaded via Fl_PNG_Image or dynamically created callback data, may be overlooked. Common sources of leaks include:

- Failure to delete heap-allocated widgets or to remove them from their parents before app termination.

- Unreleased image data when using Fl_Image subclasses.

- Untied event callbacks holding references to objects no longer in use.

- Circular references in user-defined container widgets or models holding pointers to each other.

Leak detection is most effective by combining heap profiling with code instrumentation. Overriding new/delete operators or utilizing smart pointers can help track allocations and deallocations explicitly. Additionally, leveraging FLTK's Fl::add_at_exit() facility ensures clean-up callbacks to dispose of persistent resources.

Employing `valgrind --leak-check=full` not only reports leaks but provides stack traces for allocation points:

```
valgrind --leak-check=full ./fltk_app
```

The output enables pinpointing missing `delete` calls or abandoned widget trees.

Practical Techniques to Minimize Memory Consumption

Minimizing memory usage in FLTK applications requires strategic design choices, both at the GUI and resource management layers.

Widget Reuse and Lazy Initialization Creation of widgets should be deferred until necessary. Lazy initialization reduces up-front memory allocations, especially for complex dialogs or infrequently used interface elements. Additionally, reusing widget instances instead of destroying and recreating them can minimize allocation overhead and reduce fragmentation.

Compact Widget Hierarchy Limiting the depth and breadth of widget hierarchies has direct benefits on memory consumption. Each widget carries its own data structures; thus, avoiding redundant nesting and employing container widgets judiciously conserves heap space.

Image Resource Optimization Since image management is memory-intensive, compressing images and minimizing their dimensions to what is strictly necessary reduces usage. FLTK's image classes such as `Fl_PNG_Image` can leverage internal caching, but developers should explicitly destroy or replace images when they become obsolete.

Explicit Destruction of Unused Widgets Removing widgets from their parent groups and deleting them when no longer needed prevents lingering memory consumption. Proper use of `remove()` and `delete` sequences, combined with nullifying pointers, ensures the absence of dangling references.

Minimizing Dynamic Allocation in Callbacks Long-living callback states or closure objects should avoid heap allocations unless essential. Instead, using stack-allocated or static structures reduces memory churn and simplifies lifetime management.

Embedded System Considerations

In embedded contexts, the challenges intensify due to stricter memory budgets and potentially missing advanced debugging tools. Developers should profile on representative hardware with system-friendly tools such as `gprof` or runtime instrumentation suitable for the target platform.

Code should be compiled with debugging symbols and minimal runtime overhead. Since FLTK is designed for efficiency, using its lightweight event and rendering system reduces the baseline memory footprint compared to heavier GUI frameworks.

Static analysis complements runtime profiling by detecting potential leaks or misuse of memory. Tools like `cppcheck` or Clang Static Analyzer can flag improper resource management early.

Allocating large buffers or textures off the heap and into reserved memory regions may improve predictability and reduce fragmentation. Careful design of screen update frequency and limiting widget redraws also indirectly diminishes temporary memory peaks.

- Employ heap profiling tools appropriate to the development environment, emphasizing call stack collection and detailed snapshots.

- Monitor widget creation and destruction patterns rigorously to avoid latent leaks; leverage FLTK's parent-child model correctly.

- Optimize image use through compression, explicit destruction, and careful sizing.

- Use lazy loading and widget reuse to constrain dynamic mem-

259

ory allocation.

- In embedded deployments, supplement runtime profiling with static analysis and allocate resources conservatively.

Applying these considerations systematically yields FLTK applications with controlled memory footprints, improved stability, and enhanced performance across diverse platform constraints.

8.2. CPU Profiling and Hotspots

CPU profiling is a fundamental approach to identifying computational bottlenecks and inefficient code paths within a software system. By systematically measuring the execution characteristics of a program, profiling enables developers to discern which routines consume the most processing time, thereby guiding optimization efforts towards the most impactful areas. Profiling is particularly crucial in performance-critical applications, where judicious management of CPU cycles can substantially improve responsiveness and throughput, whether in user interface (UI) threads or background processing tasks.

Profiling techniques generally fall into two broad categories: instrumentation-based profiling and sampling-based profiling. Instrumentation profiling inserts code into the program to monitor the entry and exit of functions, recording precise timing and call counts. This method offers fine-grained insights but tends to impose significant overhead, potentially distorting program behavior and execution timing. Sampling profiling, in contrast, intermittently interrupts program execution to capture the current stack trace, providing statistical approximations of CPU usage across code paths with much lower overhead. Sampling is favored in contexts requiring quick assessments or when minimizing impact on system behavior is critical.

Profilers designed for CPU analysis often expose call graphs or flame graphs, vital visualization tools for interpreting profiling data. Flame graphs represent stack traces as horizontal bars stacked according to call hierarchy, where the width of each bar correlates with time spent in that routine and its descendants. This visualization rapidly highlights "hotspots," or code regions where the CPU spends a disproportionate amount of cycles. These hotspots typically correspond to performance bottlenecks and are prime candidates for optimization. Advanced profilers integrate sampling methods with call graph reconstruction, enabling developers to focus on critical paths without exhaustive instrumentation.

Effective CPU profiling requires careful consideration of context, especially when differentiating between UI and background processing workloads. UI threads demand low-latency responses to user interactions; thus, identifying and mitigating delays caused by expensive synchronous operations, blocking calls, or inefficient rendering algorithms is essential. Profilers must be able to capture short-duration events and offer high-resolution timing data to isolate UI bottlenecks effectively. Conversely, background processing optimizations might focus on throughput and resource utilization, often benefiting from aggregate profiling over extended intervals to expose inefficient loops, redundant computations, or suboptimal data structures.

Modern profiling tools support contextual recording to distinguish between these execution domains. For example, tagging samples with thread identifiers or categorizing samples according to system-defined priority classes allows developers to isolate CPU usage specific to UI components or background services. This facilitates targeted interventions, such as migrating expensive operations off the UI thread, restructuring task scheduling, or applying concurrency improvements.

Profiling best practices encompass iterative measurement and analysis cycles. Initial coarse-grained profiling identifies dominant hotspots, followed by refining data collection to understand the underlying cause of inefficiencies. Employing tools with adaptive sampling rates can optimize the trade-off between overhead and granularity. In addition to raw CPU time, inclusive metrics that account for the cumulative cost of downstream calls provide a holistic perspective helpful in assessing the ripple effect of optimizations within call chains.

Source-level correlation of profiling data is another critical factor. Integration with debugging symbols and source code annotations facilitates direct mapping of hotspots to specific code lines or routines. This significantly accelerates diagnostics, enabling developers to contextualize inefficiencies within algorithmic design or implementation details. Profilers that support inline assembly inspection or hardware performance counter correlation can provide further depth by revealing compiler inefficiencies, pipeline stalls, or cache misses that contribute to CPU overhead.

Addressing performance-critical routines identified through profiling often involves multiple strategies. Algorithmic improvements, such as employing more efficient data structures or reducing computational complexity, yield the most substantial benefits. Code vectorization and loop unrolling can exploit modern CPU architectures, while concurrency techniques like running parallelizable work on multiple threads or utilizing asynchronous programming frameworks reduce serial bottlenecks. It is imperative, however, to balance optimization aggressiveness with maintainability and system stability.

In UI applications, reducing CPU time in rendering or event-handling code is frequently achieved by avoiding unnecessary computations, memoizing results, or decoupling expensive operations from the main thread. Profilers that capture frame rates or UI thread stall metrics can complement CPU time profiling to refine user experience optimizations. Background tasks may benefit from improved workload partitioning, batched processing, or hardware-specific enhancements like utilizing SIMD instructions or offloading to specialized accelerators.

Profiling also serves as a validation tool for optimization efforts. Post-optimization profiling confirms whether changes yield expected reductions in CPU usage and do not introduce regressions or new bottlenecks. Continuous profiling within development pipelines, facilitated by automated tools, ensures sustained performance improvements and assists in detecting emergent issues early.

Common pitfalls in CPU profiling include misattributing overhead caused by profiling instrumentation as part of the program workload, interpreting statistical samples as exact measures without accounting for variance, and overlooking interdependencies between CPU-bound and I/O-bound operations. Profilers that provide confidence intervals and allow filtering or aggregating samples by various criteria mitigate these risks, promoting more accurate interpretations.

Furthermore, an understanding of the underlying hardware architecture enhances profiling efficacy. CPU-specific features such as frequency scaling, hyper-threading, branch prediction, and cache hierarchies influence profiling results and optimization potential. Incorporating hardware performance counters in profiling supplements CPU time measurements with metrics on cache misses, branch mispredictions, and instruction-level parallelism, revealing low-level causes of hotspots that pure software timers cannot capture.

Profiling strategies must align with the software development lifecycle stage. Early development might prioritize broad performance trends and high-level bottlenecks, while later stages focus on fine-tuning critical code paths validated through extensive testing. In production environments, lightweight sampling profilers minimize overhead and support ongoing performance monitoring, complementing offline detailed profiling conducted in staging.

CPU profiling is an indispensable technique for uncovering hotspots that degrade application performance. Leveraging appropriate profiling tools, understanding their methodologies, and applying rigorous best practices enable precise identification and effective remediation of CPU bottlenecks in both UI and background processing contexts. Mastery of profiling and hotspot analysis is a cornerstone for developing high-performance software systems in demanding computational environments.

8.3. Efficient Redraw and Event Dispatch

Optimizing the rendering pipeline fundamentally requires the reduction of redundant redraw operations and the refinement of event dispatch mechanisms. Excessive repaints degrade performance and energy efficiency, while inefficient event handling can compromise application responsiveness. The strategies to address these concerns revolve around precise scheduling of repaints, intelligent batching of rendering updates, and careful prioritization of event processing.

Minimizing Unnecessary Redraws

Redraw operations are often triggered by state changes in the user interface, such as property modifications, animations, or direct user input. A naive rendering engine repaints the entire interface upon any detected change, producing redundant workload, especially when multiple changes occur within a short timeframe. This inefficiency can be mitigated by differentiating between *invalidated regions* and the entire render area.

The concept of *damage rectangles*-small bounding boxes representing areas affected by state changes-enables partial repainting. By tracking these regions during the update cycle, the rendering pipeline restricts rasterization to only those pixels needing refreshment. The aggregation of these regions into a minimal set of rectangles further reduces the complexity of redraw operations.

Another key optimization involves *deferred painting*, where repaint requests do not immediately trigger rasterization. Instead, invalidations are queued and processed at a designated time, typically aligned with the vertical synchronization signal (vsync). This deferral ensures that multiple invalidations arising within a single frame interval are combined into a single redraw command, thereby minimizing redundant work.

Scheduling Repaints

Efficient repaint scheduling must balance minimizing latency and avoiding excessive rendering calls. Two principal approaches are commonly employed:

- **Frame-based scheduling:** Repaints are synchronized to the display refresh rate, often managed by an internal compositor or scheduler. This approach leverages vsync timing to issue repaint commands at consistent intervals (e.g., 60 Hz), reducing visual artifacts such as tearing and stuttering.

- **Event-triggered scheduling with throttling:** In cases with variable event frequency (e.g., rapid user input or animations), repaints are triggered by event occurrences but throttled to ensure minimum intervals between frames. This throttling prevents the rendering thread from being overwhelmed.

A hybrid strategy frequently combines these models: event-driven invalidations mark regions for redraw, while an internal frame coordinator enforces repaint timing aligned with refresh cycles.

```
class RenderScheduler {
  Rectangle invalidatedRegion;
  bool repaintPending = false;

  void invalidate(const Rectangle& region) {
```

```
    invalidatedRegion = invalidatedRegion.union(region);
    if (!repaintPending) {
      repaintPending = true;
      scheduleRepaintAtNextVSync();
    }
  }

  void onVSync() {
    if (repaintPending) {
      repaint(invalidatedRegion);
      invalidatedRegion.clear();
      repaintPending = false;
    }
  }
};
```

This approach guarantees that multiple invalidations between vsync events are consolidated into single repaints, reducing overhead and avoiding excessive context switching.

Batching Updates

Batching is essential for consolidating multiple state changes into a single rendering transaction. Intermediate updates are collected within a frame interval and applied atomically to the render tree before painting commences. This strategy improves cache locality during rasterization and simplifies state synchronization.

Double buffering or *layered compositing* techniques often support batching: graphical elements are rendered independently onto off-screen buffers and then composited into the final frame. Offscreen buffers can be selectively marked dirty, ensuring only their content is refreshed when underlying data changes. This hierarchical invalidation and buffering scheme further reduces repaint scope.

Consider a windowed UI with multiple interactive widgets. Each widget issues invalidate calls upon internal state changes. Rather than each widget triggering immediate redraws, the application framework batches these invalidations, eventually issuing a single repaint for the window content that merges all widget updates.

Balancing Responsiveness with Efficiency

266

A critical tension exists between repaint efficiency and input responsiveness. Immediate redrawing upon each input event achieves low input latency but may overwhelm the rendering system. Conversely, aggressive batching and deferral improve throughput but risk perceptible lag.

To navigate this tradeoff, sophisticated event dispatch systems incorporate *prioritization* and *coalescing* of input events:

- **Event Coalescing:** Multiple successive motion, scroll, or text input events are merged before dispatch, reducing event queue pressure.

- **Priority Scheduling:** High-priority events, such as direct manipulation gestures, receive immediate attention and trigger timely repaints, whereas lower-priority events are deferred or combined.

This prioritization often involves separate input threads and render threads communicating via lock-free queues or platform-specific event dispatchers. By offloading event processing to specialized threads, the system maintains UI fluidity while optimizing rendering throughput.

Event Dispatch Optimization Techniques

Event dispatch design must ensure that events are routed efficiently to their intended targets, avoiding unnecessary propagation or redundant updates. Common optimization techniques include:

- **Hit Testing Acceleration:** Spatial data structures (quadtrees, bounding volume hierarchies) quickly identify which UI elements intersect a pointer event, reducing traversal overhead during dispatch.

- **Event Filtering:** Early discard of irrelevant events pre-

267

vents unnecessary processing. Examples include ignoring input on disabled widgets or during modal dialog modality.

- **Event Bubbling and Capturing Models:** Structured propagation phases enable event handlers to intercept or consume events early in the pipeline, avoiding redundant downstream dispatch.

Case Study: Combining Redraw Minimization and Event Handling

A performant example integrates damage tracking, batching, and input prioritization synchronously:

- Input events trigger only state mutation, marking corresponding UI regions dirty.

- Input events are coalesced or filtered to minimize dispatch load.

- The render scheduler defers repaint execution until the next vsync or frame boundary.

- Only invalidated regions are rasterized using offscreen buffers, composited into the final framebuffer.

- Low-latency update paths are reserved for high-priority input interactions, dynamically adjusting batching parameters in response to detected user activity.

This design achieves both low-latency interaction and minimal rendering overhead, optimizing CPU and GPU resource use.

Optimizing redraw and event dispatch within rendering pipelines hinges on meticulous invalidation tracking, efficient repaint scheduling, and judicious event handling. Together, these techniques form a cohesive framework that minimizes wasted work, preserves user interface responsiveness, and maximizes rendering throughput. Architectures that embrace deferred and batched updates, combined with sophisticated event prioritization, establish the foundation for scalable, high-performance graphical systems.

8.4. Scaling to High-DPI and Multi-Monitor Setups

Modern display environments are characterized by a growing diversity of hardware configurations, prominently featuring high-DPI (dots per inch) screens and heterogeneous multi-monitor setups. Ensuring that graphical user interfaces (GUIs) maintain visual fidelity and functional responsiveness across such environments requires a sophisticated understanding of scaling mechanisms, viewport management, and adaptive layout strategies. This section dissects these aspects in detail, providing a technical foundation for designing interfaces that remain crisp, proportionate, and performant.

High-DPI displays, often exceeding 200 pixels per inch, present a challenge to traditional pixel-based rendering paradigms, which assume a uniform pixel density. Without appropriate scaling, UI elements appear physically smaller, rendering text and icons unreadable or interfaces cramped. The fundamental concept employed to counter this is *device-independent pixels* (DIPs) or *logical pixels*, which abstract away the physical pixel density by defining a density-independent coordinate system.

For such displays, a *scaling factor* (commonly denoted as S) is introduced, where

$$S = \frac{\text{physical pixels per unit length}}{\text{reference pixel density}}$$

Typically, the reference density corresponds to 96 DPI in most operating systems. Rendering pipelines use S to scale graphical assets and layout measurements proportionally:

$$\text{Rendered pixels} = S \times \text{logical pixels}$$

This requires graphical resources to be created or accessed at multiple resolutions. Vector-based graphics are preferable for their inherent scalability, but when raster images are necessary, multiple asset resolutions (e.g., @1x, @2x, @3x) are maintained and selected dynamically according to S.

Achieving crisp visuals on high-DPI displays necessitates pixel-perfect alignment. Misalignment by fractional pixels can cause blurring due to anti-aliasing, especially noticeable in text and iconography. A standard technique is to round layout coordinates and dimensions to integral device pixels after scaling. Formally, if L is a coordinate in logical pixels, the physical coordinate P is computed as

$$P = \text{round}(S \times L)$$

where round() denotes rounding to the nearest integer. Strict rounding avoids fractional pixel offsets that induce blurring.

However, this approach must be balanced with layout responsiveness and fluidity. Overzealous rounding can cause jitter during animations or resizing. To mitigate this, subpixel rendering techniques and hardware anti-aliasing are harnessed with calibrated gamma adjustments, preserving sharpness without compromising motion smoothness.

Multi-monitor setups introduce additional complexity due to heterogeneous monitor resolutions, DPIs, and physical arrangements. Each connected display may have a unique scaling factor S_i, requiring UI toolkits and window managers to maintain multiple coordinate reference frames.

Operating systems represent the total desktop area using a global *virtual desktop coordinate space*. In Windows, for instance, this is the *device-independent coordinate system* where all windows are positioned. The API provides mechanisms to query each monitor's DPI and scale factor individually. Applications must then:

1. Detect when a window crosses the boundary of different monitors.

2. Dynamically adjust scaling and rendering parameters to comply with the active monitor's DPI.

3. Smoothly transition rendering contexts without visual artifacts.

A common approach involves maintaining two coordinate spaces:

- **Logical space:** a uniform coordinate framework for layout calculations.

- **Physical space:** monitor-specific, scaled pixel coordinates for rendering.

When a window moves between monitors with different S_i, the UI must rescale and re-layout content in real-time. This requires notification hooks or event listeners for monitor change events and a well-structured rendering pipeline supporting adaptive asset selection and layout recalculation.

To maintain responsiveness and legibility, adaptive UI designs combine scaling techniques with context-aware layout algorithms. Key strategies include:

Constraint-Based Layouts
Define constraints relative to logical units or container dimensions rather than absolute pixels. This enables interfaces to reorganize fluidly when scaling changes, avoiding rigid layouts that break under DPI variation.

Dynamic Element Sizing
UI components adjust their sizes and spacing according to scale

factors derived from the current monitor. For instance, padding, font sizes, and control dimensions are computed as

$$\text{size}_{\text{adaptive}} = \text{base size} \times S_i$$

but bounded by minimum and maximum thresholds to preserve usability.

Multi-Resolution Asset Management

Store and dynamically select graphical assets from multiple resolutions to optimize both clarity and resource consumption. Vector formats (SVG, OpenType fonts) serve as a robust baseline, while raster images utilize naming conventions and directory structures for resolution variants.

Platform-Aware DPI APIs

Leverage operating system APIs to query DPI awareness levels and adjust application scaling strategies accordingly. Modern OSes provide APIs for per-monitor DPI awareness, allowing applications to opt into or out of DPI virtualization layers.

```
UINT dpiX, dpiY;
HRESULT hr = GetDpiForMonitor(hMonitor, MDT_EFFECTIVE_DPI, &dpiX,
    &dpiY);
if (SUCCEEDED(hr)) {
    float scaleFactorX = dpiX / 96.0f;
    float scaleFactorY = dpiY / 96.0f;
    // Use scaleFactorX/Y for adaptive layout and rendering
}
```

Scaling involves additional computation and resource management overhead. Key considerations:

- *Caching scaled bitmaps* improves performance by avoiding repeated rasterization. For frequently used assets, generate scaled instances at startup or on-demand and reuse them.

- *Hardware acceleration* through GPU shaders can offload resolution independence calculations, especially for vector graphics and font rendering.

- *Limit layout recalculations* by batching scale-related updates and employing dirty region tracking.

- *Avoid redundant scaling transformations* within rendering passes to prevent compounded blurring and performance loss.

In complex applications embedding external content-such as web views, media players, or legacy controls-uniform scaling may not be feasible. Techniques to handle these scenarios include:

- **Proxy scaling layers** that composite DPI-aware and DPI-unaware content, applying transforms only where appropriate.

- **Contextual scaling adjustment** where embedded controls report or expose their DPI capabilities.

- **User override mechanisms** to allow manual scaling adjustments when automatic scaling is insufficient.

- Use logical coordinate spaces with well-defined scaling factors to abstract physical pixel density.

- Align layout and rendering to integral device pixels post-scaling to prevent blurring.

- Support per-monitor DPI awareness with dynamic detection and adjustment of scale factors.

- Implement adaptive layout techniques with constraint-based sizing and multi-resolution assets.

- Optimize performance by caching rendered assets and leveraging hardware acceleration.

- Anticipate heterogeneous content sources and plan for mixed-DPI handling strategies.

Continuing advancements in display technologies and multi-monitor configurations will necessitate ongoing evolution of scaling strategies. Mastery of these principles equips developers and system designers to deliver visually crisp, accessible, and responsive user experiences across the broad spectrum of modern hardware environments.

8.5. Threading and Asynchronous Optimization

Modern graphical user interfaces demand responsiveness, ensuring that the user experience remains fluid even when the application performs intensive computations or I/O operations. In FLTK (Fast Light Toolkit), which operates on a single-threaded event-driven architecture, leveraging concurrency carefully is essential to optimize performance without compromising the stability or responsiveness of the UI.

FLTK's event loop-responsible for processing user input, repaint requests, and widget events-executes predominantly on the main thread. Blocking this thread for computations or long-running tasks directly leads to UI freezes and dropped events. Consequently, offloading heavy processing to secondary threads is a necessity for maintaining UI interactivity. However, since FLTK's internal data structures and drawing mechanisms are not inherently thread-safe, all interaction with widgets and FLTK API calls must be marshalled back to the main thread.

A robust approach to asynchronous execution in FLTK entails the following pattern: computationally intensive or blocking operations run in background threads, while results and UI updates are communicated back to the main thread via a thread-safe signaling mechanism.

- **Worker Threads with Callbacks.** Worker threads perform the heavy lifting-complex calculations, file I/O, network requests-while the main thread remains free to handle user input. Upon completion or at intermediate checkpoints, the worker thread posts a notification to the main thread, triggering UI updates. This can be achieved via the established FLTK callback system combined with thread-safe messaging.

- **Producer-Consumer Queues.** A common design is to implement a thread-safe queue in which worker threads enqueue results or event notifications. At periodic intervals or in response to a timer event, the main thread dequeues messages and updates the UI accordingly. This pattern decouples work production and UI consumption, providing flexibility and minimizing the risk of deadlocks.

Direct manipulation of FLTK widgets outside the main thread violates its internal invariants. Therefore, a safe synchronization channel is indispensable.

- **Fl::awake() Function.** FLTK exposes the static function Fl::awake(), which is the primary mechanism for waking up the main thread from worker threads. The typical usage involves passing a pointer to a callback function and an optional user data pointer. The main thread's event loop calls the queued function asynchronously, ensuring UI updates occur in the correct thread context.

```
void worker_thread_func(void *data) {
    // Perform heavy computation
    // ...
    // Notify main thread:
    Fl::awake(main_thread_callback, data);
}

void main_thread_callback(void *data) {
    // Safely update UI here
}
```

- **Mutexes and Atomic Variables.** To safeguard shared data, proper synchronization using mutexes (std::mutex) or atomic variables (std::atomic) is critical. Worker threads modify shared results, and the main thread reads them only within the Fl::awake() callback, which ensures consistent state and prevents race conditions.

Tailoring background task execution can further enhance performance and user experience.

- **Thread Pools.** Creating a pool of persistent worker threads avoids the overhead of thread creation and destruction for each task. When a new task arrives, it is dispatched to an idle thread in the pool. This approach maintains responsiveness while supporting high-throughput workloads.

- **Futures and Promises.** C++11 introduces std::future and std::promise, which can be integrated with FLTK's event loop using Fl::awake(). A future represents a value that will become available, allowing the main thread to query the result or wait asynchronously for completion signals without blocking.

- **Progress Reporting.** Long-running tasks benefit from progress feedback. Worker threads periodically invoke Fl::awake() with partial updates, enabling progress bars or status indicators to remain synchronized with computation state.

```
void compute_progress(void *data) {
    ProgressData *pd = static_cast<ProgressData*>(data);
    window->progressbar->value(pd->progress);
    window->progressbar->redraw();
}
```

Synchronizing events accurately between threads is pivotal for maintaining application stability.

276

- **Avoiding Deadlocks and Priority Inversion.** Deadlocks occur if both the main and worker threads wait on locks held by the other. Careful lock ordering, minimal critical sections, and preferring lock-free or atomic primitives mitigate these risks. Additionally, when synchronization involves UI updating, confine all FLTK API calls to main-thread callback contexts.

- **Non-Blocking Interface Updates.** To prevent UI stalls, updates should be incremental and lightweight. Batch updates, utilizing timers or deferred redraws, avoid excessive CPU usage on the main thread.

- **Error Propagation and Handling.** Errors or exceptions in worker threads must be communicated safely to the UI thread. Storing error states in shared data guarded by mutexes, and signaling the main thread via `Fl::awake()`, allows the UI to respond gracefully, for example, by displaying alert dialogs.

FLTK's `Fl::add_timeout()` and `Fl::add_idle()` functions complement threading techniques by providing periodic or opportunistic execution inside the main loop.

Using timeouts to poll a shared message queue from background threads allows controlled UI updates without excessive overhead.

```
static void timer_callback(void *data) {
    while (!message_queue.empty()) {
        auto msg = message_queue.pop();
        // Update UI from msg
    }
    Fl::repeat_timeout(0.1, timer_callback);
}
```

The following illustrates a minimal example combining a background thread with `Fl::awake()` to update a text display:

```
#include <FL/Fl.H>
#include <FL/Fl_Window.H>
#include <FL/Fl_Text_Display.H>
#include <thread>
```

```cpp
#include <mutex>
#include <string>

Fl_Text_Display *text_display = nullptr;
std::string shared_text;
std::mutex text_mutex;

void update_ui(void *) {
    std::lock_guard<std::mutex> lock(text_mutex);
    text_display->buffer()->text(shared_text.c_str());
    text_display->redraw();
}

void worker_thread() {
    for (int i = 0; i < 10; ++i) {
        {
            std::lock_guard<std::mutex> lock(text_mutex);
            shared_text = "Count: " + std::to_string(i);
        }
        Fl::awake(update_ui, nullptr);
        std::this_thread::sleep_for(std::chrono::seconds(1));
    }
}

int main() {
    Fl_Window window(400, 300, "Threading Example");
    Fl_Text_Display display(10, 10, 380, 280);
    text_display = &display;

    window.end();
    window.show();

    std::thread t(worker_thread);
    int ret = Fl::run();
    t.join();
    return ret;
}
```

- All FLTK widget access and API calls must be confined to the main thread. Use `Fl::awake()` to marshal callbacks safely.

- Use standard C++ concurrency constructs (threads, mutexes, atomics) for robust synchronization of shared data.

- Employ thread pools or futures to efficiently manage workload distribution without excessive thread churn.

- Implement incremental UI updates using progress reporting, timers, or idle callbacks to maintain responsiveness.

- Prevent deadlocks by minimal locking, careful lock ordering, and avoiding synchronous waits on the UI thread.

Harnessing concurrency effectively in FLTK requires a disciplined division of labor and precise synchronization between worker threads and the UI thread. When implemented properly, this approach enables computationally intensive applications to remain responsive, stable, and visually fluid, meeting the demands of modern interactive software.

8.6. Profiling Tools and Advanced Debugging Methods

Effective performance analysis and debugging of complex graphical user interface (GUI) applications demand a comprehensive approach that integrates profiling, logging, and trace correlation. The rich ecosystem of open source and commercial tools provides a spectrum of capabilities tailored to diverse application architectures and runtime environments. Achieving a granular understanding of system behavior, isolating bottlenecks, and validating optimization efforts require not only the right toolset but also disciplined workflows that exploit the complementary strengths of these technologies.

A wide variety of profiling tools focus on capturing runtime metrics at varying levels of granularity, from CPU cycles and memory utilization to GPU rendering timelines and inter-thread communication patterns. For GUI-intensive applications, tools such as `Intel VTune Profiler`, `Google PerfTools` (gperftools), and `Visual Studio Profiler` provide insightful hotspot identification through sampling and instrumentation. These profilers enable call graph visualizations and function-level attribution of resource consumption.

Linux *perf* remains a powerful open source utility for collecting hardware performance counters, software events, and tracepoints. Its ability to attach to running processes non-invasively supports real-time profiling, especially useful for debugging UI response latencies. Similarly, Valgrind's Callgrind tool simulates CPU execution to derive detailed execution paths and cache utilization patterns, although with higher overhead.

Profiling GPU workloads is indispensable when rendering pipelines dominate application performance. Tools such as NVIDIA Nsight and AMD Radeon GPU Profiler allow examination of shader execution, memory transfers, and queue utilization. Integrating CPU and GPU profiling data is critical to reveal synchronization issues and underutilized resources, often manifesting as glitches or jank in complex GUIs.

```
perf record -F 99 -p <pid> -g -- sleep 30
perf report
```

The command above attaches perf to a process identified by <pid>, samples stack traces at 99 Hz for 30 seconds, and then generates a report displaying hotspots and call chains.

Profiling data alone may provide insufficient context, especially when diagnosing systemic failures or intermittently reproducible defects. Advanced logging frameworks such as LTTng (Linux Trace Toolkit Next Generation) and ETW (Event Tracing for Windows) facilitate comprehensive, kernel-level event capture with minimal overhead. These tools log events across multiple subsystems, including window management, input handling, and rendering workloads, creating a timeline of system-wide activity.

In GUI frameworks, application-level events often become intertwined with OS-level signals and driver interactions. Correlating these diverse event streams facilitates the identification of root causes for frame drops, memory thrashing, or thread deadlocks. Data recorded by LTTng or ETW can be aggregated and visualized with tools like Trace Compass or Windows Performance

Analyzer, which provide flame graphs, dependency graphs, and customizable timelines.

```
lttng create gui-debug-session
lttng enable-event --kernel sched_switch
lttng enable-event --userspace gui_handle_event
lttng start
# Run the application workload
lttng stop
lttng view
```

Correlating trace data from different sources is foundational for uncovering subtle interactions and emergent behavior in complex GUI applications. Time synchronization and event causality form the basis of these correlations. Since traces from kernel, driver, and user-space components are recorded independently, their alignment often relies on precision timestamps, monotonic clocks, and unique event identifiers.

An effective workflow employs structured event logging with identifiable correlation IDs propagated through layers of abstraction. For example, a UI Event ID generated by the input subsystem propagates through event dispatching, rendering scheduling, and frame presentation. Leveraging such identifiers, tools can reconstruct end-to-end execution paths, allowing developers to detect delays or duplications obscured within isolated traces.

Visual exploration tools such as Speedscope and Flamegraph viewers enable navigation through large temporal datasets, highlighting anomalies and hotspots. Custom parsers and analyzers built atop log aggregation frameworks (e.g., Fluentd, ELK Stack) can further automate trend detection, threshold breach alerts, and issue clustering.

Systemic performance issues in GUI applications often arise from resource contention, priority inversion, excessive synchronization, or inefficient use of the rendering pipeline. Advanced debugger tools like GDB, WinDbg, and LLDB permit breakpoint-based investigation of race conditions and deadlocks. When combined with thread sanitizers (TSan) and memory sanitizers (MSan), these debuggers can reveal latent data races and use-after-free errors that degrade application stability.

Static and dynamic analysis complement each other in this context. Static analysis tools (e.g., clang-tidy, Coverity) can identify potential concurrency hazards and memory leaks before runtime. In contrast, dynamic tools capture runtime behavior, validating theoretical predictions and exposing environment-specific anomalies.

Real-time debugging capabilities, such as reverse debugging and time-travel debuggers present in commercial offerings like Undo or Microsoft Time Travel Debugging, afford unprecedented power to replay execution paths and inspect state changes backward in time. This technique simplifies the diagnosis of intermittent or non-deterministic failures.

Verifying performance improvements following code changes requires repeatable and measurable workflows. Selective instrumentation of critical code sections, supplemented by continuous integration profiling, ensures that optimizations deliver meaningful gains without regressions.

Example instrumentation includes measuring frame rendering times to guarantee smoothness exceeding 60 frames per second, or quantifying database query latencies affecting UI responsiveness. The use of lightweight tracing macros, such as TRACE_EVENT in Chromium projects or DTrace probes on BSD and Solaris systems, permits runtime toggling of trace points, balancing overhead and data fidelity.

```
void RenderFrame() {
    TRACE_EVENT_BEGIN("RenderFrame");
    // Rendering code
    DrawUI();
    TRACE_EVENT_END("RenderFrame");
}
```

Post-instrumentation analysis typically leverages aggregate statistics, percentile latencies, and jitter measurements. Comparing pre-

and post-optimization trace captures identifies regressions due to thread contention or cache thrashing induced by the changes.

Commercial tools generally provide polished user interfaces, advanced analytics, and vendor support. For example, JetBrains dotTrace excels at .NET application profiling with integrated timeline analysis; Intel VTune offers in-depth hardware-level metrics suited for CPU-heavy GUI computations; and NVIDIA Nsight integrates seamlessly with GPU hardware for shader performance analysis.

Open source alternatives, while sometimes necessitating steeper learning curves and manual integration, provide transparency, extensibility, and cost advantages. Tools such as perf, LTTng, Valgrind, and Trace Compass foster vibrant communities and continuous improvement. Selecting tools hinges on application domain, platform constraints, and project scale.

Embedding profiling and tracing within automated testing environments ensures early detection of performance regressions. Continuous profiling frameworks such as Pyroscope or Google Cloud Profiler can track production workloads over time, providing rich datasets for differential analysis.

Integration with issue tracking and feedback systems permits developers to prioritize fixes grounded in empirical evidence. This paradigm elevates debugging beyond ad hoc investigation to a disciplined engineering process that maintains application responsiveness and stability under evolving requirements.

Achieving robust and performant GUI applications in complex ecosystems requires deploying a heterogeneous toolset combined with sophisticated data correlation and analysis techniques. Profiling, logging, and debugging are interdependent activities that, when unified through meticulous workflows, translate raw telemetry into actionable insights. This synergy empowers developers to pinpoint elusive systemic issues, confirm optimization efficacy, and sustain a responsive user experience in increasingly intricate software architectures.

Chapter 9

FLTK in Modern and Embedded Systems

Explore how FLTK's lightweight design and cross-platform flexibility empower innovation in today's most demanding environments—from handheld devices to industrial panels and IoT gateways. This chapter lifts the hood on porting, optimizing, and extending FLTK for constrained and specialized platforms, offering a clear roadmap for creating robust GUIs wherever modern hardware takes you.

9.1. Running FLTK on Embedded Linux

The Fast Light Toolkit (FLTK) is a lightweight cross-platform GUI library well suited for embedded Linux environments due to its minimal dependency model and streamlined architecture. Deploying FLTK on embedded Linux requires careful consideration to optimize resource usage, accommodate diverse hardware constraints, and integrate seamlessly with the target kernel and windowing systems. The following text elucidates the core principles and prac-

285

tical strategies behind porting, minimizing, bootstrapping, and adapting FLTK for embedded platforms.

The foundational step in porting FLTK involves selecting an appropriate backend for display and input handling. Unlike desktop Linux systems, embedded devices frequently lack a full-fledged X Window System or Wayland compositor. Therefore, compiling FLTK with its native OpenGL or direct framebuffer support is critical. FLTK inherently supports the Linux framebuffer (`/dev/fb0`) as a target, obviating the need for heavyweight graphical stacks. This support, however, demands that the Linux kernel on the device be equipped with framebuffer drivers matching the specific display hardware. Direct framebuffer usage enables efficient rendering with minimal overhead, which aligns well with constrained CPU and memory resources typically encountered in embedded systems.

The FLTK build process permits selective inclusion of features, enabling the generation of minimal builds tailored specifically for embedded deployments. The toolkit's modular source structure facilitates exclusion of unused widgets, fonts, and input methods through configuration options. For instance, specialized applications can compile FLTK with just the core windowing, basic widget set, and bitmap fonts, discarding support for internationalization, threading, and networked input devices. Customizing the `config.mk` or utilizing CMake flags during compilation streamlines the binary size and runtime memory footprint significantly. Stripped builds also reduce attack surfaces and simplify static analysis for security-critical embedded environments.

Bootstrapping FLTK in an embedded Linux development context often requires cross-compilation. The target device's architecture (e.g., ARM, MIPS, RISC-V) and operating system version necessitate utilizing a matching cross-toolchain configured to generate compatible object code. Cross-compilation mandates explicit management of dependencies and careful configuration of system include paths and libraries. The autoconf and CMake build systems within FLTK can be adapted by defining appropriate environment variables such as CC, CXX, and SYSROOT. Creating a staged build environment may involve first compiling FLTK on the host, then transferring binaries and libraries to the target or emulated environment for validation. Cross-compilation challenges, including endianness and ABI differences, must be addressed explicitly through configuration adjustments.

On resource-constrained embedded devices, further adaptation of FLTK requires attention to memory management and optimization of rendering performance. FLTK's native double-buffering mechanism can be selectively disabled or fine-tuned to save RAM at the cost of potential screen tearing, which may be acceptable in low-speed or static UIs. Font handling is another major contributor to memory consumption. Replacing scalable TrueType fonts with bitmap fonts or subsetted fonts minimizes both storage and runtime RAM use. Defining fixed font sets and leveraging FLTK's ability to load fonts from embedded memory buffers assures rapid rendering without file system access latency. In addition, reducing color depth from 24- or 32-bit RGB to 16-bit or 8-bit indexed color modes can significantly decrease framebuffer consumption, assuming hardware and driver support.

Integration with device-specific input methods and event handling requires extending or modifying the FLTK event loop. Embedded Linux often leverages evdev or specific kernel input drivers like touchscreen or button devices, which may not generate standard X events. Adapting FLTK's input subsystem to read directly from device nodes or through middleware like tslib (touchscreen abstraction layer) is a common strategy. This approach necessitates reimplementing or overriding portions of FLTK's platform-specific window and event classes, typically residing in the src/fltk/platform directory. Employing a custom input driver module streamlines response time and avoids the overhead of complex input stacks, critical for real-time or latency-sensitive embedded applications.

Resource monitoring and performance profiling tools must be incorporated early in the porting process to quantify the impact of configuration choices. Techniques such as static analysis for code size, runtime heap and stack usage measurement, and frame rate benchmarking can inform iterative refinements. For instance, examining the impact of enabling or disabling FLTK features on program RAM growth using embedded board debugging interfaces (JTAG, SWD) can reveal memory bottlenecks. Profiling rendering paths with OpenGL ES or direct framebuffer acceleration assists in identifying CPU or GPU hotspots, enabling targeted optimizations.

The buildup of static libraries versus shared libraries in the embedded environment requires consideration of application deployment and update mechanisms. While static linking integrates the FLTK toolkit directly into the application binary, reducing runtime dependencies, it increases the binary size. Shared libraries, conversely, promote modularity and facilitate dynamic updates but rely on consistent system library versions. Embedded systems with limited or non-existent package management favor static linking for simplicity, whereas more advanced embedded Linux platforms may balance modularity with size through carefully versioned shared FLTK libraries.

Power management in embedded systems also influences FLTK adaptation. Flicker reduction strategies, including limiting repaint regions and avoiding unnecessary full-screen redraws, extend battery life and reduce thermal load. FLTK's event-driven redraw model can be harmonized with the device's low-power states by suspending GUI updates during idle conditions. This coordination may be handled within the application event loop or by hooking into power management subsystems exposed by the kernel.

Lastly, debugging and diagnostics on embedded platforms benefit from FLTK's diagnostic macros and tracing facilities, which can be selectively enabled without overwhelming resource constraints.

Logging output may be redirected to serial consoles or specialized debug interfaces, since embedded devices often lack standard output terminals. Employing conditional compilation to disable verbose logging in production builds is standard practice to preserve performance and memory.

```
CROSS_COMPILE=arm-linux-gnueabi-
CC=$(CROSS_COMPILE)gcc
CXX=$(CROSS_COMPILE)g++
SYSROOT=/opt/arm-sysroot

CFLAGS=--sysroot=$(SYSROOT) -O2 -ffunction-sections -fdata-
    sections
LDFLAGS=--sysroot=$(SYSROOT) -Wl,--gc-sections

CONFIG_OPTIONS=\
  -DFLTK_USE_FB=1 \
  -DFLTK_NO_X11=1 \
  -DFLTK_SHARED=0 \
  -DENABLE_THREADS=0 \
  -DENABLE_IMAGES=1 \
  -DENABLE_GL=0 \
  -DFLTK_NO_MULTITHREAD=1

all:
    $(CXX) $(CFLAGS) $(CONFIG_OPTIONS) -c fltk_source.cpp -o
    fltk_application.o
    $(CXX) $(LDFLAGS) fltk_application.o -o fltk_application \

clean:
    rm -f *.o fltk_application
```

```
Sample runtime output on embedded device framebuffer:

[INFO] FLTK initialized in framebuffer mode
[INFO] Device framebuffer: /dev/fb0, resolution: 800x480, 16bpp
[INFO] Input device: /dev/input/event0 (touchscreen) initialized
[WARNING] Font subsystem: using embedded bitmap fonts only
[DEBUG] Framebuffer paint completed in 15 ms
[INFO] Application main loop started
```

Enabling FLTK on embedded Linux mandates a nuanced interplay between kernel configuration, cross-compilation toolchains, minimal code footprint customization, and tailored device input/output handling. The compact design of FLTK can be leveraged to create responsive GUI applications under significant resource constraints, provided the toolkit is pruned of unneeded features, adapted to the native hardware interfaces, and integrated with an awareness of runtime performance and memory limits. This foundational understanding equips embedded developers to deploy robust FLTK-based user interfaces within the stringent confines typical of embedded Linux platforms.

9.2. Touch and Industrial Panel Integration

Modern industrial environments increasingly rely on touch-enabled human-machine interfaces (HMIs) for operational control, monitoring, and diagnostics. The integration of graphical user interfaces (GUIs) on touch screens and industrial panels necessitates meticulous design and tuning to accommodate the specific constraints and requirements inherent to these platforms. This section elaborates on practical methodologies for handling diverse input modalities, executing precise calibration, and implementing responsive design strategies tailored to industrial touch panels.

Industrial touch panels commonly utilize resistive, capacitive, infrared, or surface acoustic wave technologies, each exhibiting distinct characteristics influencing GUI interaction design. Capacitive touchscreens, prevalent in consumer devices, afford multi-touch capability with high sensitivity but may exhibit limitations with gloved or wet hands typical in industrial settings. Resistive touchscreens detect pressure-based input, accommodating stylus or gloved interaction, yet offer lower resolution and slower response times.

The effective GUI must reconcile these input differences by accommodating single-touch drag gestures, multi-touch pinch-zoom where supported, and pressure sensitivity variations. Input event handling layers should incorporate debouncing algorithms to mitigate false triggers caused by vibration or noise typical in industrial environments. Furthermore, gesture recognition systems must be optimized to filter unintentional inputs due to accidental brush or environment-induced contact.

A common practice involves implementing adaptive input filters parameterized by the touch panel technology. For instance, in a resistive panel, increasing the touch area tolerance and incorporating dwell-time thresholds improve robustness, whereas capacitive panels benefit from anomaly detection in multi-touch clusters to reject spurious inputs.

Accurate touch calibration forms the backbone of precise user interaction. Calibration transforms raw touch sensor coordinates into the GUI coordinate space, compensating for alignment discrepancies, non-linearities, and manufacturing tolerances. Calibration involves capturing known reference points and applying geometric transformations to refine coordinate mapping.

Let the raw touch input vector be denoted as $\mathbf{r} = (r_x, r_y)$, and the calibrated GUI coordinate vector as $\mathbf{c} = (c_x, c_y)$. The mapping is frequently represented as:

$$\mathbf{c} = \mathbf{A} \cdot \mathbf{r} + \mathbf{b}$$

where $\mathbf{A}$ is a 2×2 calibration matrix encoding scaling, rotation, and skew, and $\mathbf{b}$ is a translation vector. Calibration routines solve for $\mathbf{A}$ and $\mathbf{b}$ via least squares estimation based on a set of $(\mathbf{r}_i, \mathbf{c}_i)$ point correspondences.

Advanced calibration methods account for panel warping and non-linear distortions using higher-order polynomial transformations or thin-plate spline warping. Such methods reduce systematic error in large panels where planar assumptions fail. However, these come at increased computational cost and complexity.

Calibration frequency depends on environmental stability. Industrial panels exposed to mechanical stress or temperature fluctuations may require periodic recalibration or continuous self-calibration using background tasks analyzing steady-state touch patterns.

Responsive design for industrial touch panels transcends traditional scaling of interface elements. Industrial environments impose stringent usability criteria including:

- **Button and Control Sizing:** Touch targets must be sufficiently large to accommodate gloved fingers, typically exceeding 9–12 mm in diameter, surpassing consumer device standards. Moreover, spacing between interactive elements is critical to prevent accidental activation.

- **Visual Feedback and State Representation:** Given noisy operational contexts, immediate and unambiguous visual feedback upon user action reassures the operator. Techniques include dynamic highlighting, state changes (e.g., pressed, toggled), and haptic feedback integration.

- **Contrast and Lighting Adaptation:** Variations in ambient lighting from low-light to direct sunlight exposure necessitate high-contrast designs and adjustable brightness or color schemes. Employing color palettes with high luminance contrast and iconography resistant to glare effects enhances readability.

- **Error Tolerance and Confirmation Mechanisms:** Industrial systems often govern critical processes warranting fail-safes. Implementing confirmation dialogs, undo capabilities, and error correction interfaces reduces the occurrence and impact of inadvertent touches.

- **Adaptation for Multiple Input Sources:** Many industrial panels support auxiliary inputs (physical buttons, rotary encoders). The GUI must gracefully interoperate with these, ensuring consistent state representation and user experience.

Implementing dynamic layouts using scalable vector graphics (SVG) or modular GUI frameworks facilitates adaptation across varying panel resolutions and aspect ratios. Declarative UI languages supporting relative positioning and anchoring properties simplify responsive behavior without altering core logic.

Industrial touch interfaces often operate under specialized conditions imposing additional design considerations:

Glove and Tool Usage

Operators commonly wear gloves or use stylus-like tools. Capacitive screens may fail to register input correctly under these conditions, prompting the selection of specialized touch technologies or hybrid solutions. GUI elements should incorporate increased sensitivity zones, augmented activation thresholds, and potentially multi-modal input capabilities.

Harsh Environmental Factors

Dust, moisture, electrical interference, and temperature extremes can degrade touch sensor performance. Incorporating robust filtering, hysteresis in state changes, and error detection routines ensures operational reliability. For example, median filtering applied to raw touch coordinates reduces jitter without excessive latency.

Single-Handed and High-Speed Operation

In fast-paced settings, operators may interact with panels using one hand while performing concurrent physical tasks. GUIs must minimize required precision and steps, favoring large control surfaces and gesture shortcuts. Timeout mechanisms prevent unintended prolonged activations or interface lockups.

The following algorithm outlines a typical affine calibration approach:

Algorithm 1 Affine Touch Calibration

1: Given: Measured raw points $\{\mathbf{r}_i\}_{i=1}^{N}$ and reference GUI points $\{\mathbf{c}_i\}_{i=1}^{N}$

2: Construct matrix $\mathbf{R} \in \mathbb{R}^{N \times 3}$ where each row i is $\begin{bmatrix} r_{x_i} & r_{y_i} & 1 \end{bmatrix}$

3: Construct matrix $\mathbf{C} \in \mathbb{R}^{N \times 2}$ where each row i is $\begin{bmatrix} c_{x_i} & c_{y_i} \end{bmatrix}$

4: Solve for $\mathbf{T} \in \mathbb{R}^{3 \times 2}$ minimizing $\|\mathbf{RT} - \mathbf{C}\|_F^2$

5: Extract $\mathbf{A} = \mathbf{T}(1:2,:)$ and $\mathbf{b} = \mathbf{T}(3,:)$

6: Calibrate each raw point as $\mathbf{c} = \mathbf{A}^\top \mathbf{r} + \mathbf{b}^\top$

Implementation in a high-level language such as Python using NumPy might resemble:

```python
import numpy as np

# Raw touch data points (r_x, r_y)
R = np.array([
    [120, 200],
    [300, 195],
    [115, 400],
    [295, 405]
])

# Corresponding GUI coordinates (c_x, c_y)
C = np.array([
    [0, 0],
    [800, 0],
    [0, 480],
    [800, 480]
])

# Append ones to R for affine computation
ones = np.ones((R.shape[0], 1))
R_aug = np.hstack((R, ones))

# Solve least squares for T in R_aug * T = C
T, residuals, rank, s = np.linalg.lstsq(R_aug, C, rcond=None)

A = T[:2, :].T  # 2x2 matrix
b = T[2, :].T   # 2x1 vector

def calibrate_point(r):
    r = np.array(r)
    c = A @ r + b
    return c

# Example calibration
```

```
raw_point = [150, 250]
calibrated_point = calibrate_point(raw_point)
print("Calibrated point:", calibrated_point)
```

Calibrated point: [200. 150.]

Successful integration of touch interfaces in industrial panels demands a holistic approach encompassing hardware characteristics, environmental factors, user ergonomics, and application-specific workflows. Robust input handling, accurate calibration, and thoughtfully engineered responsive GUIs contribute to improving operator efficiency and minimizing errors. Consequently, designers and engineers should prioritize adaptive solutions cognizant of real-world industrial constraints rather than direct transplantation of consumer touchscreen paradigms.

9.3. Resource-Constrained Optimization

Resource-constrained optimization plays a critical role in the design and deployment of software systems operating in environments where memory, storage, and CPU usage are at a premium. These limitations often arise in embedded systems, mobile devices, IoT endpoints, and other scenarios demanding high efficiency and rapid execution with minimal resource overhead. Achieving optimal performance under such constraints requires a comprehensive approach encompassing widget selection, font and image management, and strict runtime discipline.

A principal strategy to minimize memory usage is the deliberate choice of user interface elements or widgets. In graphical user interfaces, complex widgets inherently consume greater amounts of memory due to their internal state, event handling, and rendering logic. Whenever feasible, substituting heavyweight widgets with simpler or more specialized alternatives reduces both the dynamic memory footprint and initialization overhead. For example, using lightweight custom-drawn controls instead of standard comprehensive libraries can drastically cut memory consumption at the cost of increased development complexity. Similarly, the avoidance of excessive nested controls not only reduces resource consumption but also enhances UI responsiveness by limiting redraw and event propagation layers.

Font optimization is equally influential in resource-sensitive applications. Fonts can represent a significant portion of persistent storage as well as volatile memory during runtime. To mitigate this, choosing bitmap fonts tailored to required sizes and character sets, instead of scalable vector fonts, is advisable. Bitmap fonts can be stored in highly compressed formats and loaded on demand, thus reducing both memory usage and CPU cycles spent on font rendering. Additionally, subset extraction from font files-limiting character coverage strictly to required glyphs-prevents unnecessary memory reservation and improves load times. For systems permitting vector font usage, caching rendered glyph bitmaps and minimizing the use of complex typographic features such as ligatures or kerning tables can further decrease computational costs.

Image assets also demand careful optimization. Reducing image resolution to only what is perceptually necessary conserves both storage space and RAM allocated for decompression buffers. Employing lossy compression methods with tunable quality levels, such as JPEG or WebP at moderate compression ratios, achieves substantial size reductions with acceptable visual degradation, particularly for photographic content. For icons or UI elements requiring sharp edges, lossless compression formats like PNG remain preferable, provided the color palette is optimized and transparency layers minimized. An advanced approach involves converting images into vector formats when shapes and lines dominate, enabling scalable rendering at minimal storage cost. Moreover, runtime decompression of images can be streamlined using specialized hardware acccleration when available, reducing CPU load during display operations.

Runtime optimization focuses on maintaining a lean execution environment by minimizing resource allocation and maximizing reuse of data and code components. Employing static memory allocation where possible eliminates dynamic allocation overhead and prevents fragmentation. When dynamic allocation is necessary, pooling techniques that recycle memory blocks reduce the frequency and cost of system calls. Deferring initialization of resources until explicitly needed ("lazy loading") diminishes peak memory consumption and startup latency. Profiling execution to identify bottlenecks and redundant operations enables targeted optimizations such as function inlining, loop unrolling, and reducing expensive system calls. Furthermore, avoiding runtime reflection or introspection and limiting reliance on heavyweight frameworks reduces CPU cycles and memory usage.

In environments where power consumption directly correlates with CPU load and memory activity, algorithms must be chosen not only for computational efficiency but also for their memory access patterns. Cache-friendly algorithms that maximize locality of reference reduce costly memory bus transactions. Data structures favoring sequential access and compact layouts, such as arrays over linked lists, enhance cache utilization and minimize page faults, ultimately improving both performance and energy efficiency. Additionally, minimizing background tasks and aggressive use of idle states during execution pauses prolong operational lifespan on battery-powered devices.

Programming languages and compilers selected for resource-constrained systems significantly influence optimization potential. Languages that allow fine-grained control over memory layout, such as C or C++, enable manual optimizations that higher-level managed languages often preclude. Compiler settings for size optimization (for example, -Os in GCC) reduce binary footprint by disabling inlining or removing unused functions.

Link-time optimizations eliminate redundant code and data, while profile-guided optimization adapts the executable based on actual usage patterns to improve cache behavior and instruction scheduling.

An illustrative example of resource-constrained optimization involves a simple embedded GUI application providing sensor status updates. Instead of employing a standard widget toolkit like Qt, the system might use custom lightweight controls with minimal state. Fonts are reduced to a single bitmap font containing only numeric digits and uppercase letters. Iconography is stored as monochrome XBM files compressed through run-length encoding. During runtime, the application statically allocates buffers for UI elements and sensor data, avoiding dynamic memory allocation altogether. Rendering occurs only on changes, employing dirty rectangles to minimize redraw regions. Compiled with size optimization flags and stripped of debug symbols, the binary occupies a fraction of the available flash storage, while peak RAM usage remains well within the microcontroller's capacity.

```
#define MAX_WIDGETS 5

typedef struct {
    int x, y;
    int width, height;
    char label[10];
    void (*onClick)(void);
} Widget;

static Widget widgets[MAX_WIDGETS];  // Static allocation

void initWidgets() {
    // Initialize widgets with minimal state
    widgets[0] = (Widget){ .x=10, .y=10, .width=80, .height=20, .
    label="TEMP", .onClick=NULL };
    widgets[1] = (Widget){ .x=10, .y=40, .width=80, .height=20, .
    label="HUM", .onClick=NULL };
    // ... initialize other widgets similarly
}

void renderWidget(const Widget *w) {
    // Custom lightweight rendering logic
    drawRectangle(w->x, w->y, w->width, w->height);
    drawText(w->x + 5, w->y + 5, w->label);
```

```
}

int main() {
    initWidgets();
    while(1) {
        // Update sensor data and render only if changed
        for (int i = 0; i < MAX_WIDGETS; ++i) {
            renderWidget(&widgets[i]);
        }
        sleepUntilNextUpdate();
    }
}
```

Output:

- Memory footprint for widgets: approximately 240 bytes (5 widgets × sizeof(Widget))

- CPU cycles per screen update minimized by avoiding dynamic allocations

- Reduced binary size due to static memory and compiler optimization flags

Overall, resource-constrained optimization demands rigorous analysis and methodical refinement across the entire software stack. By combining careful widget selection with font and image asset management, supported by disciplined runtime and development practices, it is possible to deliver robust applications that operate efficiently within tight memory, storage, and CPU budgets. This multifaceted approach is essential to meeting the exacting requirements posed by resource-limited platforms without sacrificing user experience or functional completeness.

9.4. Cross-Compiling FLTK Applications

Cross-compilation for FLTK (Fast Light Toolkit) applications involves generating executable binaries on a host system (typically a desktop) that are intended to run on a distinct target environment, often an exotic or embedded platform. This process requires careful orchestration of toolchains, dependency management, and deployment strategies to ensure compatibility and functionality.

The primary challenges stem from differences in processor architectures, operating systems, available libraries, and runtime capabilities between the host and target systems.

The foundation of successful cross-compilation begins with choosing an appropriate cross-compiler toolchain tailored to the target
platform. A toolchain typically encompasses a cross-compiler (e.g.,
arm-linux-gnueabihf-gcc), linker, assembler, and related utilities configured for the target architecture and ABI.

Key considerations for FLTK cross-compilation include:

- **Compatibility:** The selected toolchain must support
  the instruction set and binary format of the target device.
  For embedded Linux targets on ARM or MIPS processors,
  toolchains like the GNU Arm Embedded Toolchain or
  Buildroot-provided compilers are common.

- **Sysroot Utilization:** Establishing a proper *sysroot* directory is essential. It mimics the root filesystem of the target, containing relevant headers, libraries, and configuration
  files. The cross-compiler uses the sysroot to resolve dependencies and system includes accurately.

- **Version Matching:** Aligning the versions of the cross-
  compiler, binutils, and libc implementations (e.g., glibc vs
  musl) with those installed or intended for the target is crucial
  to avoid incompatibilities.

The configuration typically involves specifying environment variables such as CC, CXX, and passing explicit command-line options
like --sysroot to the compiler and linker. For example:

```
export CC=arm-linux-gnueabihf-gcc
export CXX=arm-linux-gnueabihf-g++
export SYSROOT=/path/to/target/sysroot

$CC --sysroot=$SYSROOT -I$SYSROOT/usr/include -L$SYSROOT/usr/lib
    ...
```

FLTK is designed to be a lightweight, dependency-minimal GUI framework, which simplifies cross-compilation considerably compared to heavier toolkits. Nonetheless, careful management of its dependencies and the build environment is required.

Static vs Dynamic Linking

Embedded systems often prefer static linking to avoid runtime library resolution issues. Statically linking FLTK and minimal required libraries reduces the runtime footprint and dependency on shared libraries residing on the target. However, static linking demands that all dependencies must be available as static libraries within the sysroot, which is not always trivial to guarantee, especially for system libraries.

Cross-compiled FLTK Libraries

FLTK itself must be cross-compiled first unless pre-built libraries for the target exist. The cross-compilation of FLTK involves running its `configure` script or leveraging CMake with precise host and target specification:

```
./configure --host=arm-linux-gnueabihf --prefix=/install/path \
  --with-x --enable-shared=no --disable-dependency-tracking \
  --with-sysroot=$SYSROOT
make
make install
```

Alternatively, CMake-based builds should define `CMAKE_SYSTEM_NAME` and `CMAKE_TOOLCHAIN_FILE` to point to the cross-compilation definitions.

Fonts and X11 Dependencies

FLTK relies on X11 and fontconfig on many Unix-like targets. If these services are not running or unavailable on the target, the application will fail. Embedded platforms might require minimal X server installations or direct framebuffer usage, which FLTK supports but entails additional build-time configuration aligned with target capabilities.

Runtime Library Configuration

The target environment's available dynamic libraries must correlate with the versions used in the cross-compiled binaries. Library version mismatches induce runtime failures, manifesting as unresolved symbols or segmentation faults. Careful synchronization of runtime environments via chroot or containerized sysroots for building and deployment mitigates such risk.

Automating cross-compilation necessitates modifications to standard FLTK build procedures to integrate the toolchain and target specifics. This typically involves:

- Injecting cross-compiler prefixes.

- Setting appropriate compiler and linker flags reflecting target-specific optimizations and capabilities.

- Disabling or replacing optional modules incompatible with the target's hardware or OS features.

- Enforcing static linking when dynamic linking leads to deployability issues.

Commonly used build systems (autotools or CMake) allow these customizations through environment variables or dedicated toolchain files:

```
cmake -DCMAKE_TOOLCHAIN_FILE=arm-toolchain.cmake \
    -DCMAKE_INSTALL_PREFIX=/install/path \
    -DFLTK_STATIC=ON \
    /path/to/fltk
```

The toolchain file defines the cross-compiler executables, sysroot paths, and target architecture flags, providing consistent build environments.

Several pitfalls arise during cross-compilation of FLTK applications that impede portability. Foremost among these are:

ABI and Endianness Discrepancies

Architectural differences can lead to ABI incompatibilities, such as differing calling conventions or endianness. Cross-compilers for architectures like ARM (little-endian) versus older PowerPC (big-endian) require binaries to respect these constraints. Source code that includes assumptions about byte ordering or uses packed structures must be audited and adapted accordingly.

Hardcoded Paths and Configurations

Applications sometimes embed absolute paths or rely on host-specific environment variables and configurations. These must be avoided or replaced by target-relative paths or dynamically obtained runtime parameters to ensure correct execution on the target.

Filesystem and Device Support

Embedded targets often feature restricted or non-standard filesystems and may lack support for certain device abstractions or IPC mechanisms present on host systems. FLTK applications dependent on such features will require conditional compilation or runtime checks to gracefully degrade functionality or select alternative implementations.

Testing and Debugging on Target

Cross-compiled binaries may fail silently or behave inconsistently due to subtle mismatches. Deploying interactive debugging tools such as `gdbserver` or logging mechanisms is recommended. Lightweight remote debugging facilitates diagnosing runtime issues specific to the target environment.

After successful compilation, deploying the FLTK application to the target necessitates fidelity to the target's filesystem layout, permissions, and library availability.

File Packaging

Applications and their dependencies are often packaged into

firmware images, root filesystem tarballs, or container formats. Strip debugging symbols from release binaries to reduce size, unless these symbols are specifically required.

```
arm-linux-gnueabihf-strip fltk_app
tar czvf fltk_app.tar.gz fltk_app /usr/lib/libfltk.a ...
```

Runtime Environment Preparation

The target must provide a compatible runtime environment including necessary device drivers, X server configurations, and font services. In minimal embedded Linux systems, this may require integrating libraries and services via package managers or build systems (e.g., Yocto, Buildroot).

Cross-Compiled Auxiliary Tools

Sometimes, utilities or scripts for initialization or configuration must also be cross-compiled or carefully scripted to function appropriately on the target.

Mastering cross-compilation for FLTK applications demands thorough understanding of the target platform's architecture, operating system nuances, and runtime dependencies. Synchronizing compiler toolchains, sysroots, and build environments prevents common incompatibilities. Additionally, addressing portability pitfalls proactively through modular design and thorough testing streamlines deployment. Consequently, cross-compiled FLTK applications can leverage the lightweight and efficient nature of FLTK for rich graphical interfaces across diverse and resource-constrained systems.

9.5. Security and Lifecycle in IoT GUIs

The security and lifecycle management of graphical user interfaces (GUIs) in the Internet of Things (IoT) environment present unique challenges distinct from traditional desktop or mobile applications.

304

When leveraging the Fast Light Toolkit (FLTK) for IoT device interfaces, the imperative to safeguard both the GUI and the underlying system intensifies, particularly given the constrained resources and diverse threat vectors. This necessitates a comprehensive approach encompassing sandboxing, secure update mechanisms, and lifecycle strategies, including over-the-air (OTA) updates, to maintain trustworthiness and operational continuity throughout a device's deployment.

Sandboxing FLTK Interfaces for IoT

Sandboxing is a foundational security measure that isolates applications to limit the impact of potential vulnerabilities, a principle crucial for IoT devices where GUIs often handle sensitive control and monitoring functions. Deploying FLTK-based interfaces within sandboxed environments helps minimize exposure to system-level compromise by restricting permissions and interactions with critical system resources.

On IoT platforms, sandboxing can be implemented using lightweight containerization or operating system-level isolation techniques. Containers such as Docker or podman are applicable where the device's OS supports them, packaging the FLTK interface and its dependencies into a confined environment. For more constrained systems, sandboxing frameworks such as Seccomp (Secure Computing Mode) or AppArmor enforce granular access controls on system calls, reducing the attack surface available to a compromised GUI process.

From a development perspective, the FLTK interface design should adhere to the principle of least privilege, avoiding unnecessary access to hardware interfaces or system files. Explicitly restricting input/output channels and configuring secure inter-process communication (IPC) paths further confine the sandbox. For example, GUI components interacting with sensors or actuators should communicate through well-defined, authenticated channels rather than direct hardware manipulation.

Secure Software Update Mechanisms

IoT devices must remain updatable post-deployment to address vulnerabilities discovered after release and to enhance functionality. Securing these update mechanisms is especially critical for FLTK-powered GUIs, as injection of malicious code or tampering with interface logic can mislead operators or disrupt device operations.

A robust secure update pipeline involves cryptographic signing of update packages and verification on the device prior to installation. Typically, a public key infrastructure (PKI) is employed so that updates are signed by the vendor's private key. The device stores the corresponding public key to verify authenticity and integrity. This ensures that only authorized updates are accepted and mitigates risks from supply chain attacks.

The update package must be transmitted using secure transport protocols such as TLS to guarantee confidentiality and protection against man-in-the-middle attacks. Additionally, update metadata should include versioning and rollback information to prevent downgrade attacks.

FLTK applications must support atomic update strategies whereby a corrupted or incomplete update does not leave the GUI or device in an inoperable state. Employing dual-partition systems or transactional file systems enables fallback to a known-good state on failure. The update process should trigger integrity checks and signature verifications integrated tightly with the GUI startup routines to avoid execution of compromised interfaces.

Device Lifecycle Management and Over-the-Air Updates

Managing the lifecycle of an IoT device extends beyond the initial deployment to encompass continuous updates, monitoring, and eventual decommissioning. The GUI layer constitutes a critical interface for administrators and users to interact with device lifecycle operations, making its security and reliability paramount.

Over-the-air (OTA) updates provide a scalable mechanism to distribute patches and upgrades without physical access to devices. When implementing OTA updates for FLTK interfaces, the processes must be efficient, reliable, and resistant to attack. Constrained bandwidth and intermittent connectivity common in IoT contexts demand careful design considerations such as differential updates, compression, and resumable downloads.

Key to managing device lifecycle via OTA is monitoring update status and ensuring visibility into device health and GUI state. Integration with device management platforms can provide telemetry that includes GUI responsiveness, error reports, and usage analytics. This information supports proactive maintenance and targeted updates, reducing downtime and improving security posture.

Lifecycle management also necessitates secure decommissioning. End-of-life devices should receive updates that sanitize stored data, revoke cryptographic keys, and disable network access. The GUI can facilitate guided workflows for secure decommissioning, ensuring compliance with organizational policies and data protection regulations.

Mitigating Specific Attack Vectors in FLTK IoT GUIs

FLTK-powered GUIs in IoT are exposed to a range of specific attack vectors, including but not limited to code injection via input fields, exploitation of graphical resource handling, and denial-of-service (DoS) attacks through interface flooding.

Input sanitization is essential to prevent injection flaws. GUIs must validate and constrain user input rigorously, especially when commands or parameters propagate to embedded device logic. When FLTK interfaces handle scripting or configuration files, sandboxed execution environments for these scripts minimize risk.

Memory safety is critical given FLTK's reliance on C++. Use of modern C++ standards with bounds-checking, smart pointers, and static analysis tools can reduce vulnerabilities such as buffer overflows that attackers might exploit via crafted graphical elements or malformed data files.

To counter DoS scenarios, interfaces should implement rate limiting and prioritize essential tasks to maintain responsiveness. Watchdog timers integrated with the FLTK event loop can recover GUI operations from deadlocks or crashes, preserving stability in hostile conditions.

Integration of Security Policies and Access Controls

In many IoT applications, the FLTK GUI forms part of a larger system requiring multiple tiers of access control. Role-based access control (RBAC) or attribute-based access control (ABAC) policies can be integrated within GUI logic to restrict sensitive functions to authorized users only.

Authentication mechanisms must be robust and compatible with IoT constraints. Lightweight authentication protocols such as OAuth 2.0-based tokens or hardware-based attestation provide scalable security without excessive resource consumption. The GUI should reflect authentication status clearly and enforce session management rigorously to prevent unauthorized actions.

Logging and audit trails generated within the GUI offer additional layers of security assurance. Secure transmission and storage of logs allow forensic analysis post-incident and help detect anomalous behavior related to interface use.

Summary of Best Practices

- Enforce sandboxing at the process and system-call levels to compartmentalize GUI execution.

- Use cryptographic signing and transport security for software and interface updates.

- Design OTA update processes to be atomic, resumable, and verifiable to reduce operational risk.

- Adopt lifecycle management policies that include secure provisioning, continuous monitoring, and safe decommissioning through GUI interactions.

- Implement strict input validation, memory safety measures, and protections against DoS to mitigate attack vectors.

- Embed robust authentication and access control within GUI workflows, supported by logging and audit mechanisms.

Adhering to these principles facilitates secure, resilient, and manageable FLTK interfaces that align with the stringent demands of contemporary IoT device deployment and operation.

9.6. Case Studies: Real-World Embedded FLTK Deployments

Several embedded systems have successfully integrated the Fast Light Toolkit (FLTK) to fulfill demanding graphical user interface (GUI) requirements. The following case studies present detailed analyses of diverse FLTK deployments, emphasizing design decisions, architectural adaptations, and pragmatic solutions to platform constraints. These examples serve as benchmarks for crafting maintainable, performant UI solutions on resource-constrained embedded platforms.

Industrial Control Panel for a Smart Manufacturing Line

In the implementation of an industrial control panel for a smart manufacturing line, FLTK was chosen to deliver a lightweight, responsive GUI on a custom ARM-based embedded board. The device required real-time feedback from sensors and control over actuators with minimal latency.

Design Decisions: The development team prioritized a minimal memory footprint and real-time responsiveness. Leveraging FLTK's small binary size and low overhead, the GUI was designed with a simplified widget set focused on buttons, sliders, and numeric displays. Its event-driven model was integrated directly with the platform's real-time operating system (RTOS) event queue.

Graphical assets were rasterized offline to raw bitmap data compatible with the device's framebuffer, circumventing the CPU expense of on-the-fly rendering. The application architecture separated UI logic from sensor data acquisition using a producer-consumer threading model, mitigating blocking operations in the UI thread.

Challenges and Solutions: A major challenge was maintaining low latency while updating displays with high-frequency sensor data streams. FLTK's default redraw behavior was optimized by subclassing key widgets to implement partial and region-based redraws, reducing CPU utilization by 30%. Additionally, direct framebuffer memory mapping was employed to minimize context switching during redraws.

Interfacing FLTK's event loop with the RTOS posed synchronization challenges, resolved by adapting FLTK's Fl::wait() function to accommodate RTOS-specific signaling primitives without resorting to busy-wait loops. This ensured low-power idle states between UI updates.

Reusable Patterns:

- *Decoupled UI and data acquisition threads* allowed smooth real-time updates without UI freezes.

- *Custom redraw optimizations* demonstrated that carefully tailoring paint regions could enhance embedded GUI efficiency.

- *RTOS integration for event loops* highlighted the necessity of adapting FLTK primitives to non-POSIX environments.

Medical Imaging Device Interface

A high-end medical ultrasound device employed FLTK to implement a complex diagnostic imaging panel with multiple simultaneous display windows and interactive controls. The system ran on a Linux-based embedded platform with a PowerPC CPU and a 24-bit color LCD.

Design Decisions: Due to the critical role of clarity and performance, the GUI prioritized smooth rendering and accurate user input handling. FLTK's native support for OpenGL was leveraged to integrate hardware-accelerated rendering for ultrasound image previews alongside the standard FLTK widgets.

A modular UI design was adopted; each imaging mode corresponded to distinct FLTK window instances interconnected via a centralized controller class. This structure allowed independent updates of imaging views while preserving a consistent overall interface.

Challenges and Solutions: Balancing FLTK's immediate mode widget system with OpenGL's retained mode demanded careful synchronization of redraw sequences. Custom FLTK widget subclasses embedded OpenGL canvases, overriding the draw() method to issue OpenGL commands while maintaining FLTK control event handling.

Another critical challenge was ensuring the display did not flicker during rapid image refreshes. Double buffering was implemented by configuring the FLTK OpenGL windows with the appropriate flags and tuning the refresh rates to match hardware vertical sync signals.

Performance profiling revealed bottlenecks in numeric input responsiveness when processing patient data. Integrating asynchronous input validation and deferring heavy computations to background threads improved the perceived latency significantly.

Reusable Patterns:

- *Integration of OpenGL canvases within FLTK widgets* to combine 3D accelerated content and traditional UI elements.

- *Modular window-controller architecture* for managing complex GUI states.

- *Asynchronous input processing* techniques to maintain UI responsiveness under heavy computational loads.

Vehicle Infotainment System

An embedded vehicle infotainment system incorporated FLTK for its UI core running on an ARM Cortex-A platform with a Linux OS. The display encompassed media control, navigation, and vehicle diagnostics with a capacitive touchscreen interface.

Design Decisions: The project emphasized user experience, with fluid animations and clear information hierarchy. FLTK's inherent lack of built-in animation support was addressed by coupling its event loop with a timed callback mechanism, enabling incremental graphical updates for animation frames.

To address the multitouch capabilities, a customized input event adapter was developed to translate Linux evdev touch events into FLTK-compatible events. Widget hit-testing was extended to support gesture recognition such as pinch and swipe, supplementing FLTK's standard mouse and keyboard event handling.

A flexible theming system was constructed by subclassing FLTK's themed widget base classes, permitting dynamic switching of UI palettes and fonts based on ambient lighting conditions detected via onboard sensors.

Challenges and Solutions: The primary challenge was the integration of multipoint touch inputs and gesture recognition into FLTK's primarily single-pointer event model. Extending the core event handling mechanism required deep modifications to the

Fl_Event enumeration and dispatch logic to preserve compatibility with existing widgets.

GPU-accelerated compositing was introduced through an EGL context on the Linux framebuffer to enhance graphical performance, necessitating custom bridging code for surface management between FLTK and EGL.

Power consumption constraints mandated that the UI enter low-power standby states without impeding rapid user reactivation. Implementing intelligent event loop dormancy through adaptive timers in Fl::wait() optimized power usage.

Reusable Patterns:

- *Event adapter layers* effectively map platform-specific input systems into FLTK event models.

- *Timed-callback driven animation loops* extend FLTK for smooth, low-overhead GUI animations.

- *Theming via subclassed widgets* supports dynamic UI customization in embedded contexts.

- *Power-aware event management* techniques for embedded user interfaces sensitive to energy consumption.

Wearable Device Health Monitor

This case involves a wearable health monitor with a small 320×240 pixel display, limited CPU at 100 MHz, and constrained memory resources. FLTK was chosen for its minimal runtime requirements and straightforward build system.

Design Decisions: A custom minimal subset of FLTK widgets was selectively compiled using C++ preprocessor flags, reducing binary size by removing font handling and unused widgets. The project adopted a statically compiled embedded bitmap font system, eliminating runtime font rasterization.

The UI layout utilized a compact grid system implemented via custom container widgets derived from Fl_Group, enforcing size constraints and pixel-perfect placements. The graphical style emphasized low-contrast UI elements to conserve display power on an OLED screen.

Challenges and Solutions: Memory constraints precluded traditional dynamic memory allocation; thus, widget instances and UI elements were statically allocated and reused during operation. This entailed redefining widget constructors and destructors to accommodate placement in fixed memory regions.

Event handling was simplified by bypassing FLTK's internal event queue, instead directly dispatching touchscreen interrupts to registered callback handlers. This minimized latency and run-to-run variability in UI response.

Rendering speed limitations led to the implementation of aggressive partial redraws, leveraging FLTK's damage() mechanism. Only changed widget regions were redrawn each frame, reducing CPU utilization by more than 50%.

Reusable Patterns:

- *Selective compilation of FLTK components* to minimize binary footprint.

- *Static allocation and reuse of UI components* suitable for systems without dynamic memory.

- *Direct event dispatch bypassing FLTK queues* to achieve deterministic UI latency.

- *Aggressive partial redraw optimizations* to conserve CPU cycles on low-power devices.

Automated Teller Machine (ATM) Interface

An ATM interface running on an Intel x86 embedded board under

GNU/Linux utilized FLTK for a stable, maintainable transaction UI that operates reliably in high-availability environments.

Design Decisions: The ATM UI was structured around a multi-window hierarchical design, enabling seamless navigation between banking transactions. Reliability considerations drove the choice of stateless UI widgets where possible, minimizing dynamic state retention across screens.

FLTK's focus on native look and feel was leveraged to provide a consistent user experience across different hardware batches. The system incorporated secure PIN entry via a custom FLTK widget with masked input and tamper-detection logic embedded.

Challenges and Solutions: Security constraints imposed restrictions on GUI responsiveness during sensitive transactions; thus, FLTK's idle and timeout functions were modified to lock the UI after inactivity. Custom input method spoofing protections were implemented at the OS level and reflected in the FLTK event handling pipeline.

The necessity to support multiple languages with complex scripts led to integrating a third-party text rendering engine alongside FLTK's standard font system. This hybrid rendering approach maintained performance while enabling full localization.

Debugging intermittent input device errors revealed sporadic event drops during high CPU load. Introducing prioritized event queuing within FLTK's core event loop ensured critical input events were not lost.

Reusable Patterns:

- *Stateless widget designs* improving UI reliability.

- *Secure input widget extensions* protecting sensitive user data entry.

- *Hybrid text rendering integration* for multilingual embedded applications.

- *Event prioritization* within the event loop to guarantee critical input processing.

Common threads arise through these case studies. Foremost is the flexibility of FLTK's minimalistic, event-driven architecture, which permits effective adaptations to vastly differing embedded requirements, from ultra-low-memory wearables to GPU-accelerated medical instruments. Methodical decoupling of UI logic from data processing ensures responsive interfaces despite platform constraints.

Optimization of redraw mechanics and event handling represents a recurrent theme; embedded FLTK deployments benefit substantially from customized damage-region management and tightly integrated event loops with native OS or RTOS primitives. The extensibility of FLTK's widget set enables targeted enhancements, encompassing touchscreen gestures, secure inputs, and embedded OpenGL content.

Reusable design patterns discovered span both architectural and low-level implementation domains, offering engineers a toolkit of strategies for maintaining performance, readability, and reliability in complex embedded UI systems. Emphasizing modularity, resource-awareness, and precise event control decisively improves the user experience on resource- and power-limited devices.

These real-world deployments underscore FLTK's capabilities as both a lightweight and extensible GUI framework, shaping embedded system UI designs where performance constraints and usability demands converge.

Chapter 10

Best Practices, Advanced Patterns, and Community Extensions

Ready to push your FLTK expertise to the next level? This chapter distills years of experience and innovation into a toolkit of proven practices, battle-tested patterns, and extensibility techniques. Dive into advanced design strategies, robust testing, and fearless participation in the thriving FLTK community— unlocking the insights to create maintainable, secure, and future-ready applications.

10.1. Architectural Patterns for Large-Scale FLTK Apps

Designing large-scale applications using the Fast Light Toolkit (FLTK) demands rigorous architectural strategies to manage complexity effectively and ensure long-term maintainability. The relatively lightweight, event-driven nature of FLTK provides excellent performance and simplicity for small to medium applications; however, scaling such projects into substantial codebases requires deliberate modularization, clear decoupling, and proven design patterns that accommodate feature expansion without sacrificing code clarity or stability.

Modularization for Manageable Codebases

Modularization is fundamental for dividing a monolithic FLTK application into comprehensible units, facilitating teamwork, code reuse, and isolated testing. In FLTK, modularization can be approached on several levels:

- **Widget Encapsulation**: Wrapping complex UI components into self-contained widget classes that inherit from Fl_Widget or its derivatives enables abstraction of low-level event handling and drawing logic. For example, a composite widget managing multiple child widgets (buttons, sliders, text inputs) can provide a clean interface exposing only relevant state changes and actions.

- **Feature-Based Modules**: Organizing source files and classes by discrete application features or domains prevents tangled dependencies. Each module can include core UI components, logic handlers, and data models pertinent to that functionality. C++ namespaces are effective in avoiding symbol collisions and clarifying boundaries.

- **Separation of UI and Logic**: Extracting business logic from UI code reduces coupling. FLTK's signal-slot style callback system lends itself well to a Model-View-Controller (MVC) or Model-View-Presenter (MVP) approach, where widgets handle presentation while controllers or models govern application state and behavior.

Modularization applied consistently reduces compilation times, promotes incremental builds, and enhances developer productivity by limiting cognitive load.

Decoupling via Event-Driven and Observer Patterns

Maintaining low coupling in an event-driven framework like FLTK is critical. Direct, hard-coded widget-to-widget interactions lead to brittle code that is difficult to extend or debug. Instead, the following mechanisms promote decoupling:

- **Callback Indirection**: FLTK uses a callback registration system where widgets notify clients of events. Utilizing functors, lambdas, or member function pointers wrapped in lightweight adapters abstracts callback targets and permits flexible reassignment.

```
button->callback([](Fl_Widget* w, void* data) {
    auto app = static_cast<MyApp*>(data);
    app->handle_button_click();
}, this);
```

- **Observer Pattern**: Implementing observer or publish-subscribe mechanisms decouples event producers from consumers. Observers register interest in particular state changes or actions, and subjects notify them asynchronously. This is invaluable for propagating UI state changes, logging, or triggering side effects without widgets knowing each other explicitly.

```
class Subject {
public:
    void attach(Observer* obs) { observers.push_back(obs);
    }
    void notify() {
        for (auto* obs : observers) obs->update();
```

```
    }
private:
    std::vector<Observer*> observers;
};
```

- **Message Queues and Event Dispatchers**: In highly modular FLTK applications, introducing a dedicated event dispatcher or message queue enables loose coupling. Modules send messages or events through the dispatcher without direct references to recipients, which improves testability and enables runtime configuration of handlers.

Architectural Patterns Supporting Maintainability

Several well-established architectural patterns provide scalable structures for FLTK apps, allowing feature growth and independent evolution of components.

- **Model-View-Controller (MVC)**: MVC cleanly separates application concerns into three parts:

  - *Model*: Encapsulates data logic and business rules, independent of UI representations.
  - *View*: FLTK widgets rendering the model's data and handling basic user input.
  - *Controller*: Mediates user interactions, updating the model and instructing views to refresh.

  This division minimizes dependencies and allows parallel development of UI and logic. The observer pattern typically realizes the communication from model to view, enabling automatic updates when data changes.

- **Model-View-Presenter (MVP)**: A variation on MVC tailored for event-driven GUIs, MVP places the presenter as an explicit mediator between the view and the model with a well-defined interface, easing unit testing and handling more complex user interaction logic.

- **Service-Oriented Architecture (SOA) within the application**: For applications interacting with multiple back-end or utility modules (e.g., data acquisition, logging, network communication), encapsulating these as services with clearly defined interfaces allows the FLTK GUI to remain agnostic of underlying implementations. Dependency injection can provide concrete service instances at runtime.

- **Command Pattern for User Actions**: Wrapping UI commands into objects supports undo/redo functionality and macro recording-valuable for sophisticated FLTK applications such as editors or configurators.

```
class Command {
public:
    virtual ~Command() {}
    virtual void execute() = 0;
    virtual void undo() = 0;
};

class RenameCommand : public Command {
    // Implementation details
};
```

Techniques for Handling Cross-Cutting Concerns

Large FLTK codebases must address recurring concerns such as state persistence, error reporting, configuration management, and logging without entangling core logic.

- **Aspect-Oriented Approaches**: While C++ lacks native aspect-oriented programming support, careful use of wrapper classes and macros can modularize logging or validation code, separating it from application logic. For instance, decorating callbacks with error-handling proxies improves robustness.

```
auto safe_callback = [](auto f) {
    return [f](Fl_Widget* w, void* data) {
        try { f(w, data); }
        catch (const std::exception& e) {
            // log error, show message
```

```
        }
    };
};
```

- **Configuration and Resource Management**: Centralizing configuration loading and resource management (icons,
  fonts) in dedicated modules prevents duplication. Injecting configuration references into widgets or controllers improves consistency.

- **State Management Strategies**: Leveraging state
  machines or state pattern implementations clarifies
  complex widget behaviors based on application state. Such
  patterns reduce scattered conditional logic within event
  handlers.

```
class State {
public:
    virtual void handle_event(AppContext& ctx, Event e) =
    0;
};

class EditingState : public State {
    void handle_event(AppContext& ctx, Event e) override {
        // handle editing-specific events
    }
};
```

Practical Implications and Tooling Support

Effective architectural patterns must be complemented by tooling
and processes to enforce the intended modularity and decoupling:

- **Static Analysis and Code Structure Visualization**:
  Tools for dependency graph generation aid in identifying
  cyclical dependencies and enforcing layering constraints
  within FLTK projects.

- **Unit and Integration Testing**: Modular designs facilitate
  rigorous testing at multiple levels. Separation of UI and logic
  permits unit tests to focus on non-GUI components with

mock interfaces, while integration tests validate widget interactions.

- **Continuous Integration (CI) Pipelines**: Incremental builds supported by modularization, combined with automated tests, ensure regressions related to architectural patterns can be detected early.

- **Documentation and Coding Standards**: Consistent adherence to architectural guidelines is vital. Code reviews and documentation specifying interface contracts, callback ownership, and expected module interactions reduce accidental coupling.

Summary of Architectural Design Motifs

The recurring motifs for creating maintainable, scalable FLTK applications include:

- *Layered architecture*, separating UI, business logic, and data layers.

- *Communication via interfaces and callbacks*, avoiding direct pointer manipulation across modules.

- *Encapsulation of widgets and UI composition*, promoting reuse and isolation.

- *Observer and event-driven patterns* enabling asynchronous state propagation.

- *Use of command and state patterns* to manage user interaction complexity.

- *Separation of concerns through service abstractions* for auxiliary subsystems.

These patterns and techniques collectively empower the development of large FLTK applications with clear code organization, easier feature addition, and sustainable maintenance over the software lifecycle.

10.2. Advanced Testing and QA

A rigorous quality assurance (QA) regime is paramount for delivering reliable, maintainable, and robust software systems. Advanced testing methodologies extend beyond basic unit and integration tests by introducing layered strategies that provide comprehensive coverage, timely defect detection, and meaningful insights into software behavior throughout the development lifecycle. This demands a disciplined orchestration of multiple test types, sophisticated tooling for automated verification-including graphical user interface (GUI) testing-and seamless integration with continuous integration (CI) pipelines to foster rapid feedback and continuous quality improvement.

Layered testing, often conceptualized as a testing pyramid, balances speed and depth by structuring tests across different scopes and execution times. The foundation comprises fast, isolated unit tests targeting individual functions or methods to validate correctness at the smallest code granularity. These tests enable developers to detect regressions or logic errors immediately after code changes, ensuring low-level functionality integrity.

Above the unit tests lie integration tests, which evaluate the interaction among multiple components or subsystems. Unlike unit tests, integration tests verify the correctness of interfaces, data flows, and service contracts under realistic conditions. They often exert higher resource consumption and longer execution times, thus suggesting judicious scope selection-focusing on critical interfaces or potentially error-prone integrations.

At the apex, system tests validate the software in an environment simulating production-like conditions, encompassing the entire application stack, including databases, external services, and user interfaces. System tests are essential for verifying compliance with functional requirements and nonfunctional attributes such as performance, security, and usability. Despite longer execution durations, they provide confidence in the software's holistic behavior before release.

Complementing this hierarchy, acceptance tests embody customer-oriented scenarios, typically written in domain-specific languages (DSLs) to express expected behaviors declaratively. These tests facilitate alignment between business requirements and delivered features, enhancing traceability and stakeholder trust. Modern behavior-driven development (BDD) frameworks automate acceptance tests, converting natural language specifications into executable test cases.

GUI testing poses unique challenges due to the inherent dynamism, event-driven nature, and complexity of user interfaces. Manual testing of GUIs is labor-intensive, error-prone, and difficult to scale, making automated GUI verification indispensable in contemporary QA.

Robust automated GUI testing tools operate at various abstraction levels. At a low level, they simulate user actions such as clicks, keystrokes, and gestures to exercise interface components. High-level frameworks provide domain-specific APIs to encapsulate interface elements and expected workflows, abstracting away raw event simulations and improving test readability and maintainability.

Key considerations for GUI automation include:

- **Element Identification**: Reliable selectors or locators must uniquely identify UI elements across varying states and configurations. Strategies include using stable attributes

(IDs, labels) or employing hierarchical navigation in the interface tree.

- **Synchronization**: Automated tests must account for asynchronous UI updates, such as animations or network-induced delays. Explicit or implicit waits are used to synchronize test execution with application state changes.

- **Test Stability**: Flaky tests-tests that intermittently fail without code changes-undermine confidence and productivity. Minimizing flakiness involves robust element identification, appropriate synchronization, and deterministic test data setup.

- **Cross-Platform and Cross-Browser Coverage**: Web applications require testing across diverse browsers and devices. Tooling supporting parallel execution and environment abstraction enhances coverage and efficiency.

Widely adopted GUI testing frameworks and tools include Selenium WebDriver for web applications, Appium for mobile platforms, and platform-specific frameworks like Microsoft's Coded UI Tests or Apple's XCTest. These tools enable scripting of complex user flows, capturing screenshots and logs for diagnostics, and integrating assertions to validate visual and functional correctness.

```
from selenium import webdriver
from selenium.webdriver.common.by import By
from selenium.webdriver.support.ui import WebDriverWait
from selenium.webdriver.support import expected_conditions as EC

driver = webdriver.Chrome()
driver.get("https://example.com/login")

username = WebDriverWait(driver, 10).until(
    EC.presence_of_element_located((By.ID, "username"))
)
password = driver.find_element(By.ID, "password")
login_button = driver.find_element(By.ID, "login")

username.send_keys("testuser")
password.send_keys("securepassword")
login_button.click()
```

```
welcome_message = WebDriverWait(driver, 10).until(
    EC.presence_of_element_located((By.ID, "welcome-message"))
)
assert "Welcome" in welcome_message.text

driver.quit()
```

```
Sample output upon successful test execution:

[INFO] Starting Chrome WebDriver
[INFO] Navigated to https://example.com/login
[INFO] Entered username and password
[INFO] Clicked login button
[INFO] Verified welcome message presence
[INFO] Test passed, closing browser
```

The advent of continuous integration has transformed QA from a predominantly manual gatekeeping function into a continuous, automated process tightly integrated with development. This integration enables rapid detection and resolution of defects, higher deployment frequency, and improved software quality.

A well-architected CI pipeline encompasses automated testing as a foundational stage. Upon code check-in or merge requests, pipelines trigger a battery of tests organized in logical sequences and parallel executions:

- **Pre-commit and Commit-Stage Testing**: Fast-running tests, typically unit and lightweight integration tests, validate code correctness before the integration proceeds. Such tests act as quick sanity checks to prevent breaking the build.

- **Post-commit and Pre-deployment Testing**: Lengthier system, acceptance, and performance tests execute after initial validations to verify software behavior in a production-like environment.

The integration with test tooling requires orchestrating environment provisioning, test execution, and artifact collection.

Infrastructure-as-code (IaC) solutions and containerization (Docker, Kubernetes) enable consistent, reproducible test environments, minimizing environment-specific failures. Test results are aggregated and reported via dashboards or notifications, providing rapid visibility to developers and QA teams.

Ensuring traceability between code changes, build artifacts, and test outcomes is crucial. Modern CI platforms support versioned pipelines, failure analytics, historical trending, and integration with issue tracking systems. This holistic feedback loop accelerates root cause analysis and remediation.

```
stages:
  - build
  - test

build_job:
  stage: build
  script:
    - ./build.sh

unit_test_job:
  stage: test
  script:
    - pytest tests/unit
  artifacts:
    reports:
      junit: test-reports/unit.xml

integration_test_job:
  stage: test
  script:
    - pytest tests/integration
  artifacts:
    reports:
      junit: test-reports/integration.xml
  dependencies:
    - build_job

gui_test_job:
  stage: test
  script:
    - xvfb-run -a python gui_tests.py
  artifacts:
    reports:
      junit: test-reports/gui.xml
  dependencies:
```

```
    - build_job
```

Upon pipeline execution, test summaries with pass/fail counts and timings
are displayed, along with detailed logs and test reports in JUnit XML format
for downstream analysis and reporting.

Strategically, test suites may be optimized using test impact analysis and prioritization to reduce pipeline runtimes while maintaining coverage. In addition, employing parallelization, distributed test execution, and caching mechanisms enhances throughput efficiency.

Advanced QA methodologies benefit from complementary techniques such as mocking and service virtualization for isolation during integration testing, enabling stable test execution despite unavailable or expensive external dependencies. Code coverage analysis instruments the measurement of executed code lines during tests, illuminating potential gaps in coverage and guiding test suite improvements.

Mutation testing, which introduces programmed faults to assess test effectiveness in detecting defects, provides deeper insight into test quality beyond coverage metrics. Security testing and static code analysis tools embedded within the QA framework identify vulnerabilities and enforce coding standards early in the development cycle.

Performance benchmarking integrated with system-level tests ensures that software meets latency, throughput, and scalability requirements. These benchmarks inform tuning decisions and validate infrastructure provisioning.

Collectively, the synergy of layered testing, automated GUI verification, and tight CI integration enhances software quality, reduces risk, and accelerates delivery cycles. An investment in comprehensive, automated, and maintainable QA frameworks yields long-term returns in software reliability and stakeholder confidence.

329

10.3. Security Hardening and Defensive Coding

Robust security within Fast Light Toolkit (FLTK) applications demands a multilayered approach, integrating secure input handling,
comprehensive threat modeling, systematic code audits, and deliberate architectural choices that anticipate and mitigate exploit vectors. These combined strategies form the cornerstone of a resilient
graphical user interface (GUI) framework capable of withstanding
diverse adversarial efforts.

Secure Input Handling

User input remains the most prevalent attack vector in desktop applications, where FLTK's event-driven model necessitates particular vigilance. Input fields such as text boxes, file dialogs, and custom widgets that consume user data must be rigorously sanitized
and validated before processing or storage. Defensive coding starts
by constraining input types at the widget level; for instance, employing Fl_Input subclasses with defined character sets or length
restrictions reduces risk exposure.

Beyond widget-level constraints, all input data should be treated
as untrusted regardless of source. Common vulnerabilities arise
from improper handling of buffer boundaries, format strings, and
encoding. Explicit length checks prior to buffer copying, use of safe
string functions, and canonicalization to a normalized character
encoding (e.g., UTF-8) are imperative. The following illustrative
pattern exemplifies secure input copying in C++ within an FLTK
callback:

```
const char* raw_input = input_widget->value();
char safe_buffer[256];

// Explicitly limit the length of input to avoid buffer overflow
size_t len = strnlen(raw_input, sizeof(safe_buffer) - 1);
memcpy(safe_buffer, raw_input, len);
safe_buffer[len] = '\0';
```

Input filtering should also extend to preventing injection attacks; for instance, if user input interfaces with SQL databases or command-line invocations, parameterized queries and explicit escaping routines are mandatory. FLTK applications that utilize external interpreters or scripting engines must rigorously compartmentalize input and employ sandboxing or strict API boundaries.

Threat Modeling for FLTK Applications

Systematic threat modeling guides the identification and prioritization of risks specific to GUI toolkits. FLTK, while lightweight, exposes attack surfaces primarily via its event handling loop, widget callbacks, file operations, and integration points with backend processes or networking services.

A recommended approach begins with enumerating assets-user data, session tokens, configuration files-and interfaces susceptible to malicious influence. The STRIDE framework (Spoofing, Tampering, Repudiation, Information disclosure, Denial of service, Elevation of privilege) provides a structured taxonomy for classifying potential violations. For example:

- **Spoofing**: Unauthorized manipulation of GUI elements to impersonate user actions.

- **Tampering**: Malicious modification of input event data or internal state variables.

- **Repudiation**: Lack of auditing in user-triggered commands within the application.

- **Information Disclosure**: Exposure of sensitive data via debug logs or improperly restricted widget states.

- **Denial of Service**: Infinite loops or resource exhaustion triggered through malformed inputs.

- **Elevation of Privilege**: Exploits leveraging callback vulnerabilities to invoke elevated operations.

Mapping these threats onto the FLTK application codebase involves detailed analysis of the event dispatch mechanism, callback registration routines, and data flow from input widgets to business logic layers. Threat modeling must also consider underlying OS and hardware security properties since GUI applications operate in complex runtime environments.

Code Audits and Static Analysis

A disciplined audit process is essential for uncovering latent security defects inherent in GUI frameworks. Important targets include unchecked pointer dereferences, improper resource management, race conditions within event handlers, and insecure memory handling.

Static analysis complements manual reviews by automatically detecting patterns such as buffer overflows, use-after-free conditions, and format string vulnerabilities. Tools capable of analyzing C++ constructs and idioms pertinent to FLTK's style-such as Clang Static Analyzer, Cppcheck, and Coverity-should be integrated into the development pipeline.

Consider analyzing an FLTK callback handling user-submitted filenames for loading images:

```
void LoadImageCallback(Fl_Widget* w, void* data) {
    const char* filename = (const char*)data;
    // Potential flaw: no validation of filename string or
     existence check
    Fl_PNG_Image* img = new Fl_PNG_Image(filename);
    if (img->fail()) {
        fl_alert("Failed to load image.");
        delete img;
        return;
    }
    display_widget->image(img);
    display_widget->redraw();
}
```

An audit reveals absence of validation for filename integrity, absence of whitelist or blacklist controls, and lack of exception handling for resource allocation failures. To fortify, rigorous checks must precede image instantiation, including path normalization, existence verification, and exception-safe memory management.

Memory-use profiling tools (e.g., Valgrind) and fuzz testing can further expose runtime anomalies, especially given FLTK's reliance on raw pointers and manual memory management. Additionally, integration of AddressSanitizer and UndefinedBehaviorSanitizer during development phases strengthens detection of security-critical runtime errors.

Designing for Resilience Against Exploit Techniques

Strategic architectural decisions can dramatically improve application robustness against exploitation. Employing defense-in-depth principles in FLTK applications often involves layering protective mechanisms and minimizing trust boundaries.

Immutable and Least-Privilege Patterns

Restrict data mutability and limit privilege scope within widget and callback implementations. For example, designing callbacks that operate on immutable copies of user data rather than shared mutable state prevents race conditions and unintended side effects.

Callback Isolation

Avoid monolithic or overly complex callback functions. Decompose event handlers into minimal units with explicit error handling and validation paths. This modularity enables easier auditing, debugging, and containment of failures.

Use of Safe Wrappers and RAII

Leverage Resource Acquisition Is Initialization (RAII) idioms in C++ to manage lifetime of resources such as dynamically allocated images, font handles, or file descriptors. Smart pointers, scoped guards, and exception-safe constructs enhance predictability and reduce leaks or dangling pointers.

Memory Safety Enhancements

Although FLTK inherently involves low-level pointer management, integrating modern C++ standards (C++11 and beyond) features within FLTK codebases can reduce susceptibility to memory safety bugs. For instance, replacing raw arrays with `std::array` or `std::vector`, and preferring `std::string` over C-style strings for temporary buffers, provides built-in bounds checking and reduces manual error.

Input Event Sanitization Pipeline

Develop a centralized input sanitization pipeline that preprocesses all incoming events or user data before propagation to the core business logic or rendering subsystems. This not only limits exposure but also enforces uniform validation standards.

Error Handling and Logging Discipline

Incorporate comprehensive, informative yet secure error reporting targeting both developers and users. Avoid exposing sensitive internal state or system details in error messages. Secure logging-potentially encrypted and with access controls-supports forensic analysis without introducing information leakage.

Protection Against Common Exploit Techniques

Address common exploit classes explicitly:

- **Buffer Overflows**: Utilize length-limited operations and robust memory management.

- **Format String Attacks**: Disallow user-controlled formatting strings or sanitize input before passing to functions like `printf`-style APIs.

334

- **Use-After-Free**: Employ smart pointers and careful lifecycle management.

- **Race Conditions**: Synchronize access to shared resources across event handlers and background threads.

- **Code Injection**: Restrict dynamic scripting or macro functionality or enforce strict sandboxing.

Integration with Operating System Security Features

FLTK applications can benefit from operating system protections by adhering to best practices such as privilege separation (running with least necessary permissions), utilizing secure file system permissions, and operating within sandboxed contexts where supported. Where possible, enabling address space layout randomization (ASLR), data execution prevention (DEP), and control-flow integrity (CFI) mechanisms further hardens the runtime environment.

Continuous Security Validation

Security hardening is dynamic; continuous integration pipelines must include automated security regression tests, fuzz testing of GUI inputs, and dependency vulnerability scanning. These measures ensure that the FLTK application evolves with maintained defenses, promptly addressing newly discovered vulnerabilities both within the application code and the underlying FLTK library.

Throughout these measures, maintaining rigorous documentation of security decisions, threat assessments, and auditing results contributes to a resilient development culture, empowering teams to anticipate and prevent emergent security challenges typical in complex GUI applications.

10.4. Extending FLTK with Plugins and Third-Party Libraries

The Fast Light Toolkit (FLTK) lends itself naturally to extensibility through both plugin architectures and integration with diverse third-party C++ libraries, enabling developers to build highly modular and scalable graphical applications. An extensible application architecture facilitates dynamic addition of new features without modification to core code, improving maintainability and fostering a vibrant ecosystem of reusable components. Exploiting FLTK's minimalistic design paired with modern C++ idioms allows developers to leverage the wider ecosystem effectively while maintaining application responsiveness and compact footprint.

A foundational strategy to enable plugin-based extensibility within an FLTK application is to design well-defined interfaces abstracting the plugin's input, output, and interaction mechanisms. Utilizing pure virtual classes as plugin interface contracts—commonly known as abstract base classes—promotes decoupling between the core application and plugins. Plugins implement these interfaces and are dynamically loaded at runtime using platform-specific mechanisms such as dlopen on UNIX-like systems or LoadLibrary on Windows. The dynamic loading process generally includes discovering plugin shared libraries placed within a known directory, opening these libraries, and resolving initialization functions or factory methods that instantiate plugin objects conforming to the interface.

```
class IPlugin {
public:
    virtual ~IPlugin() = default;
    virtual const char* name() const = 0;
    virtual void initialize() = 0;
    virtual void execute(Fl_Widget* parent) = 0;
};
```

In this example, the interface IPlugin defines crucial lifecycle and interaction functions. The execute method accepts a pointer to

336

an Fl_Widget that can act as a container for plugin-driven UI elements, enabling seamless integration within the host's widget hierarchy. The core application manages plugins through smart pointers to ensure exception safety and proper resource release.

Loading these plugin objects dynamically requires precise control over symbol resolution. A typical idiom defines a factory function with external C linkage to prevent name mangling:

```
extern "C" IPlugin* create_plugin();
```

Each plugin shared library exports this function, allowing the host to retrieve an instance:

```
#include <dlfcn.h>
void* handle = dlopen("plugin.so", RTLD_LAZY);
auto create_plugin = reinterpret_cast<IPlugin* (*)()>(dlsym(
    handle, "create_plugin"));
IPlugin* plugin = create_plugin();
```

Robust error handling remains critical to gracefully recover from missing symbols or library loading failures.

Leveraging this approach permits separation of concerns: all core application logic remains independent of plugin implementations, which can be developed, updated, or replaced independently. Furthermore, runtime discovery of plugins supports extensibility in deployed environments without recompilation.

Integration of third-party libraries extends application capabilities far beyond native FLTK components. FLTK primarily caters to lightweight GUI rendering and event handling but often requires complementary functionality such as image processing, networking, advanced text rendering, or database interactions. Many established C++ libraries can be incorporated by careful design of adapter classes that bridge their APIs with FLTK's event-driven environment.

For example, image processing frameworks like OpenCV or graphics rendering libraries such as Cairo can be integrated into FLTK by wrapping their drawing operations within custom Fl_Widget subclasses. The widget's draw() method provides a natural override point to invoke these libraries' render calls, composing their output onto FLTK's drawing context. When combining disparate libraries, attention must be paid to thread safety and event dispatch conventions—FLTK's single-threaded event loop requires external asynchronous operations to synchronize carefully with the UI thread, often by posting custom FLTK events or employing thread-safe queues.

A practical recipe to incorporate a third-party library involves:

1. Encapsulating library initialization and resource management in a dedicated C++ class.

2. Designing or subclassing FLTK widgets to invoke library APIs within their rendering or interaction callbacks.

3. Mapping application-specific data models to the library's data structures to preserve synchronization.

4. Managing lifecycle events—loading and unloading of resources—coherently with FLTK's widget destruction to avoid leaks.

An example integrating a JSON parsing library such as nlohmann/json into an FLTK application might provide a configuration panel where user input is serialized or deserialized from JSON structures. This decouples UI code from configuration persistence details, enabling straightforward adoption of alternate formats or storage backends.

```
#include <nlohmann/json.hpp>

class ConfigManager {
public:
    void load(const std::string& filename) {
        std::ifstream file(filename);
        file >> configJson;
    }
```

```
void save(const std::string& filename) {
    std::ofstream file(filename);
    file << configJson.dump(4);
}

void setOption(const std::string& key, const nlohmann::json&
 value) {
    configJson[key] = value;
}

nlohmann::json getOption(const std::string& key) const {
    if (configJson.contains(key))
        return configJson.at(key);
    else
        return nullptr;
}
private:
    nlohmann::json configJson;
};
```

To integrate with FLTK widgets, changes in the configuration can directly trigger widget state updates and vice versa, facilitating an interactive, persistent user experience.

When combining FLTK and external libraries' event or main loops, particular care is required. Some libraries provide their own threading models or event pumps (e.g., Boost.Asio or Qt within plugins). To avoid blocking or race conditions, the FLTK event loop should act as the master main loop. External operations may execute in background threads, signaling FLTK through thread-safe mechanisms such as Fl::awake()—a safe approach to notify the main thread to process queued UI updates.

Managing dependencies is another crucial aspect, as some libraries introduce complex build requirements or platform-specific configuration. Utilizing modern C++ package managers like vcpkg or conan facilitates version compatibility and cross-platform consistency. When designing plugin architectures involving third-party libraries, it is often advantageous to isolate these dependencies within plugin boundaries, keeping core application dependencies minimal.

339

Extending FLTK applications through plugins and third-party library integration enables rapid scalability of capabilities while preserving the lightweight and efficient nature of FLTK itself. Designing clear plugin interfaces, employing dynamic loading with abstract factory patterns, and encapsulating external libraries in clean adapter layers promote modularity and ease of maintenance. The combination of FLTK's streamlined GUI framework with robust C++ ecosystems empowers developers to craft responsive, richly featured applications adaptable to evolving user requirements and technology landscapes.

10.5. Future Directions for FLTK

The Fast Light Toolkit (FLTK) has maintained its relevance over decades by prioritizing simplicity, portability, and efficiency. Looking forward, the toolkit is positioned to evolve in multiple dimensions driven by emerging trends in software development, hardware capabilities, and user expectations. These future directions emphasize enhanced functionality while retaining FLTK's core attributes, ensuring it remains a viable solution for lightweight graphical user interfaces (GUIs) amid a rapidly changing ecosystem.

A primary focus area for ongoing development is improving modern graphical capabilities without sacrificing the minimalist design philosophy. The integration of hardware-accelerated rendering, particularly through OpenGL and Vulkan backends, is a critical trajectory. While FLTK currently leverages OpenGL for some components, future enhancements aim to further abstract GPU acceleration layers, enabling smoother and more complex graphical effects with minimal developer intervention. This includes broader support for contemporary display features such as high-DPI (dots per inch) scaling and HDR (high dynamic range) rendering. The challenge lies in balancing these advances with FLTK's lightweight footprint, ensuring that new capabilities do not introduce undue complexity or dependency bloat.

Cross-platform consistency remains a fundamental priority. FLTK's appeal is partially rooted in its ability to produce portable applications with minimal modification across various operating systems, including Unix/Linux, Windows, and macOS. However, emerging platforms and changes in existing OS architectures necessitate ongoing adaptation. For instance, evolving windowing systems such as Wayland on Linux require FLTK to update and optimize its native backend implementations. Moreover, expanding support for mobile and embedded platforms presents both an opportunity and a challenge. FLTK's light resource demands align naturally with constrained environments, but the diversity of input methods and form factors introduces new design considerations. Anticipated future work includes refining touch input integration, gesture recognition, and runtime adaptability for screen orientation changes.

The modern software development landscape emphasizes interoperability and integration with contemporary languages and frameworks. While FLTK is traditionally C++ centric, ongoing efforts are targeting improved bindings and interfaces for languages such as Python, Rust, and Go. These bindings aim to expose FLTK's robust widget set and event-handling mechanisms while ensuring idiomatic usage within each language ecosystem. Enhanced foreign function interfaces (FFI) and automated binding generation are areas of active exploration. This strategy not only broadens FLTK's potential user base but also facilitates its integration into complex applications leveraging multiple languages.

User interface paradigms have shifted towards more declarative, reactive, and data-driven architectures. FLTK's event-driven, callback-based model is simple and effective but can become cumbersome for large-scale applications with complex state management. Future initiatives may explore incorporating components inspired by modern GUI frameworks that support

341

declarative UI definitions and state synchronization. Such enhancements could include optional layers or libraries emphasizing reactive programming patterns, signal-slot mechanisms, or binding frameworks that facilitate synchronization between data models and widgets. Importantly, these developments must coexist harmoniously with FLTK's existing imperative style, providing developers with flexibility rather than mandatory paradigmatic shifts.

In the area of widget design and extensibility, expanding the native widget repertoire is an ongoing priority to support richer application scenarios. While FLTK's current widget set covers most common interface elements, there is interest in adding specialized controls such as advanced text editors with syntax highlighting, modern tree views with incremental search, and complex layout managers capable of adaptive and responsive design. Furthermore, enhancing accessibility support to meet modern standards (such as ARIA roles and keyboard navigation improvements) is vital to broaden FLTK's applicability in professional-grade software.

Development workflows and tooling around FLTK also continue to progress. Improved support for integrated development environments (IDEs), including project templates, debugging utilities, and UI design tools, facilitate faster and less error-prone application creation. A significant direction is the evolution of FLUID, the native FLTK GUI designer, to offer enhanced functionality such as a live preview, real-time property adjustment, and export options compatible with modern build systems. Additionally, the incorporation of continuous integration and automated testing strategies tailored to GUIs influence ongoing work to ensure stability and regression safety in new releases.

FLTK's open-source community and governance play crucial roles in its sustainable growth. Encouraging contributions through clearer documentation, more approachable code bases, and community-driven roadmaps ensure that innovation is not only developer-led but also responsive to user feedback and real-world application needs. Collaborative efforts, including harmonization with related projects and libraries, help leverage synergies-sharing improvements in areas such as graphics rendering, event handling, or internationalization.

Security considerations in GUI toolkits have gained prominence with increasingly networked and data-sensitive applications. FLTK's lightweight nature inherently reduces attack surface, but future enhancements will likely address secure input handling, mitigation against injection vulnerabilities in scripting interfaces, and compliance with security best practices across supported platforms.

Finally, long-term viability will rely on maintaining simplicity and modularity to facilitate embedding FLTK within larger systems. The toolkit's small size and clear architectural boundaries enable its use as a component in complex software stacks or even within unconventional environments such as virtual reality displays or IoT devices with graphical frontends. Anticipated research and prototyping are investigating such novel deployment scenarios, potentially exposing new interactions between FLTK and system APIs.

Future directions for FLTK revolve around striking a delicate balance between innovation and tradition: modernizing graphical capabilities and platform support, enriching developer experience and language interoperability, and expanding widget and accessibility features, all while preserving the toolkit's hallmark lightness and clarity. This roadmap secures FLTK's role as a resilient, versatile foundation for cross-platform GUI development in the decade to come.

10.6. Open Source Best Practices and Community Engagement

Effective participation in the FLTK (Fast Light Toolkit) community is predicated on understanding and respecting open source best practices that foster collaboration, maintain code quality, and sustain project vitality. The FLTK project, as with many open source initiatives, operates through a distributed network of contributors and maintainers who rely on clear communication, structured workflows, and shared governance principles. Adhering to these principles ensures that contributions are integrated smoothly, issues are tracked systematically, and the project evolves in a sustainable manner.

Open Source Etiquette in FLTK

The FLTK community culture is fundamentally built on respect and constructive communication. Contributors and users alike must approach discussions—whether on mailing lists, issue trackers, or code review forums—with professionalism and patience. Responses to questions or critiques should be factual and constructive, avoiding confrontational language or assumptions about others' expertise or intentions. Recognizing that participants are often volunteers balancing varying time commitments encourages empathy and smoother interactions.

Technical inquiries should be precise and well-researched prior to engagement. Presenting clear problem descriptions, including minimal reproducible examples or logs, accelerates diagnosis and resolution. When introducing new ideas or design changes, supporting rationale with references to documentation, standards, or precedents within the FLTK codebase or GUI toolkit ecosystem enhances credibility and facilitates consensus.

Maintainers and reviewers should provide detailed feedback with explanations geared toward both the immediate contributor and the wider community, enabling shared learning. A consistent, welcoming tone benefits retention and growth of contributors, particularly those new to C++ GUI libraries or FLTK's particular design philosophy.

Issue Tracking and Management

The FLTK project employs an issue tracking system as a central repository for bug reports, feature requests, enhancements, and tasks. Effective utilization of this system improves project visibility and prioritization. Contributors submitting new issues are expected to classify them correctly using tags such as "bug," "feature," or "documentation," and provide comprehensive information covering environment details, FLTK version, steps to reproduce, and expected versus actual behavior.

Maintainers triage issues by verifying reproducibility, categorizing, and prioritizing based on impact and resource availability. Users tracking issues through the system benefit from transparent change logs and milestone markers that describe target releases or phases associated with particular fixes or features.

Cross-referencing pull requests or patches with related issue numbers maintains traceability. When issues are resolved or rendered obsolete, closure comments documenting the outcome and any further considerations strengthen institutional knowledge. Contributors should monitor their issue submissions for feedback or requests for additional details to facilitate timely progress.

Contributing Patches and Code Reviews

Contributing patches to FLTK requires adherence to established coding standards and submission procedures to maintain codebase consistency and robustness. The FLTK source follows idiomatic C++ practices with a focus on minimalist design and portability. Contributors should familiarize themselves with the project's style conventions, including indentation, naming, comment format, and header inclusion policies.

345

Prior to submission, code changes must be tested across supported
platforms to ensure uniform functionality and avoid regressions.
For diagnostic or new feature code, accompanying documentation
updates and unit tests are highly encouraged or required. The in-
troduction of new GUI elements or API modifications undergo rigorous scrutiny to safeguard backward compatibility and adherence
to the toolkit's overarching architecture.

Patch submissions are most commonly performed through a version control system pull request or patch file attached to the issue
tracker. Each submission should contain a clear and concise commit message delineating the nature of the change, motivation, and
any relevant references to issues or discussions. Modular, atomic
commits simplify review and potential reversion if necessary.

Code review is an integral part of the collaborative process, involving feedback from one or more maintainers or senior contributors.
Review comments typically address functional correctness, security, code clarity, performance implications, and documentation
completeness. Iterative refinement based on this feedback leads
to acceptance and merging of the patch. Contributors benefit from
engaging openly with reviewers' recommendations and queries, as
this process enriches understanding and project alignment.

```
# Clone the FLTK repository and create a feature branch
git clone https://github.com/fltk/fltk.git
cd fltk
git checkout -b feature/your-feature-name

# Make code changes, then stage and commit
git add .
git commit -m "Implemented feature X; fixes issue #123"

# Push branch and create a pull request
git push origin feature/your-feature-name
```

```
On GitHub, navigate to your branch and submit a pull request,
linking to issue #123 and providing a detailed description.
```

Release Management

Release management within the FLTK project emphasizes stability, incremental improvement, and coordinated distribution. Releases are typically scheduled to incorporate a batch of validated bug fixes and enhancements, balancing the need for timely updates with the rigor of testing and documentation.

Pre-release versions (alphas, betas, release candidates) provide early feedback mechanisms for the community. Contributors testing these snapshots report regressions or shortcomings which inform final release stabilization. Tagging releases in the version control system ensures reproducibility and archival.

Change logs accompany official releases, describing new features, behavioral changes, deprecated functionality, and critical fixes. This documentation supports downstream users and distributions relying on FLTK by enabling informed upgrades and compatibility planning.

Release managers coordinate community contributions, verifying that the merge queue is stable, does not introduce regressions, and that related documentation is complete. They also engage with packagers and distributors to announce new versions, addressing any platform-specific caveats.

Project Governance and Decision-Making

FLTK governance reflects an open meritocracy shaped by consensus and sustained stewardship. Core maintainers hold commit rights and act as custodians of the project's vision, architecture, and quality bar. These individuals emerge through demonstrated expertise, sustained contributions, and trusted judgment.

Significant technical decisions undergo community discussion, typically on mailing lists or forums, allowing diverse viewpoints to surface. Design proposals benefit from concrete prototypes or detailed analyses, enabling informed evaluation by maintainers and contributors. When consensus is elusive, maintainers adjudicate decisions prioritizing project coherence, usability, and long-term sustainability.

Governance also encompasses management of external dependencies, release cadence, intellectual property considerations, and community codes of conduct. Transparency in these domains fosters trust among contributors and end users alike.

Mechanisms such as regular virtual meetings, roadmap publications, and issue milestone definition provide structured coordination. Contributor acknowledgment through maintainership invitations or formal crediting reinforces motivation and community identity.

Effective engagement with the FLTK community depends on adherence to open source etiquette, systematic issue tracking, disciplined patch submission and review workflows, deliberate release management, and respect for established governance structures. These elements collectively enable FLTK to maintain its lightweight design ethos while evolving to meet contemporary graphical user interface development demands.

www.ingramcontent.com/pod-product-compliance
Lightning Source LLC
Chambersburg PA
CBHW061234220326
41599CB00028B/5423